GLIMPSES OF THE PROFOUND

Glimpses of the Profound

Four Short Works

Chögyam Trungpa

EDITED BY JUDITH L. LIEF

SHAMBHALA
BOULDER
2016

Shambhala Publications, Inc.
4720 Walnut Street
Boulder, Colorado 80301
www.shambhala.com

9 8 7 6 5 4 3 2 1

Printed in United States of America

♾ This edition is printed on acid-free paper that meets
the American National Standards Institute Z39.48 Standard.
♻ This book is printed on 30% postconsumer recycled paper.
For more information please visit www.shambhala.com.
Distributed in the United States by Penguin Random House LLC
and in Canada by Random House of Canada Ltd

Library of Congress Cataloging-in-Publication Data
Names: Trungpa, Chögyam, 1939–1987, author. | Lief, Judith L., editor.
Title: Glimpses of the Profound: Four Short Works / Chogyam Trungpa;
edited by Judith L. Lief.
Description: Boulder: Shambhala, 2016. | originally published as four
separate volumes by Vajradhatu Publications. | Includes index.
Identifiers: LCCN 2015013654 | ISBN 9781611803037 (paperback: alk. paper)
Subjects: LCSH: Trungpa, Chögyam, 1939–1987—Sermons. | Buddhist sermons. |
BISAC: RELIGION / Buddhism / Tibetan. | RELIGION / Buddhism / General (see
also PHILOSOPHY / Buddhist).
Classification: LCC BQ7612 .T73 2016 | DDC 294.3/420423—dc23
LC record available at http://lccn.loc.gov/2015013654

Contents

Editor's Introduction

IT IS AN HONOR to be introducing this collection of teachings by the Vidyadhara Chögyam Trungpa Rinpoche, based on a set of five pivotal seminars he conducted between 1972 and 1975.*

TRUNGPA RINPOCHE'S EARLY SEMINARS

The Glimpses series was originally published by Vajradhatu Publications in five small volumes, each one consisting of a lightly edited transcript of both the main seminar talks and the discussion periods that followed. The intent of these books was to bring the reader as much as possible into the experience and ambiance of these early teachings, presented when Trungpa Rinpoche was first introducing the dharma in North America.

Trungpa Rinpoche came to North America in 1970 and embarked on a very vigorous teaching schedule that continued for seventeen years, until his death in 1987. He traveled extensively, giving individual talks and lecture series and three- to five-day seminars, as well

*The other seminar in the Glimpses series, *Glimpses of Abhidharma*, is published separately by Shambhala Publications and has been in print since 2001. Consisting of nine talks given at Tail of the Tiger in August 1971, it covers Buddhist psychology and the nature of ego and contains extremely helpful and fundamental teachings that lay a groundwork for the teachings found in this volume.

as conducting longer retreats, such as the three-month-long Vajra-dhatu Seminary programs.

In presenting the dharma, Trungpa Rinpoche's preferred format was the ITS, or "Intensive Training Seminar," and he was always careful to conduct his talks within an environment of meditation or sitting practice. For instance, a weekend ITS would typically begin with a Friday-night talk and continue with two full days of sitting and walking meditation, each followed by an evening talk. Residential programs, such as those held at Tail of the Tiger (now Karmê Chöling) or Rocky Mountain Shambhala Center (now Shambhala Mountain Center), would also include work shifts.

With the ITS format, participants do not simply listen passively to a series of talks: they are encouraged to engage with the material through discussion groups, reflection, and questioning, and they do so in the context of group meditation practice. Trungpa Rinpoche talked often about the "container principle," the idea that setting up a proper container, or atmosphere, as an individual and as a group can draw down the power of the teaching. The most essential component of establishing such a container is meditation practice. Through such practice, an environment can be created in which the openness of the students and the benevolence of the teacher are brought together. That connection is what makes genuine dharma possible. So establishing a proper container is crucial.

Trungpa Rinpoche's emphasis on group sitting practice was unique among Tibetan teachers. In his encounter with the West and its various spiritual traditions, he had seen how conceptual and heady people tended to be. He once remarked, after observing a Holy Communion ritual, how beautiful the ceremony was but how unfortunate it was that so few of those participating were really fully present. He realized that for his students to hear the dharma, they would first need to settle down, learn how to work with their minds, and be more present. As a model for how to approach this, he turned to the Zen tradition.

In the early seventies Trungpa Rinpoche met many of the leading Zen teachers who were active in the United States. He made a particularly close connection with the great Zen master Shunryu Suzuki Roshi of the San Francisco Zen Center. As Trungpa Rinpoche developed his own centers, he drew on a number of Zen forms, particularly the form of extended group meditation practice that alternated sitting and walking meditation for extended periods of time, from one day to an entire month. He was innovative in his use of Zen forms in conjunction with traditional Tibetan Buddhist teachings on mindfulness and awareness. By his emphasis on the container principle, and by alternating study and practice in his teaching programs, he was able to help students develop both mind and heart, both intellect and intuition.

THE GROUND OF SITTING MEDITATION

It is hard to overstate the importance Trungpa Rinpoche placed on sitting practice. Repeatedly, after almost every talk, he would remind students—even implore them—to practice. He went so far as to say that without sitting practice, study is a waste of time. Here are a few examples:

> We're having a *nyinthün* tomorrow, which is whole-day meditation practice. I feel it is extremely important for those who take part in the seminar to have that kind of discipline, that way of handling ourselves, of meeting ourselves personally. So, for anyone who takes part in this seminar, I hope they take part in this nyinthün tomorrow, which is extremely important in order to experience a complete seminar.[1]

Although this is a short seminar, still I would like to encourage people to try as much as they can to take part in the practice of meditation. We feel it is important that you do not become too heady through the seminar, and that we are not transplanting further samsara in your head and in our scene.[2]

Some technical or intellectual understanding is important, and your experiential situation is also important. Working those two together is extraordinarily possible. . . . So please take part in the discussion groups and also the meditation practice with our community here; that is also part of the seminar. It is very important to give in to the irritations and frustrations that take place in meditation practice.[3]

Trungpa Rinpoche talked about sitting meditation in terms of two aspects—*shamatha* (mindfulness) and *vipashyana* (awareness)—and he encouraged his students to see the two as complementary and inseparable. The mindfulness aspect of meditation, he taught, is to tame and settle the mind, and the awareness aspect is to brighten the mind and cultivate clarity and inquisitiveness. Through direct experience, his students began to see how study undertaken in the context of mindfulness and awareness takes on an entirely new dimension, how the nonconceptual nature of sitting meditation opens ways of understanding that are inaccessible by mental facility alone.

The meditation technique Trungpa Rinpoche taught was deceptively simple: You take a comfortable upright posture and then proceed to place attention lightly on your breath as it goes out and dissolves into the space around you. If distractions such as thoughts, sensations, or emotional dramas arise, you simply note them and return attention to the breath without comment or judgment. He emphasized dissolving outward rather than centering inward.

As you study the material in this book, it will be much richer if you take some time to first settle your mind and do some meditation practice. You could imagine yourself as a full participant in these vital seminars: practicing with your fellow students, engaging in discussions and dialogue, listening to the talks, and offering your questions and insights.

CONTENT OVERVIEW

GLIMPSES OF MAHAYANA

The first seminar presented in this book, originally titled "The Complete Teachings of Mahayana," was given at Tail of the Tiger in Barnet, Vermont, in March and April 1973. Consisting of six talks, it centers on a discussion of buddha nature—its discovery and characteristics. Trungpa Rinpoche touches on loving-kindness and compassion and their application in daily life, as well as the aspiration that leads us to commit to these buddha activities in the form of the bodhisattva vow.

GLIMPSES OF SHUNYATA

The four-talk seminar "Glimpses of Shunyata" was presented at Tail of the Tiger in Barnet, Vermont, in April 1972. It is a highly experiential evocation of the central mahayana teaching on emptiness, or *shunyata*. Trungpa Rinpoche talks about shunyata in terms of ground, path, and fruition—the nonexistent ground being egolessness, the nonexistent path being unconditioned openness, and the nonexistent fruition being ceaseless space.

GLIMPSES OF SPACE

The section on unconditioned space contains two seminars. The first, "The Feminine Principle," took place in four talks at Karmê Chöling in Barnet, Vermont, in January 1975, and the second, the six-talk "EVAM," took place at Karma Dzong in Boulder, Colorado, in April

1976. These two seminars were closely linked. In fact, students who wanted to attend the EVAM seminar were not allowed to do so unless they had first attended the feminine principle seminar. For students who had not been able to attend that seminar, Trungpa Rinpoche recruited four of his senior students to lead a series of workshops so that those students could review the feminine principle teachings prior to the EVAM seminar.

The Feminine Principle

Trungpa Rinpoche begins by pointing out that the feminine principle is not a sociological idea but has to do with meditation and the nature of reality. He talks about a kind of basic atmosphere that is completely accommodating and has the potential to give birth and thus could be referred to as "feminine"; prajnaparamita, known as the mother of all the buddhas, is considered to be an expression of that unconditioned space. The body of this seminar is about how manifestation arises from unconditioned space, which Trungpa Rinpoche describes in terms of three characteristics: unborn, unceasing, and like the sky.

EVAM

The EVAM seminar is unusual in that Trungpa Rinpoche was able to consult with his teacher, Dilgo Khyentse Rinpoche, who was in Boulder at the time he was preparing his talks. Trungpa Rinpoche talks about the EVAM principle as extraordinary vastness. In EVAM, E represents vastness, and VAM is what is contained within that vastness; this seminar is about the interplay of the two. Trungpa Rinpoche also discusses the EVAM principle in terms of the three stages of the path: hinayana, mahayana, and vajrayana.

GLIMPSES OF REALIZATION

The six-talk seminar "Glimpses of Realization," originally titled "The Three Bodies of Enlightenment," took place at Karma Dzong in Boulder, Colorado, in February and March 1975. Once again, it is about space and manifestation, this time in terms of what are called the three bodies of enlightenment: dharmakaya, sambhogakaya, and nirmanakaya. Trungpa Rinpoche begins by talking about the birth of a split between the enlightened and the unenlightened, and the notion of a path from one to the other. Once that basic split has taken place, there is a descent, as he describes it, from the space of dharmakaya to the energy of sambhogakaya to the bodily manifestation of nirmanakaya. He brings this all together by pointing out how the potential for awakening is everywhere and that it manifests in every aspect of our lives.

Titling these texts "Glimpses" may seem to imply that the teachings they contain are superficial or incomplete. But many of our most profound discoveries come about in just that way: as sudden glimpses. In fact, the task of the teacher is to provoke such glimpses. Instead of adding to our drone of subconscious gossip, never-ending preoccupations, and habitual obsessions, the wise teacher interrupts that samsaric momentum, gently or abruptly, and points us to the heart of the matter.

It is my wish that this book provokes glimpses of all kinds: glimpses that inspire you to look further, glimpses that give you confidence, glimpses that upset the apple cart, glimpses that open your heart, glimpses that undermine falsity, glimpses that awaken you to your boundless potential.

NOTES

1. "Message of Milarepa" seminar, Talk 3, Tail of the Tiger, Barnet, VT, July 1973.

2. See page 149 of this volume.

3. Chögyam Trungpa, *Orderly Chaos: The Mandala Principle* (Boston: Shambhala Publications, 1991), 13–14.

GLIMPSES OF MAHAYANA

1

Bad News and Good News

THE SUBJECT OF this seminar is mahayana Buddhism. It is about spirituality as a discipline and how we can exercise that discipline in day-to-day life. We are not purely discussing religious theory; we are talking about actual experience. I would like to make that quite clear. It is a spiritual approach rather than a religious one. Ego, or confused neurosis, always tends to find new crutches to support its own existence. So taking up particular religious ideas might only serve to enrich that tendency to prop up the self-existence of ego.

Both the hinayana and the mahayana* are processes of cutting through that basic tendency of ego, which is called spiritual materialism. Although different techniques might be involved, the basic approach is the same. It is based not on becoming higher, greater, or better persons but on finding tendencies of "awake" that exist within us. It is an uncovering process rather than an expanding out. At the same time, there are differences between the hinayana and the mahayana. We need some kind of footing as to those differences, to make the basic pattern clear.

In the hinayana, we work with the basic characteristics of neurosis

*In this discussion, the terms *hinayana* and *mahayana* refer to stages on the three-yana journey of hinayana, mahayana, and vajrayana rather than to the different schools of Buddhism.

as a way of cutting down the unnecessary chaos that arises from ego's mentality. It is a cutting-down process. The hinayana could be called narrow-minded, in that it does not make any allowance for entertainment or therapy. It is direct, definite, stubborn. No therapy and no entertainment in the ego-oriented style are permitted at all.

Hinayana presents the narrow path in order to develop an understanding of the open path, or open way, of mahayana. The narrow path is to experience that life is pain: it is dwelling in pain and growing up in pain. The whole process of life is wrapped up in pain because the basic tendency of ego is to yearn so much toward pleasure. We try to ward off pain and the notion of pain. However, by doing so and by yearning toward pleasure, the notion of pain gets a lot of attention. Consequently, our pain is increased, because it is being teased and fiddled with so much. It's like scratching a wound—by doing so, we only get it more infected. The hinayana way is to realize that situation. We accept the fact that we have a wound, but we don't have to scratch it even if it itches. Instead we relate with our wound. We accept that we have a wound: it is part of our bodily chaos and irritation. Hinayana is about accepting that life situation.

Without the hinayana, without a good foundation, we can't build the fortress of mahayana. It is important to know that life is so much to the point. On the one hand, we might say that life is very complicated and chaotic. It's difficult to keep up with all the problems we go through. On the other hand, life is extremely simple. It can be simplified into one phrase: ego pain. Existence is based on the continual birth and death of pain—and ego tries to make that process continuous and to hang on to it. Unless we realize the narrowness of life—*narrow* in this case meaning that we can't escape from those two basic things, ego and pain—we can't develop the greater vision of mahayana, the great vehicle, at all. We have to start from one atom, one basic point, which acts as a catalyst for the larger world.

Someone told me that ten years ago he had read a book on Buddhism and found it extremely depressing. He said to himself, "Who wants to get into this?" Instead he joined a love-and-light path. However, he found himself asking that same question again later, which brought him back to the basic meaning of pain. Sooner or later we have to realize that life is very simple, extremely simple. Life consists of the notion of escape, or trying to avoid pain, and the notion of giving one's existence an identity, or trying to increase ego. In order to understand mahayana and its ideals, we have to understand that matter-of-fact situation.

Mahayana is the inspiration of the open way of allegiance to buddha, or "awake." You associate yourself with buddha; that is the mahayana way. Hinayana is allegiance to samsara, associating yourself with samsara and relating with the samsaric process, which is called renunciation. In other words, buddha cannot exist without samsara; nirvana cannot exist without samsara; awake cannot exist without asleep.

At the beginning we have to realize the meaning of life, which consists of erroneous beliefs of all kinds. That is what led us to this point and to our search for the teachings—which could be an erroneous belief as well. We are here because we made lots of mistakes, piles and piles of mistakes. That we happen to be here discussing this matter together is a result of such mistakes. Whether it is the right mistake or the wrong mistake, it is still an accident that happens to be bringing us together in this life, discussing the whole question of spirituality.

Spirituality is experiencing the narrowness of life. We no longer have any areas to escape to or areas to improvise. It's like birth: we can only come out of one channel from our mother's womb; there's no way of improvising. Having realized that situation fully and completely, having worked on the discipline of relating with pain, impermanence, and suffering, then we might have a new area to explore, which is that life is not as grim as it seems. There are sparks of light happening here and there, sparks of intelligence. For the very reason that we are agitated by our life, there is a spark of intelligence. There is hope—the hope for enlightenment. The reason we are dissatisfied with our life is that the message of mahayana is coming through.

In traditional language, that spark of intelligence is referred to as *bodhichitta*, which means "awakened heart," "the heart of enlightenment." Bodhichitta is always there. Because of that heart of enlightenment, instead of constantly cutting ourselves down and condemning ourselves, or purely seeing the negative aspects of life, we come to another conclusion, which is that we are already awake. We have within us *tathagatagarbha*, which means "the essence or seed of enlightened mind," or "buddha mind." That is the good news. But it seems that you cannot create good news without bad news to begin with. So the hinayana approach deliberately creates the bad news: that we are trapped, we are hopeless, we are helpless, and the meaning of life is pain.

The mahayana approach, the good news, is that even if life is pain and you are trapped in samsaric imprisonment, how do you *know* that? If you know that, if you have some notion of discovering that, maybe there is something in you that is actually able to see that— which is good news. From that point of view, hinayana and mahayana are reciprocal. The mahayana is based on a sense of self-respect, openness, and hope. The hinayana is based on a sense of hopelessness, narrowness, that there is no other way, no alternative. That is equally important, extremely important.

This notion of buddha nature, embryonic enlightenment, is one of the dominant inspirations of the mahayana. It is embryonic because it is still looked at with suspicion—it may not happen. It is still conditioned by the hope of becoming solid or getting into some solid situation. Buddha nature is also very pragmatic. In order to acknowledge such an embryonic situation, you have to work on it and awaken it. Contemplating or theorizing alone doesn't help—it takes a tremendous energy boost to exercise the buddha nature as if you had already awoken.

Although you may be half asleep, you still have to wake up and acknowledge your buddha nature as if you were completely awake. That is trusting in the heart. You believe that you could relate with yourself and your potentialities in spite of your imprisonment in samsara. You could still make love to yourself. You could love yourself and appreciate yourself because those two situations do exist in you. One of the basic principles or foundations of mahayana is that life is workable after all; it can be handled. But a certain amount of warmth and sympathy is necessary—toward yourself to begin with. And again, in order to develop the mahayana, it is necessary to begin first with the hinayana.

Student: Is the seed of enlightenment you spoke of always alive in us, or can it perish?

Chögyam Trungpa Rinpoche: As long as there is a question about the subject, it can't have perished. Acknowledging the restlessness of life is the seed. Seeking pleasure and warding off pain is the seed. In other words, unless you are a robot or a jellyfish, something is happening, which is the seed. Even a jellyfish might have buddha nature.

S: Rinpoche, you spoke of hinayana as being the way of renunciation, and renunciation as being the way of relating to samsara. Could you say more about that?

CTR: Renunciation is completely relating with the fact that you are trapped in an extremely strong prison. The only way of dealing with that situation is not to try to get out but to try to make yourself at home communicating with the things that caught you. It is like having a net around you. The whole thing is very narrow. Escape is not possible; therefore a better, more pleasurable situation is not possible. Renunciation is accepting that you have only one or two situations to work on. There are no other areas that you can dream up—and even if you dream, your dream is cut down. Renunciation means realizing the nuisance of yourself.

S: In our daily life it's possible to experience both narrowness and openness. What does one do?

CTR: The first step is to acknowledge the narrowness. Then, having acknowledged that, you have to take some kind of leap to bring that realization to a functional level. That is to say, first you feel the narrowness, the imprisonment. You feel that there is no alternative in life, that life has only one track, which is suffering and ego. Then, realizing that, you dance on that one track. So that one track isn't purely further depression, but it is further excitement as well, because you have no alternatives to play around with.

S: But what if you experience both states at the same time? Do you dance with both of them?

CTR: Sure. I think that's possible.

S: That becomes quite a confused space.

CTR: Then explore the confusion, which is also a dance.

S: You said something about compassion toward ourselves. How much compassion should we have toward ourselves? Are we too harsh with ourselves?

CTR: Generally, we are too *compassionate* with ourselves. We constantly seek pleasure, so we try to be overly kind to ourselves and delude ourselves. We try to shield ourselves from our mistakes as if nothing had happened. The hinayana way begins with the realization that everything is very serious, that you have no alternatives. In your attempt to be too kind to yourself, you have trapped yourself in your idiot compassion, which creates further pain.

If you become more familiar with that pattern and realize the alternativelessness, then you could become more compassionate. I think that is why hinayana is important at the beginning—to realize that you can't just treat yourself as if you were what you would like to be. To begin with, you have to cut down your indulgence. You have to realize that if you indulge yourself, that only creates further pain. That realization itself is hopeful. It brings more encouragement. Compassion does not mean creating pleasure but rather creating a sense of trust in yourself and not condemning. This kind of compassion can be developed if you have the relative intention to do so.

S: Isn't it indulgent to try to improve your situation at all, to move geographically or try to get a better job? If you give up alternatives, do you simply stick with the boredom of your current situation?

CTR: Changing jobs doesn't have anything to do with it. Moving from an armchair to the sofa, which is more comfortable, or drinking tea instead of coffee—those don't have anything to do with the larger situation. In talking about indulgence, I don't mean that you have to punish yourself constantly. Changing your physical situation doesn't make any difference. Indulgence is the general attitude of wanting to achieve a state of solid pleasure. That is the basic point. It is a psychological issue, a question of trying to secure your being.

S: There might be a point where you need to make a choice.

CTR: Choice is related to the present situation. You have only one situation at a time; you cannot have two situations happening simultaneously. You have the present situation and you have a possibility. When you make a choice, you start with the present situation rather than the possibility of some hypothetical situation that hasn't yet materialized. That seems to be the point of having ground.

S: By loving oneself more, do you mean not judging yourself for being in samsara, for being pleasure-seeking or involved in ego pain, but just accepting that that's where you are?

CTR: That seems to be the point. Loving oneself means accepting both the positive and the negative, whatever there is. It is not only loving but also regarding the whole thing as fertile ground, as a workable situation—like a field with manure on it.

S: You talked about trust in the heart providing the energy that stirs you toward enlightenment. That is confusing because what we experience is so totally dependent on the confusion of our moods, on insubstantial stuff. I don't really know how to get to the heart. It seems to suggest a ground.

CTR: It does suggest a ground, but the ground doesn't have to be flat ground. The ground could be the current that flows through, the ocean as ground as opposed to the land as ground. The ocean goes up and down, but it is still ground. Likewise, dissatisfactions could be regarded as ground. It's a question of whether you are relating with the situation as workable or whether you are taking advantage of frivolity. Even frivolity could be related to as ground, somewhat, but you shouldn't be possessed by it because in frivolity you are no longer experiencing the seriousness of the pain. Frivolity does not relate with anything except its own irony or foolishness. It is a mask. By relating with it, you might crush the mask. That seems to be the only way to relate with it.

You can't really start with an ideal situation. In fact, as a product of discriminating intelligence, which compares grounds, you may find that the present ground is completely insubstantial—but there is still some energy going on that could be worked with. I think you have to allow yourself to have some kind of stepping-stone. It may not be as solid as you would like, but it is still a stepping-stone.

2

A Golden Buddha

IN THE MAHAYANA, inspiration comes from experiencing the spark of intelligence or enlightenment in us. Discovering that potential is one of the fundamental characteristics of the mahayana. Having looked into our feelings of inadequacy, pain, and confusion, we see them as neither good nor bad, but as *workable*. In our day-to-day life, we find that the search for pleasure, either materialistic or spiritual, is unconvincing. Behind that whole approach is a sense of dissatisfaction and continual struggle. Recognizing that dissatisfaction and struggle is the discovery of the first noble truth, the truth of suffering, or *duhkha*. However, that discovery of the universality of pain is the discovery of buddha nature as well. That realization is not stupid or ignorant, but intelligent. So the struggle we go through is an expression of enlightened mind. The bad news in itself is good news.

The enlightenment potential, or buddha nature, has two components: fundamental intelligence and basic warmth. Fundamental intelligence, or discriminating awareness, allows us to look at situations in life critically—hopefully even to the point of searching for spirituality, the ultimate goal. Basic warmth means that even though we may condemn ourselves as bad, weak, or confused, by its very nature, such condemnation is an expression of warmth, strangely enough. By looking at ourselves critically, we expect something good

will come of it, so there is a sense of ambition. Condemning ourselves is the ultimate hope, in fact.

Such virtues may be entirely spiritually materialistic or psychologically materialistic. Nevertheless, the driving force behind them, the
very existence of such potential, is the buddha nature operating. At
the same time, that potential is entirely dependent on the realization
of pain. We start from that. So pain becomes a kind of crutch or stepping-stone to buddha nature. But at this point, buddha nature is still
embryonic or potential. It is embryonic because it is *glimpse* of hope
rather than an actual experience of complete hope.

The great teacher Taranatha talks about the embryonic awakened
state of mind being solid, eternal, permanent. His approach is challenged by others, who say that is not the experience of real buddha
nature but of ultimate ego. They say that it is precisely the function
of ego—to be ambitious, to strive toward achievement, and to try to
associate with what is solid, positive, and hopeful.

On the one hand, it is true that buddha nature could be regarded
as ego. Enlightened mind becomes ego because a sense of security is
imposed on it, a feeling that we will live forever. Ego is all those attitudes that are imposed on buddha nature. Buddha nature, or basic
sanity, is exploited and used as backing to reassure us of our existence. Buddha nature is used to reassure us that we are secure and
healthy, that we will never experience death. On the other hand, if
there is no sense of permanent security, no sense of using buddha
nature as a pawn, no sense of maintaining a relationship with sim-
ple-minded hope and fear—then buddha nature becomes just simple
straightforward buddha nature, or enlightenment mind. So, on the
whole, buddha nature, the attitude directed toward enlightenment,
is very solid, very continuous. It is extremely definite, without any
mistakes.

Buddha nature, or tathagatagarbha, has many attributes: it is
unborn, unobstructed, and it does not dwell on anything. To begin

with, it is continuous and solid because it is unborn. It is not based on or reinforced by something that already exists. Buddha nature does not have to be given birth to by effort or preconception, in the way that giving birth to a child requires a father and a mother. In this case, parents are synonymous with preconceptions. Buddha mind or enlightened mind is not dependent on such preconceptions; therefore, it is unborn, unoriginated.

Another attribute of buddha nature is that it is unobstructed. Its flow cannot be prevented by any causal characteristics that depend on karmic chain reactions. So it is free from karma. Our intelligence, our restlessness, does not need nursing or securing. It is constantly, intelligently, critical of pain. Our restlessness is unobstructed and does not need to be nursed.

Another attribute of buddha nature is that it does not dwell on anything, which means that we cannot categorize it as being associated with good or bad, pleasure or pain. Enlightened intelligence shines through both pain and pleasure; in other words, through any kind of cognitive mind. So the unconditioned cognitive mind that functions in our basic being is the true enlightened mind. There's nothing very obscure about this. It has nothing to do with mystical experience or anything like that at all. It is functional, simple, direct, intelligent, sane, and pragmatic.

The basic point about buddha nature is that this restless mind is the buddha nature. Because it is so intelligent, therefore it is restless. It is so transparent that we can't put any patch on it to mask over the irritation—if we do, the irritation still comes through. We can't hold the irritation back or maintain ego-style comfort anymore. The purpose of ego is to search for permanent, solid comfort. Even though this search might cost a lot in terms of temporarily sacrificing and inflicting pain on ourselves, we hope that in the end we will finally achieve ultimate comfort or security—but each time we begin to achieve that, something else goes wrong.

In tantric literature, buddha mind is referred to as a lamp in a vase. If a vase is cracked, the imperfections of the vase can be seen because of the light shining through from inside. In mahayana literature, a popular analogy refers to enlightened mind as the sun and ego's security as the clouds that prevent the sun from shining through.

The idea of buddha mind is not purely a concept or a theoretical, metaphysical ideal. It is something extremely real that we can experience ourselves. In fact, it is the ego that feels that we have an ego. It is ego that tells us, "My ego is bothering me. I feel very self-conscious about having to be me. I feel that I have a tremendous burden in me, and I wonder what the best way to get rid of it is." Yet all those expressions of restlessness that keep coming out of us are the expression of buddha nature, the expression of unborn, unobstructed, and nondwelling.

It is said in the *Guhyasamajatantra* that all sentient beings are good vessels for the mahayana teaching, that we can exclude nobody. Therefore, we should take delight and cheer up. Also, in one of his opening speeches, so to speak, the Buddha discussed which vessels are appropriate to receive the teachings, who could be excluded and who could be included. He said, "Let everyone come and join. Invite *everybody!*" This approach of seeing buddha nature as all-pervading is one of the basic threads of tantra as well as of the mahayana. That upsurge of the energy of awakened mind is energy one can use and transmute in the tantric teachings.

In taking the bodhisattva vow, we are acknowledging that we have a great many family characteristics of the family of the Buddha. We are acknowledging that potential, or buddha nature. In fact, any kind of ambition we might have in our life, such as trying to maintain or advance ourselves, could be regarded as an expression of enlightened mind. It has been said that even the most vicious animals have the instinct to take care of their young and be loving to them, which is an expression of buddha nature.

When people have a glimpse of buddha nature, it is not a glimpse in the sense of viewing something: it is a gap rather than a glimpse. That gap is the experience that comes out of seeing through the veils of ego. But whether we have a glimpse of it or not, the buddha mind is still functioning in us all the time. It occurs in the most bizarre, cheap, and confused styles we might present, as well as in whatever extremely profound, dignified, and wise experiences we might have. All of those are the expressions of buddha nature.

One of the foundations of the mahayana approach to life is the realization that completely perfect enlightenment, *samyaksambuddha*, is no longer a myth—it is real. For the hinayanist, enlightenment is pure myth. First one has to attain the arhat stage, which is a stage of absorption, and from there one has to advance to the enlightened attitude. But in the mahayana approach, as Taranatha puts it, everybody carries in his or her heart a perfectly produced image of the Buddha, beautifully made, cast in gold.

Everybody has such an image in his or her heart. That seems to be true. It's very real, delightfully real—and the unreality makes things *more* real! That is the ground of the great vehicle: before you think big, you have to think real. That seems to be the starting point of the Lion's Roar, the proclamation of mahayana. Mahayana starts with the faith and conviction that nobody is condemned or confused.

Student: Because of our confusion, because we don't understand life, we may sit down to read a book on Buddhism. Are you saying that the impulse to try to find greater clarity or truth that prompts us to pick up the book is enlightened mind coming through?

Chögyam Trungpa Rinpoche: Yes. Whether you understand it or not, that very attempt is buddha nature.

S: Then where would the ego come in?

CTR: Ego's approach is the mentality of the lucrative, the profitable: "I should be getting something out of this book; otherwise my effort is wasted." It's an unrealistic, businesslike mentality, the idea that if things don't make sense, your search is wasted.

S: You said that the ego is buddha nature. Could you also dwell on your ego *without* having buddha nature involved?

CTR: If you are trying to separate them, that is the work of ego. That very project becomes ego's project. The impulse to go forward is buddha nature—any afterthoughts are ego. The first impulse, the first clear driving force, is buddha nature. If you lay an affectation over basic sanity, it becomes neurosis. Whether your attitude is that there is nothing good in ego, that there is no buddha nature, or you try to make things better or more solid, it is still an affectation.

S: What attitude *would* bring forth buddha nature?

CTR: Having *no* attitude, just being simple and straightforward.

S: Can it become dangerous to believe that one has had a glimpse of buddha nature? At what point does trust in the heart become dangerous?

CTR: It could become dangerous if you begin to use it as a credential, as a way of expanding your power over either yourself or others. The same thing applies to any kind of practice. If your practice is just pure, direct practice, that seems to be very simple. But if your practice becomes somewhat heroic, or connected with finding definite proof, it is dangerous.

S: Rinpoche, you said that the impulsive afterthought is ego, while the immediate thought is buddha nature. How do you distinguish between impulsiveness and spontaneity?

CTR: To begin with, impulse is not spontaneous. It may *seem* spontaneous, but it doesn't have the relaxed quality of spontaneity. Impulse comes out like a sneeze, as the result of pressure, whereas spontaneity is like yawning: it has less pressure, and it takes its time. A glimpse of buddha nature is not violent; whereas impulse is very violent, desperate. Spontaneity is buddha nature, and impulse is ego. Impulse never reaches the first stage; impulse always trails behind. Impulse is never up to date; it is the rebound. First you see, then you react. Impulse never comes firsthand; it is a reaction.

S: It sounds as though buddha nature is intermittent.

CTR: The restlessness is the sharpest and most immediate situation we experience, whereas buddha nature itself is something we can't catch hold of and put in a container. That is why it is associated with light. Buddha nature is happening constantly, but ego doesn't have a chance to register it. Buddha nature is constantly ahead of you, you being ego at this point. It is constantly ahead of you.

S: So you are continually dissatisfied?

CTR: Yes. The intelligence is always shining through.

S: Could you relate buddha nature with the image of falling, of having no ground at all?

CTR: That seems to be the whole point: buddha nature brings the realization that there is no ground.

S: But it doesn't seem as if you are seeing anything.

CTR: It isn't *seeing*, really, in terms of reporting back to your brain or anything like that. I don't know what word you could use. The usual word for this is *jnana*, or knowing—but you don't even *know*. I suppose we could make a distinction between looking and seeing. You see first; you look afterward.

S: Could you say that buddha nature sees that there is no ground because it sees the ego coming up over and over again?

CTR: Buddha nature is not regarded as another kind of cognitive mind functioning. It is part of our cognitive mind, but it supersedes cognitive mind. It naturally sees the fruitlessness of struggle—as well as encouraging struggle in order to prove its fruitlessness. The whole thing is sort of an automatic, inbuilt, natural mechanism which is trying to wear itself out. In other words, without buddha nature, ego cannot exist. Ego is constantly teased by buddha nature into activating itself, so either it is perpetuating itself or wearing itself out.

S: Rinpoche, when you talk about having no ground, it seems to imply that there are no rules about what to do, or about whether what you are doing at a certain moment is good or bad. That seems very confusing. It leaves you hanging on a cliff.

CTR: That seems to be the whole point, that you don't have any reference point to hold on to. And the fear is the fear of losing ego. But losing ego doesn't mean that you wouldn't know how to brush your teeth or make a cup of tea. In fact, you would probably do those things better. However, it is quite fearful, even in theory—and the *experience* is going to be even heavier.

S: Why do we have to concern ourselves with this? It seems to happen spontaneously as we go along. If we are practicing and learning and becoming more aware of our groundlessness, why do we have to discuss buddha nature?

CTR: I don't know why, but we find ourselves questioning ourselves. You could ask why we question at all, but that in itself is a question.

S: Rinpoche, if an individual is not into Buddhism, or a spiritual path, if he's a businessman, restless and ambitious to make more money, to make his life better, if he is not aware of ego or of duality— is his restlessness still considered a spark of intelligence, or buddha nature?

CTR: Yes, I think so, in the long run. This seems to have been happening in this country already. Your father, your great-grandfathers, and your great-great-great-grandfathers were all preoccupied with building a brand-new world—so they built it. Then the whole thing turned around, and now we are talking about buddha nature. Without missionaries, or people proselytizing these ideas in this country, the country itself is awakening to this idea of buddha nature. It might take a long time for people to realize their buddha nature, and businessmen might have to freak out. Nevertheless, the effort is not wasted, although it might take several lifetimes to come about. In fact, this whole question has come up as a result of that restlessness and as a result of those people putting in their effort.

S: Rinpoche, how about the case of traditional societies that seem to go along their leisured way and don't change very much, societies in which people seem content to do things the way their forefathers did them?

CTR: Generally, you can't have an ideal solid society operating for thousands of years, although I suppose you could say that Tibet was close to it. When I left my country recently, it was still a medieval society, but then a force from the outside thrust us out. Since we didn't make any new discoveries, somebody else made a new discovery for us. We were pushed out. So there can be no such thing as a permanent traditional society as long as people desire to be comfortable and happy. But I suppose the more speed there is, the more buddha nature is coming through. We could say that.

S: If we are aware of buddha nature, isn't that a type of security in itself?

CTR: It could go either way. If we are aware that we have a buddha nature, that is security—but we are also aware that we might lose our ego by being involved with buddha nature, and that is not security. Knowing that you cannot witness your own burial is quite uncomfortable.

S: You said that ego tries to use buddha nature to ensure its own security.

CTR: Ego tries anything it can lay its hands on.

S: But ego itself is buddha nature, right?

CTR: Yes. That is why it can be used up. Otherwise it would become a war between buddha nature and ego.

S: It seems confusing that buddha nature as ego would try to use buddha nature.

CTR: Yes, isn't that absurd?

S: Ego and buddha nature in this case are almost the same. Isn't that a paradox, the notion that buddha nature and ego are interchangeable?

CTR: It is like a healing wound. When your wound is healed, the scab falls away; but at the same time, the scab is part of the wound. The fundamental idea is something like that.

3

Awakening Buddha Nature

IN REGARD TO buddha nature, the question seems to be: How can we provoke or awaken that basic potential? Traditionally, the aspiration to develop compassion comes from experiencing the misery and pain that we and our fellow beings are going through; from allegiance toward the spiritual friend; and from a sense of dedication, in that we are not afraid to apply our experience in working with sentient beings.

Buddha nature is not regarded as a peaceful state of mind or, for that matter, as a disturbed one either. It is a state of intelligence that questions our life and the meaning of life. It is the foundation of a search. A lot of things haven't been answered in our life—and we are still searching for the questions. That questioning is buddha nature. It is a state of potential. The more dissatisfaction, more questions, and more doubts there are, the healthier it is, for we are no longer sucked into ego-oriented situations, but we are constantly woken up. We may feel that we are able to relax, let go, and take pleasure out of our life—but that becomes more and more momentary. We are woken up constantly by that unrest. Whether we are in a greater dramatic situation or a smaller petty situation, that same pattern goes on.

The beginning point of buddha nature seems to be the development of *maitri*, which could be translated as "love," "kindness," or "a friendly attitude." Having a friendly attitude means that when you make friends with someone, you accept the neurosis of that friend as well as the sanity of that friend. You accept both extremes of your friend's basic makeup as resources for friendship. If you make friends with someone because you only like certain parts of that friend, then it is not complete friendship, but partial friendship. So maitri is *all-encompassing* friendship, friendship that relates with the creativity as well as the destructiveness of nature.

Maitri is not only maitri toward others, it is also maitri toward ourselves. In fact, the first step of awakening buddha nature is friendship with ourselves. This tends to help a great deal. We don't have alternatives or sidetracks anymore, because we are satisfied with ourselves. We don't try to imitate anyone else because we hate ourselves and we would like to be like somebody else instead. We are on our own ground and we are our own resources. We might be fantasizing that there is a divine force or higher spiritual energy that might save us, but even that depends on our recognition that such a thing exists. Finally we end up just relating with ourselves. So friendship, or maitri, means the complete acceptance of our being.

The agitation of buddha nature coming through, questioning and dissatisfied, at the same time produces all kinds of insightful discoveries. We begin to settle down to our situation—not looking for alternatives at all, but just being with that. So the first step of the process of awakening buddha nature, embryonic enlightened mind, is trust in the heart, trust in ourselves. Such trust can only come about if there is no categorizing, no philosophizing, no moralizing, and no judgments. Instead there is a simple, direct relationship with our being.

One reason our being becomes workable is that we are constant people. We are completely, all the time, constant and predictable. We are predictable in the sense that there is a continual upsurge of energy and a continual upsurge of wanting: wanting to change, wanting to grasp, wanting to find out the details of life, wanting to seek pleasure. That happens constantly, and that constant unrest and energy could be regarded as a stepping-stone. We could work with that.

We might feel that we go through ups and downs: we feel highly excited and good and then we feel terribly depressed and shaky. But whatever we might be going through, we are still in the same situation all the time. We are constantly questioning, doubting, looking from this angle, looking from that angle, looking from a slight distance or from completely close up. All those games that go on are not regarded as bad, particularly, at all. Rather, they are expressions of our agitated enlightened mind trying to foment a revolution. Our agitated enlightened mind is trying to throw off the seeming expressions of ego. As long as we are able to relate with that as workable—and very real, in fact—then there is tremendous potential in us. We could make friends with ourselves. We could develop maitri.

Having managed to do such a thing, we could begin to relate with others. We could relate with our father and our mother, the people who taught us how to walk, how to talk, how to behave. We could relate with our friends and we could relate with our enemies. We could relate with people who taught us the unpleasantness of life as well as the people who taught us how pleasant life is. We feel that we have inherited so much from the people around us right from childhood.

If we develop friendliness to ourselves, we could extend that friendliness to others—in a sense it is others; nevertheless, it is *us* at the same time. It is a very dubious relationship: it is not exactly the *other* other, but the *seemingly* other, which constantly bounces back on us. So extending to others is predominantly and basically a way of making friends with ourselves. Obviously, our father, mother, brother, sister, friends, and enemies have done their best to relate with us. We have become their product in some sense. But their product, *their* other, means *us* at the same time.

Expanding maitri cuts the neurosis of wishful thinking, the idea that you should be a good person only. Maitri is *intelligent* friendliness that allows acceptance of your whole being. It doesn't exclude friend or enemy, father or mother. It does not matter whether you regard your father as a friend and your mother as an enemy, your brother as a friend and your sister as an enemy, your friend as a friend, your friend as an enemy, or your enemy as a friend. The whole situation becomes extraordinarily spacious and is suddenly workable. Maybe there is hope after all.

It is tremendously delightful that you could make friends with your parents and yourself, make friends with your enemies and yourself. At the same time, creativity still goes on. Something is beginning to break through. It is actually becoming real rather than imaginary. It is real because we don't have any hypothesis about how a good person should be or how we should improve ourselves. It is no longer hypothetical—it is real. Something actually does exist: relationships exist; love and hate exist. Because they exist, we are able to work with them as stepping-stones.

We begin to feel that we can afford to expand, that we can let go without protecting ourselves. We have developed enough maitri toward ourselves that we are no longer threatened by being open. At that point, we are inspired to spirituality. In this case, the idea of spirituality is nothing religious or sacred; it is purely relating to something beyond ourselves. Spirituality is relating to something beyond the simple level of me and my pen, me and my relatives, me and my friends. It is going slightly beyond that. We can go beyond the limitations of our familiarities. We see that there are further areas to explore. That becomes important—prominent, in fact.

This is the level where we begin to relate with the "spiritual friend," or *kalyanamitra*. In other words, unless the fortifications of home ground have been broken down, we can't relate with the spiritual friend at all. The spiritual friend is somebody else, some other person quite different from our parents, relatives, or friends. He or she is the epitome of a foreigner. The spiritual friend is not our father, not our mother, not our friend. He represents what is outside of home ground—an entirely new area, a new perspective.

At the beginning, the idea of relating with such a person may be rather frightening. We prefer to come back home and relate with our own people, those whom we are used to having relationships with. That feels very safe—and this idea seems a bit dubious, uncertain. Nevertheless, there is inspiration; and that inspiration is constantly expanding. The radiation of maitri is still happening, so we can't just keep holding on to incestuous and stagnant relationships, alternating from father to friend, friend to enemy. That becomes a bit too localized, too simplified. Instead, we develop the tendency to explore a greater area. In fact, that is precisely what *mahayana* means: it is the "great vehicle," encompassing a greater area and a sense of exploration.

At this point an odyssey begins to take place. Although we don't want to, we still can't keep ourselves from relating with the kalyanamitra. We finally begin to make the right mistake; we fall into the right accident. We feel uncomfortable, but at the same time it is so tempting that we *have* to step out of our old realm and get into a new approach, a new perspective. We cannot help it. We feel that we are being very naughty, but we can't help it. We can't help being naughty. Our people, our friends, might say, "Don't talk to those foreigners, we don't know about *them*, they could be dangerous." But we still want to find out more about those foreigners, for the very reason that they think differently, they behave differently, and their style is outlandish and fascinating.

The reason we refer to such a person as a spiritual friend rather than a guru is because the popular idea of a guru is of a person who possesses spiritual power and insight and is omniscient and wise. A guru is someone who has enormous understanding about life in the world and of reality and also has tremendous power and skill. A guru could cause the world to turn against us if we were on the wrong side of that person—in contrast, we ourselves feel embarrassingly small and stupid, undignified and frivolous.

Feeling so small ourselves and being in the presence of such a large situation is so threatening. Even if we have received spiritual instructions from such a guru, we still feel uncertain as to how to handle that message. We feel so unaccommodating, so poverty-stricken, that we couldn't possibly digest it. We can't even hold it in our hands. Our vision is so limited, our hearing is so limited, our brains are so small and inadequate, that we feel that we can't do anything. We might try, but it still feels as if nothing is really communicated. It is like a flea trying to study with an elephant and one day trying to become one. That seems to be the wrong notion of guru. That idea of guru is a myth.

The right approach, according to Shantideva, Gampopa, and Buddha, is that a spiritual friend, or kalyanamitra, is much more powerful than a hierarchical guru. A kalyanamitra brings a sense of friendship. The spiritual friend is extending friendship to you as you have done already. You have made friends with yourself; you have prepared yourself to search for a spiritual friend—and you find somebody who is the spokesman of the world outside your home ground. You can work with him and talk to him. He speaks your language. That person is a human being, a full-fledged human being. He needs food to sustain himself, he needs to take a rest at night, he gets up in the day, has breakfast as we do, lunch as we do, dinner as we do, wears clothes and breathes like we do. The spiritual friend is a human being.

One of the attributes of Buddha is that he is referred to as the supreme being among men. Literally, the text says, "the supreme being among two negative ones"—which is referring to humans rather than birds. The Buddha is never referred to as a heavenly being outside of this world. He is referred to as the teacher of human beings, a leader of men. He is a man himself—but he is an extraordinary one, a healthy one. Nevertheless, we can still communicate. So the spiritual friend is not a person who undermines our existence and our neurosis, but a person who speaks the same neurotic language we speak. He or she is an extraordinarily adaptable person. It is workable to relate with such a person.

The spiritual friend represents the dharma, "the teachings," the message of enlightenment. By judging this particular person we find that enlightenment may not be as far out as we had imagined. This person is a spokesman, soaked in this particular awake state of being himself, yet he speaks and behaves as we do. He has something to teach us, and he seems to be friendly as well—although at the beginning we may still be suspicious. That is the meaning of spiritual friend: you are working with a human being, the son or daughter of a human.

Relating with such a spiritual friend is our first introduction to the realization that our adventure is not a bad one after all. The spiritual friend does not speak our petty domestic language—but in a very strange combination he is able to speak our language while at the same time not being wrapped up in the things that we usually get wrapped up in ourselves. It is a very strange kind of performance. You could almost call it magic: being a human being and not being caught up in the pettiness. It's an extraordinary thing.

We often wonder whether somebody doing that is an accomplished actor. Maybe it is our own fantasy. Maybe we are seeing somebody we want to see, but it is not actually happening. Those thoughts flicker in our minds naturally. I don't see anything wrong with that at all. Such things are necessary. They give us a break from the heavy-handedness of our spiritual friend. We have a little snack, a little break, an intermission—which is good. We don't expect to be heavy-handed ourselves or transform ourselves completely.

According to the scriptures and my own personal experience, a kalyanamitra, or spiritual friend, is a good person, good and trustworthy; and relating with a spiritual friend is a trustworthy situation. It is trustworthy because whenever there is doubt or fear, the spiritual friend does not try to justify himself, but bounces that back on you to remind you to awaken buddha nature. The spiritual friend is a very powerful mirror—a mirror that can reflect back your own reflection with super-clarity to the point of irritation. Even if you try to escape from that embarrassing encounter, that notion of escape is also recorded. It bounces back on you as well, so you can't get out of it. You find yourself on the path in an encounter with a spiritual friend who will let you escape—but that escape itself becomes another encounter.

The spiritual friend can perform miracles purely by working with the ordinariness of life. It is nothing fabulous or magical, but a question of how much one is involved with the ordinariness of life. You would be surprised how much magic there is if one is being completely ordinary, if one is thoroughly and fully experiencing the highest quality of ordinariness or simplicity of life. While you are taking off into some fantasy, which you think is your ground—when you think that you have your ground already set up—that person who is at the ordinary level pops us. At the beginning you think it is a miracle, that somebody has conjured up chaos. But in fact it is not a miracle in terms of magic; it is a miracle in that self-existing energy has been connected. The spiritual friend is very powerful because he or she has direct access to the ordinariness of life, nothing fanciful.

Relating with the spiritual friend brings us out from our home ground of seemingly domesticated maitri to the level of compassion, or *karuna*. That seems to be the turning point of commitment to the teachings and to the agent of the teachings, who is the spiritual friend. The teaching is not a myth anymore; it is real, livable, workable, and pragmatic. At the same time, the intelligence of our buddha nature begins to function.

Student: It seems that sitting practice exercises maitri, that it gives us room. I have been following my breath, sort of shutting out the chaos, but I'm a little confused about this.

Chögyam Trungpa Rinpoche: Shutting out chaos is necessary at the beginning. Then, when you let go of the technique, you find that you have more space than you imagined. So the technique creates a situation, rather than the technique being valid in itself. It is like dropping your crutches—you begin to bounce. The idea of technique is to accentuate whatever comes afterward.

S: How does one develop maitri and really accept oneself?

CTR: When you talk about *how* to do it, you are asking for a technique that won't bring you into an uncomfortable situation but at the same time will achieve what you want to achieve. Instead of using your hands, you want to use some machine, a pair of pliers or gloves. You are not willing to relate with things directly. So it seems that there is no *how* to do it, you have to *push* yourself. If you are pushed into the water, it may create a situation of panic—but, at the same time, you automatically swim.

S: How does one relate to the spiritual friend when one cannot accept friendship with oneself or one's family?

CTR: The relationship with the spiritual friend demands a relationship with yourself, so it works two ways at once. You have to learn to relate with yourself, because the spiritual friend is trying to make sure that you have no other choice. The heavy-handedness of the spiritual friend is also bouncing back a mirror reflection on you, so you are also your friend, as well as the spiritual friend being your friend. Also, if you have a relationship with a spiritual friend, that automatically means that you have done some work already; otherwise you wouldn't look for such a person at all. That must mean there's something going on inside you.

S: You said that buddha nature is not a peaceful state, that it's still searching for questions. That kind of confused me.

CTR: In describing buddha nature, I used the analogy of a revolutionary who is trying to throw off the expressions of ego. So ego is still there, of course. A revolutionary might act as if there's no authority, but he still has to fight with the authorities. As long as buddha nature is "nature," or *garbha*, it has to try to break out. The function of buddha nature is breaking out of the shell.

Buddha nature has cognitive mind, because it is "nature"; it is imprisoned within boundaries. So cognitive mind is buddha nature. In other words, you cannot have a revolution in a country if there is no suppressor. Suppression and revolution work together as an integral situation. It is like Mao Tse-tung's theory that you have to have a cultural revolution repeating every ten years or so to make sure that things are refreshed. Without any person to attack, you can't renew your revolution. This is an interesting point of tension, that an upsurge needs suppression. That's exactly the job of buddha nature, seemingly.

S: Does the bodhisattva transcend the whole struggle of samsara and nirvana?

CTR: There are ten stages of the bodhisattva path, and each stage is a struggle, so I don't think the bodhisattva transcends struggle. You can't get rid of struggle at the start; you need struggle, otherwise there's no journey.

4

Sudden Glimpse

THE WHOLE APPROACH of loving-kindness, or maitri, is one of expanding. We are taking steps outward instead of internalizing, or developing maitri in ourselves alone. This is a crucial point in the bodhisattva path and the philosophy of mahayana altogether. Mahayana is a way of expanding, and the spiritual friend acts as the entrance to that journey. Having made a relationship with a spiritual friend already, that suggests that we relate not only with that one friend alone, but with many friends. There are friends everywhere, either seemingly threatening or seemingly attractive.

In bodhisattva language, the definition of *friend* is the idea of a guest. There is a phrase, "inviting all sentient beings as your guests." An interesting point about the word *guest* is that when we invite a guest we have a sense of the importance of the relationship. We wouldn't invite a guest unless that guest brought some highlight, some important friendship or exchange of hospitality. Guests are usually fed specially cooked food and receive special hospitality. The life of a bodhisattva is relating with *all* sentient beings as guests. He or she is inviting everyone as a guest, constantly offering a feast.

Inviting all sentient beings as our guests is the starting point of the application of compassion. In viewing sentient beings as guests, the bodhisattva has a constant sense of the impermanence of the relationship—not that the guest is going to turn into an enemy, but that the guest is going to leave. So we view this as an opportune time, and there is constant appreciation. We don't want to seduce our guests into our territory and hold them with us for our benefit, nor do we want to go along with our guests when they leave our home in order to ease our loneliness. We don't take a journey with our guests; we stay at home.

Our guests come. We entertain them and relate with them. Afterward the guests thank us, we say good-bye, and we go back to running our home. There is a sense of the preciousness and the impermanence of the relationship, a sense of that relationship being extremely special. Our guest may be our husband, our wife, or our child—everybody is the guest of everybody. Although nobody completely lives up to his credentials, on a day-to-day level each relationship is based on relating with one's guests constantly.

Compassion is a combination of maitri and generosity. It is a journey outward, communication. On one level, compassion is feeling friendly toward ourselves. On another level, it is experiencing a sense of richness, that we can expand that warmth toward ourselves to other sentient beings. Compassion, from this point of view, is quite different from sympathy. Sympathy involves looking down on someone with the attitude, "I am in a secure situation, but you couldn't live at my level, so you need to be helped. You should be raised up to my level, helpless little person." Unlike sympathy, compassion is the radiation of mutual warmth to ourselves and to others.

We could look into the details of the nature of compassion, that sense of communication, how we *feel* compassionate. It is said in the scriptures that as fish cannot live without water, likewise compassion cannot develop without egolessness, without the experience of emptiness, or shunyata. That may bring up the idea that compassion is quite abstract, a logical conclusion of logical mind, rather than literal. It may seem that compassion is somewhat abstract because you just feel a sense of awareness. In fact, compassion is the heart of the practice of meditation in action.

We feel the presence of compassion as a sudden glimpse, a sense of clarity and warmth simultaneously. That is the notion of *recollection*, the awareness we might experience after intense sitting meditation practice. During the sitting practice of meditation, we find ourselves completely chaotic. All kinds of things are going on, and we try to swim through those overcrowded situations of this and that, subconscious mind, discursive thoughts, and so on. Physically, sitting meditation is supposedly quiet and simple—psychologically, it is quite a nightmare. At the least it is annoying and rather inconvenient. There's a sense of rediscovering hidden corners, uncovering all sorts of areas that we haven't discovered before. And when we try to solve all the problems that arise, that only creates further problems.

That is what we might find in sitting practice—and all of that is a result of holding on to definite ideas, a result of not having enough maitri and compassion, enough security and warmth. When we sit, we feel that we are attacking and dealing with problems. We are trying to get something out of it. However, when the sitting meditation is completed, when the gong rings and we decide to stop, we find that we are experiencing *better* meditation. At that point all those struggles have gone and all the chaos is dissolved. There is a sense of relief. It is as if we were entering into nirvana—and our *meditation* was a samsaric act.

At that moment there is an absence of struggle, a sense of warmth and freedom. If we deliberately try to create that, it is impossible. Instead we come upon it by accident. The crescendo created by sitting meditation practice brings that kind of release and freedom. The nature of awareness—the real meaning of *satipatthana*, or the practice of recollection—is that feeling of presence, that feeling of relief. At that point you could say that compassion and the shunyata experience are happening simultaneously.

In daily life we don't have to *create* the concept of letting go, of being free, or anything like that at all. We can just acknowledge the freedom that was already there—and just by the memory of it, just by the idea of it, there is a quick glimpse. A sudden glimpse. That sudden glimpse of awareness that occurs in everyday life becomes the act of compassion. We don't have to keep up with that or hold it for a long time. It is just a quick glimpse, which goes on always. It's almost a sense of experience without time to label anything, without time to feel good or bad or compassionate or empty or whatever. Just *that* happens—constantly. We could create that situation right now, at this very moment—a quick glimpse—just to see that there is awareness that is not watched or confirmed. Just awareness. A quick glimpse.

The scriptures talk about bodhisattvas who develop compassion and awareness instantly, at the same time. Even if such bodhisattvas are about to lose their awareness and go into the chaos of a samsaric situation, they can correct themselves in the process of doing so. It's like a healthy person with good balance who slips or skids: in the process of slipping, he can correct himself without falling. The force of the slipping is used as a way of rebalancing. That doesn't require any mystical experience—it is just one look, then let go.

According to the scriptures, that glimpse, if you analyze it, takes one-sixtieth of a second. It is so fast and so sharp. The sharpness is the *intelligence* of the compassion. Compassion also means being open and communicable. It contains *warmth*, because you have the desire to do such a thing. We could split that one-sixtieth of a second into sixty parts, as in the analogy of sixty flower petals being suddenly punctured with a needle. If you look at that in slow motion, you first see the needle touching a petal; then penetrating through that petal; then, having completely penetrated, getting into the next petal; again you see it touching the petal, piercing through, and going on to the next. Likewise with compassion: first there is the sense of warmth, or maitri, in oneself; then there is a sense of cutting neurosis; and finally, there is a sense of openness. So the whole thing falls into three parts. It's very quick!

The whole thing is very abrupt. That's why what is known as the postmeditation experience, or meditation in action, is regarded as a highly powerful thing. There is no time to analyze; no time to work with it or hold on. At the same time there is a gap. In other words, there is no time to refer back to oneself as "I am doing this." There is no time to relate with *me* or ego awareness at all. It is just *awareness*, simple awareness. That awareness is regarded as the heart of meditation in action. It is compassion.

A person might develop the patience to repeat that many times in a day. By doing so, that glimpse of compassion and shunyata cuts the chain reaction of karmic causal characteristics. At the same time, you are communicating fully and completely. When the penetrating is going on, when the puncturing is going through, when you are cutting the chain—you are catching a quick glimpse of buddha nature at the same time. If that act is divided into three sections, first there is maitri, trusting in the heart; second, there is a gap in which you experience the openness of tathagatagarbha, or buddha nature; third, there is a sense of communication in that, having already woken up at that level, there is a sense of freedom to expand and to relate with your actions, whatever you are doing. That seems to be how to develop compassion. The problem is that if we begin to hold on to that, or begin to analyze it, then the analytical mind begins to pollute the freshness of that sudden glimpse.

In a sense, we don't have to develop compassion. We simply acknowledge a situation that is already there: we are just seeing it, looking at it. One of the analogies used in the text *Entering a Path of Enlightenment*, or the *Bodhicharyavatara*, is that of seeing a picture of the Buddha. If a person in a state of rage sees a picture of the Buddha painted on the wall, the merit of seeing a picture of the Buddha is not wasted. In reference to the idea of compassion, when we see a picture of the Buddha, it has all kinds of associations, such as the idea of friendliness. Seeing that compassionate Buddha creates a sudden glimpse in our mind, which cuts through the rage and aggression. It might not cut through completely or ideally. We may not just flop like a punctured balloon—that would be expecting magic. But at least it de-intensifies the pressure of neurotic speed.

Compassion also brings a sense of communication with other people. You are constantly relating with other people in everyday-life situations, not only when you have developed a state of extreme emotional upheaval. That awareness constantly flashing again and again produces friendliness. In other words, subconsciously you begin to realize that you are no longer as vulnerable as you thought you were. There is something going on behind the facade of emotions and protections, something going on behind that whole thing. Subconsciously or consciously you begin to develop a sense of confidence, that you can afford to be openhearted. You can afford to invite all those guests into your territory and work with them, entertain them.

Compassion is not only the logical conclusion that you are going to be okay. It is almost a subconscious trick, you might call it, to deliberately create that sudden glimpse constantly. Looking back or looking forward, there is openness. Seemingly, such looking destroys the ground of ego—but surprisingly, that doesn't become a state of loss or a state of shock from the point of view of ego. Instead, it becomes something fundamentally sane, fundamentally workable and smooth.

This type of compassion is what bodhisattvas practice, and it seems that we can get into it ourselves. We can do so very simply—as long as we don't try to re-create past experiences or future expectations of the glimpse, but just look. Look! Look! The idea of compassion is direct. We might realize that the idea of becoming enlightened beings one day is not very far ahead, if we are not enlightened already. It becomes very real and very direct—it ceases to be a dream.

As that basic ground of compassion is set on the path, then magically, I suppose we could say, there is a sense of openness, almost ambition. It is ambition in the positive sense, that you would like to extend an invitation to your guests all the time. Gentleness becomes powerful. You are not afraid to cut down, and you are not subject to idiot compassion anymore at all.

Fundamentally, the pressure of ego's speed is what causes aggression and stupidity, because you don't have a chance to examine anything when you are carried away by such great speed. As you drive yourself along through this speed, you collect all kinds of garbage, which is passion. This sudden flash of compassion cuts that speed, or at least slows it down. Somebody had to decide to puncture your car tire—which is *you!* As a result, you collect less dust, less garbage, on your woolly tail. The whole situation becomes more spacious and workable.

This applies not only to us as individuals personally, but it expands to working with other people as well. For instance, you might develop a sense that you want to help somebody. You feel very bad about someone and you want to help. You feel so excited about helping that person that you become very ambitious about that particular project. You want to make a clean sweep, create a new person; but your style is so ambitious, so speedy, that you fail to realize the details of what kind of help that person actually needs.

From the point of view of that person, you become a clown pretending to help him; there is no respect—and from your point of view, there is no time. You want to make a clean sweep, but instead you only create a thicker skin for that person, who begins to see through you and your speed. Seemingly you are acting in the name of compassion, but there is no room to be compassionate. So, in fact, it is an uncompassionate act. There is no time taken, and no patience. That kind of situation can be saved by a sudden glimpse, through looking. Such looking, such a compassionate glimpse, becomes extremely powerful, naturally workable.

Student: Could you briefly describe idiot compassion?

Chögyam Trungpa Rinpoche: Idiot compassion is the highly conceptualized idea that you want to do good to somebody. At this point, good is purely related with pleasure. For instance, somebody might say that a person needs an operation, and you defend him from the operation, saying, "He's sick already so why do we have to cut his body? We don't want to hurt him." But that is very primitive: we are trying to cure him, not destroy him. Idiot compassion also stems from not having enough courage to say no. Saying no means saying yes in the long run, but you are afraid to say that. It's like what often happens in Mexico and India. When you ask people the way, they don't want to say no to you; instead they say, "Yes, yes. It's very close. You turn right and turn right again and you'll be there." They don't say, "I don't know." That's a primitive form of idiot compassion.

S: I'm getting the sense that one should try to open oneself and be fully compassionate at least three times a day.

CTR: The idea of opening yourself is quite different from the primitive approach of repeating God's name or thinking higher thoughts a few times a day. It is abrupt awareness, awareness which looks at yourself. It doesn't have to be strategized, but it is abrupt, a glimpse. Krishnamurti referred to this experience as "choiceless awareness." You don't have to choose it—it comes to you. However, it seems that it is not as simple as that. You have to make some effort to decide to look, but not hold on to it.

S: Rinpoche, when you were analyzing this sudden glimpse the first time, you said that it has three stages: the first is warmth, or maitri; the second is cutting through neurosis; and the third is openness. Then a little later you went through it again and you gave the three stages slightly differently: the first as maitri; the second as gap or openness, tathagatagarbha; and the third as communication.

CTR: Piercing the chain of karma is regarded as creating a hole, so to speak, creating a gap, which is openness. But at the same time communication is also a form of openness. It is openness in the sense of not just creating a gap between you and your neighbor but going out toward it, which is saying the same thing.

S: Is the transition between the stages automatic?

CTR: At this point it is almost useless to talk about three stages, because the glimpse is so quick and so sudden that there is no point in taking notice of it. There is no point in analyzing it. The nature of the experience is that it does have those three stages. But it's not especially important to take notice of them. It just happens.

S: It seems possible that the awareness of the open space might be so attractive that you would want to stay there.

CTR: At that point you have to be able to give up. You have to deliberately push the experience away, disown it. That is extremely important. Otherwise you kill the whole thing. I mean, this glimpse is very simple. Just look! That's it. There's no problem with that.

S: Are we cognizant of the glimpse?

CTR: You are aware at the beginning and at the end, obviously. When somebody takes your photograph with a flashbulb, as it flashes you don't think, "Now my photograph is being taken"; you are just dazzled by the flash. *After,* you say, "Now my photograph has been taken"; and *before,* you say, "My photograph *will* be taken." But that is okay; we can't start perfectly.

S: Earlier you said that you just had to recall the idea, but later on you said that you can't use the past to try to re-create the glimpse.

CTR: The point is that you have a recollection that such a situation exists. Then you look, but you don't hold on to it. Rather than trying to re-create the experience you had yesterday, thinking it was a better flash than today's flash, recollection is a boundary, an outline. Deliberate action exists only at the boundary. Once you are *inside* the boundary, there is no point in making *further* boundaries. In fact, you can't—it is so quick. Before you even think you have made a boundary, you have lost it already. You haven't lost it, but it has passed away. It is very sudden.

S: It seems to me that it is so fast that it almost has a foolproofness to it; it's so fast you couldn't do it wrong.

CTR: That's the whole point. You can only go wrong at the beginning, by preparing too much. In that case your flash would be a very clumsy one. Actually, you are fooling yourself, you are not flashing. And at the end, you may congratulate yourself, trying to hang on to the tail of it.

S: When neurotic patterns get set up between people, they often become a vicious circle. All you have to do is cut that circle at one point, because once the circle is cut, there's a way out.

CTR: Once you cut the circle at one point, there is a possibility of setting chaos to the whole circle. But you still have memories of the circle, so you will still go on. The way out has to be repeated many times. The circle has to be sliced thoroughly all over.

S: Talking about idiot compassion, you were saying that you should *not* do everything for everybody. But Shantideva said he would do everything for everybody, more or less.

CTR: Of course you should do everything for everybody; there is no selection involved at all. But that doesn't mean to say that you have to be gentle all the time. Your gentleness could have heart, strength. In order that your compassion doesn't become idiot compassion, you have to use your intelligence. Otherwise, there could be the self-indulgence of thinking that you are creating a compassionate situation when in fact you are feeding the other person's aggression. If you go to a shop and the shopkeeper cheats you, and you go back and let him cheat you again, that doesn't seem to be a very healthy thing to do for others.

S: Is it better not to help people if you are in a speeded-up state and you don't have the awareness and the gap? Is it better to do nothing at all? Or is it possible that the gap can be created in the process of helping people?

CTR: That's it. You try to create a gap as you are helping people. You shouldn't give up.

S: You shouldn't go away and prepare yourself?

CTR: Everything happens on the spot, so there really is nothing to prepare. In any given situation, as things are exposed to you, the preparation and skillful means happen simultaneously.

S: When you reach a climax of hope and fear, there's a sudden relaxation. There's a really vivid moment of intense relaxation and emptiness. You are only likely to stay in it for a couple of seconds. Although it is very dramatic, it might last only for a few moments, like a flash in sitting. Is that the kind of experience you are talking about?

CTR: I think so, yes. It happens with any kind of clarity. The experience of clarity might last for half a day or half an hour, but you can't repeat it. That sudden glimpse is an aspect of clarity. It has a similar quality to the sudden glimpse of compassion.

S: Within the experience of clarity, are there gaps between the moments of clarity, or is it one whole thing?

CTR: It is one sudden thing you can't define. The scriptures talk about touching and penetrating and releasing compassion, but that almost becomes a myth because it happens so fast.

S: Is the time between glimpses a state of pure hell?

CTR: Whatever you would like to call it. It is *this.*

S: Would you say that the glimpse is stepping out of the whole wheel of life?

CTR: Not necessarily. The glimpse is just cutting the umbilical cord. Just that. Seeing the no-man's-land.

S: If you don't let go of the experience, I suppose that would make everything worse afterward. You would be struggling to get back there.

CTR: Yes, very much so. Then the experience becomes a trip. You keep trying to get higher and higher, better and better. Quite possibly we could categorize this by serial numbers—glimpse one, glimpse two, glimpse zero—which becomes a big trip.

S: How does this relate to the levels of absorption, or *dhyanas*, in hinayana?

CTR: The dhyana states are less abrupt—they are different intensities of rest. There is no flash of clarity, simply a kind of absorption. It's like being concerned with whether you had a good sleep, a bad sleep, or a relatively good one. The sudden glimpse cuts through those absorptions as well. So there are two levels: developing the experience of the realm of the gods, which is the dhyana states, and transcending the dhyana states, which is the development of wisdom. According to Buddhism, wisdom transcends the god realm. From this point of view, it is nirvana experience, rather than samsaric experience.

5

Leap of Confidence

SO FAR, we have not studied the bodhisattva path thoroughly; we have just had a preliminary glimpse of the bodhisattva path. We have an idea of the basic psychology of the bodhisattva, or the bodhisattva's mentality, and how one develops it. Now we could discuss the idea of commitment to the bodhisattva path and the bodhisattva vow.*

The bodhisattva's mentality consists of two aspects. The first aspect is the *general meditative state of mind*, the awareness or glimpse that we discussed in chapter 4. That is referred to as the absolute aspect. The second, or relative, aspect is *the actual application of this in our day-to-day life*. So the commitment of a person's whole being to the bodhisattva path involves not only a commitment to the basic sanity of the bodhisattva, but also the commitment not only to contemplative practice, but to working with situations that require decisions and the function of discursive thoughts to make the right decisions.

Joining the bodhisattva path is not by faith alone—there should be a sense of conviction and intelligence, almost to the level of intellect. It is important to be able to sort things out, to distinguish between

---

*This talk was given after the bodhisattva vow ceremony. The text of the bodhisattva vow is included as an appendix.

skillful means and unskillful means. You need to know how to work with situations, how to handle them. If you regard the bodhisattva path as purely following some preexisting law, with headlines of this and that, unless you know the bodhisattva's bible by heart, you cannot keep track of all that. But if you begin to see the bodhisattva path as an existing feeling or basic understanding, you realize that skillful means is not based on prescriptions in books but on prescriptions given by your own innate nature or basic understanding.

Having taken the bodhisattva vow and committed yourself to the bodhisattva path, there's a tremendous sense of excitement. You want to do everything and handle every situation extraordinarily. You feel that you could save people on the spot, that you could help people by sacrificing your next meal or your next nap. But that doesn't seem to be quite enough. In fact, quite possibly, if you do not take care of your own body and energy, your bodhisattva action will become very sloppy and tedious as a result of your being too tired. You have been putting too much energy into working with other people without regard to your own basic health. So the bodhisattva's skillful means does not only go outward; it also involves tremendous concern for one's own body, one's own basic being. There is a sense of responsibility in all directions.

The sense of excitement can be an obstacle on the bodhisattva path. You feel so excited that you want to convert everybody to your trip. You would like to make everyone a replica of yourself. This is one of the first big mistakes that an adolescent bodhisattva can make. There is so much inspiration, so much energy, that you begin to feel that you could conquer the whole world. There is so much conviction that the bodhisattva could be blinded by it. You are not able to see the situation beyond that emotional conviction and sense of excitement.

At the same time, that conviction should be nursed. The idea is not just to play it safe. Security is not in question, particularly. What is lacking in that approach is vision. Your vision is limited; you are unable to see. Rather than developing the panoramic vision to see how the whole thing works, you are purely interested in converting other people to the bodhisattva path. But in the bodhisattva path there is a sense of totality. There is *comprehensive* vision, seeing what needs to be done in the present situation, but at the same time, not being rushed into it. There is a sense of experiencing what comes next, an emphasis on the future and on creating the right atmosphere or working base for that. It is about relating with other people.

The question is whether or not the bodhisattva's attitude is involved with the ambition of ego. Even if the bodhisattva's ego is associated with enlightenment, it is still ego; so it is subject to spiritual materialism. On the bodhisattva path there is a sense of giving away and destroying your ambition at the same time as you are building your inspiration. That is one of the basic points of skillful means: you have enough power to exert your energy, but at the same time you have enough gentleness to change your decisions to suit the given situation.

The bodhisattva's approach is a gentle but powerful effort, which is based on prajna. Here prajna involves both skillful means and knowledge. Developing basic prajna is almost like becoming an enlightened politician. You are aware of the surrounding situation, but at the same time you are also aware of your version of it. So you don't just give in to what is happening, but your version has something to do with it as well. Every corner has been seen with the skillful means of the bodhisattva approach.

Texts such as *Forty-six Ways in Which a Bodhisattva Fails,** which describe the bodhisattva discipline, talk about not presenting the dharma if the listener is uninterested, not associating with heretics,

---

*This traditional text on the many ways a bodhisattva may fail to practice the six paramitas, translated by the Nālandā Translation Committee, can be found in the book *Training the Mind and Cultivating Loving-Kindness* by Chögyam Trungpa (Boston: Shambhala Publications, 1993).

and not refusing an invitation to teach. All those guidelines, if you look at them very generally, may seem to be illogical and confusing. But once you begin to look at them as they apply to real, definite situations, you can see that they have a logical working basis. When there is a pull toward ego, that could be cut. When there is hesitation to step outside of ego, to loosen one's grip, one could let loose and go. When there is hesitation about not being able to make a correct decision, one could push oneself into the situation so that the direction comes about naturally.

Skillful means, from the point of view of prajna mentality, could be said to be slightly paranoid or fearful of consequences. This is a product of egolessness, because if you have nothing, if there is no project to achieve, if you are not drawing things in your direction, then there is a sense of ambition. That empty-heartedness could be said to be paranoid. At the same time, there is the inspiration to deal with situations perfectly and directly. So there is also a sense of pride. This is not pride in the pejorative sense, but pride in the sense of clear perception—seeing what needs to be done, what should be fulfilled. So the bodhisattva mentality of skillful means consists of a sense of ambition and also a sense of tentativeness. Tentativeness means allowing suggestions to come to you from outside, so that you can utilize situations. You are not afraid to do so, because that whole process is one's basic inspiration.

There seems to be a tremendous subtlety of perception in the bodhisattva path. That subtlety comes from a sense of basic warmth, a compassionate mentality, along with the shunyata mentality of openness—compassion and openness operating simultaneously. It seems to be extremely difficult to develop that just by magic. We cannot develop it by doing some unrelated technique like standing on our heads or reciting certain formulas that supposedly provide sympathetic vibrations toward that practice. According to the bodhisattva's way, we have to get into it—we have to *do it!* It is as if we had all those faculties such as generosity, patience, discipline, energy, meditation, and knowledge already in us. On the whole, some kind of leap seems to be necessary—leap in the sense of developing basic confidence. We might feel that we are inadequate, but nevertheless we pretend we can do it. We push ourselves into that situation. It is similar to taking the bodhisattva vow. There is tremendous pretense involved. We are uncertain whether we are able to tread the bodhisattva's path or not, but we still decide to do it. This confidence is known as *pranidhana*, which means "vision."

Fundamentally there is hope. There is space for vision, space where vision could be worked through and distributed. Looking back and looking to the future are equally necessary, particularly in actually practicing the bodhisattva's way in day-to-day living. There is a sense of fearlessness, that there is a solid working basis. We don't have to shy away from what is happening, and, at the same time, we don't have to exaggerate it either. We could just accept the given situation and work with it directly and simply as it happens.

Student: The bodhisattva has committed himself to save all sentient beings, yet he himself is a sentient being. How is he different?

Chögyam Trungpa Rinpoche: The bodhisattva has vision. He is already inspired, whereas the others are not—so he has to work with them. As far as he is concerned, his salvation is there already; he doesn't particularly have to cultivate it. What he has to cultivate is working with others who might lack his openness.

S: Rinpoche, you said that a bodhisattva should take care of his body and energy in order not to overextend himself. How can he do that without living a self-centered life?

CTR: I think that comes naturally. A bodhisattva has a natural sense of the limits of his own physical strength. A bodhisattva wouldn't punish himself or say, "That's just my imagination, my comfort-oriented trip." The difference between impulse and a real need would be quite obvious.

S: Could there be a problem if a person wants to take the bodhisattva vow for the wrong reasons?

CTR: That's possible.

S: In a situation like that, would it make sense to leap over the uncertainty, or would that be a further obstacle and just add to the confusion?

CTR: If the bodhisattva has a wrong attitude, there will naturally be some chaos creating obstacles to his journey. Things won't fit together, things won't fall into a workable situation. Obviously, instead of giving away his ego-oriented ambition, he is working toward Rudrahood.

S: You talked about the seriousness of deciding to make a leap. I'm wondering if it is possible, having made that leap, to realize you were wrong. If so, could you change directions at that point, or would it be better just to continue along as you are?

CTR: I don't think you can maneuver around it. You have to make a definite break, a fresh start. The problem is that you have not been able to surrender your ego. When you suddenly try to do so and get back to the right path, you cannot do it because there has been no basic generosity or surrendering. Sooner or later you have to be humiliated. Sooner or later your ego has to be humiliated. You have to face that. That requires an operation, a big jump, a drastic change. It requires that you not continue to follow the process you are on, but acknowledge that it is not a very positive approach. It requires that you come back and change your mind.

6

Identifying with the Teachings

THE SKILLFUL MEANS of the bodhisattva extends to a sense of identifying with the practice. If there is no identification with the teachings and the practice of the bodhisattva—if a person has a purely intellectual relationship with the teachings and the hope that the spiritual friend may be able to guide him—there seems to be a discrepancy. The bodhisattva's way is one of tremendous identification with the dharma. The dharma is no longer regarded as simply following the books, the scriptures, or the doctrine—dharma is following one's own conviction. When such conviction has been awakened in the bodhisattva, the teachings become pure confirmation. That is a very important point.

If a person has not completely taken refuge in the dharma as a path and has not completely taken the vow in the way of the bodhisattva, there is still an impersonal attitude toward the teachings; so making a commitment is very complicated. In deciding whether you should commit yourself to the teachings or not, you are still thinking of it in terms of joining a club or society rather than as a real pursuit.

In relating with the teachings of the bodhisattva path, commitment means that a person has already surrendered the notion of intellectual speculation on the teachings. He or she has also surrendered the need for proof. So that person does not ask, "If I do this, what result am I going to gain?" He has given up such theorizing and searching for security. He has given up the need to know that what he is getting into is foolproof and really works. If you are buying a new gadget, there is no point in possessing that gadget if it doesn't work. But the bodhisattva's way has nothing at all to do with purchasing anything or joining a club—it is simply commitment to the practice and to the teachings. That commitment comes from the individual rather than from any external reinforcement.

The bodhisattva's way of relating to the spiritual friend is similar, in that the spiritual friend is seen as the vanguard or spokesman of the teachings. As the bodhisattva works with the spiritual friend, he is also working with his own involvement and commitment to the teachings; so the spiritual friend and the teachings are complementary. Therefore, for the bodhisattva, making a definite decision to be involved with the spiritual friend is not a big deal, or the only hope he or she can latch on to. Neither is purely dealing with the teachings without the spiritual friend a big deal. They are complementary, both ways.

Basically, we could summarize the teachings of the bodhisattva path as a way of transcending aggression. You are working with aggression, and as you begin to work with aggression, that commitment becomes part of your practice. Doctrinal studies do not bring out your aggression, although doctrinal texts talk about how to deal with aggression; living life brings out aggression and speed. Leading your life automatically shows you how to relate with the complexities of your mental activities and emotions.

Identification with the teachings also means developing a sense of friendship with the doctrine. The teachings are regarded as a friendly message rather than reading a menu. When you read a menu, you develop a businesslike mentality. How much does it cost? Which is the most delicious food to order? You are rejecting one dish and ordering another dish. With a sense of friendliness toward the doctrine, or the dharma, you cannot pick and choose. It is a complete process. You can't say, "I prefer generosity rather than patience, so I'll have that." For that matter, you cannot reject the hinayana and only accept the mahayana. You must begin with hinayana and slowly proceed along to the mahayana. If you are able to do that, that is the real demonstration of identification with the teachings.

As we identify with the teachings, at the same time we can also identify with the teacher, or the spiritual friend. However, there is a certain kind of watcher, a certain aggression, which keeps us from identifying with the teachings. It includes, for one thing, the businesslike mentality of always asking, "Which is the safest and best thing to do? What is the most efficient approach?" We watch ourselves developing or not developing, and when we get bored with what we are doing, we are always looking at possibilities of changing course. For instance, if we are bored with one class, we look into another class or another department.

There is also a sense of personal indignation, that you don't want to be reduced into a nonexistent person. Each time the penetrating words of the teachings begin to come through, you feel personally humiliated. To the extent that you did not know these things and somebody else did—that somebody else knew better than you—you are constantly challenged. There is a sense of competition. Connected with this is that you want to impress your friends, your students, and other people. You are looking for topics or subjects you can use to impress people. You wouldn't tell people, "I just read about this topic this morning," but you would talk about it as if you had known it for a long time. All those situations—such as the sense of indignation, the sense of wanting to impress other people, or the sense of wanting to choose the best one—pervert the teachings. They are based on failing to identify with the teachings.

In the hinayana path, you are pushed into disciplines and there are all kinds of recommendations. The way of identifying with the dharma is to regard the dharma as a whip. The truth of suffering is somewhat external: it pushes you like a whip behind a slave. In the mahayana, it is much more open than that. It is only by identifying with the teachings that you are inspired—that is what pushes you. You are not taking refuge in the dharma as something external or purely a command; the dharma is something you identify yourself with. If there is any discrepancy or any doubt—"Should I get into it? Should I jump into it or shouldn't I?"—that is a sign of being unable to identify with the teachings as the truth. The teachings are still regarded as taking out an insurance policy. It is still business mentality.

In the beginning of the bodhisattva path there is the development of maitri, making friends with oneself. Maitri is an experience. It is not that somebody is telling you how to make friends with yourself so you are pushed into it. That doesn't happen. Rather you find yourself making friends. You have to make friends with yourself and see the logic that you are good or bad not as praise or threat but as something you have to work on. You can work on yourself.

Finding a spiritual friend is also a way of involving yourself with the teachings. The spiritual friend acts as a mirror reflection. Your doubts and hesitations are being thrown back at you, so you feel extremely threatened and confused. Your own private parts are exposed by the medium of the spiritual friend, in that mirror reflection. In that way, you develop further involvement with the teachings.

The development of compassion and the paramita practices of generosity, patience, discipline, and so forth, are also ways of involving yourself further with the teachings. Rather than being converted into this particular trip, there is a sense of constantly being challenged and having to get yourself involved. It is like eating and drinking. When you are hungry you eat food, when you are thirsty you drink water. It is not necessary that you believe or have faith in the food and water. You have a personal demand for food and water because food protects you from hunger, and water protects you from thirst. So you create the food and you create the water, rather than someone pushing you into eating and drinking. You feel a real need.

When you feel tired, you fall asleep—you feel your need to rest. Likewise with generosity, you feel your need to open more, so you get into being more generous. With discipline, you feel you need to put yourself in situations in which you can work with the details of life rather than frivolously ignoring the whole thing. So you get into discipline. Patience is also necessary, because without something to work with to develop patience, you feel constant boredom, constant loss of the substance of life. So you get into patience because you need to create further substance and solidity in your life. In regard to energy, working hard, you feel worn out. You feel used up by the sense of constant speed. Your energy has been lost, so you need to build it up—therefore you work hard, diligently.

Meditation is likewise. When your whole experience is scattered, with no structure, and your subconscious mind of discursive thoughts and emotions is shooting out all over the place, there is no focus, no paying attention. So you develop meditation—to simplify all those complications. With prajna, or knowledge, you begin to feel that you are so vague and diffused that there's no definite understanding of things as they are. Because there is tremendous vagueness, you need to develop prajna, knowledge.

None of these paramita practices are imposed on you. It is not that somebody says it is good for you to practice the paramitas although it is painful. Paramita practice is something you feel you need. Paramita practice is like eating food when you are hungry, drinking water when you are thirsty, or resting when you are tired.

As long as we have awakened to the attitude of heroism of the bodhisattva's way, we are going to proceed along. We are not going to rest. Even when we do rest, it is part of our journey. If we are not walking but resting, that is only to regain further energy to walk. As long as there is a sense of ongoing process rather than wanting to stay in the snugness of self-indulgence of ego's neurosis, there is a constant journey taking place.

That constant journey demands certain requirements. Various skillful means are necessary. These skillful means come along as we feel we need them. On the whole this is the result of our commitment to the teachings. We feel one with the teachings as we feel one with our body. Because we feel one with our body, we feel what our body needs. Our body needs rest, shelter, clothing, food, drink. Similarly, because we feel one with the teachings, with all these skillful means and practices of the bodhisattva way, we feel intuitively what needs to be done. In other words, unless there is a sense of involvement with the teachings, complete identification with the teachings, whatever we try to do is like shooting an arrow in the dark. Most often it is ineffective, and it does not fulfill the demands we want to achieve.

On the whole we could say that the basic definition of the bodhisattva path is that sense of involvement and identification with the teachings. It is complete identification with the teachings and with life; complete identification with bodhisattva, with buddha nature, with the paramitas, and with the spiritual friend. There is something *real* about the whole thing. You are not afraid to get into it, to latch on to it.

Identification with the teachings is an important point of the bodhisattva path and the teachings of mahayana. It is not that you have to be smart so that you can choose which item is the best to have. At the same time, it is not based on blind faith either. Instead, you feel what you *need*, and you *involve* yourself in it. The mahayana is based on a sense of sympathy toward oneself, compassion toward oneself. If you don't relate with your body, with your basic being, so to speak, there is no sympathy to your being. Without sympathy, you would purely be involving yourself with a fantasy dream world, rather than actually experiencing what needs to be done—which is a very intelligent act rather than an act of blind faith.

That seems to be the summary of mahayana practice: complete identification with the teachings. Bodhichitta is implanted in your heart. Therefore, you are the embodiment of bodhichitta, the awakened state of mind. Your creation, your being is bodhichitta. You are no longer dealing with foreign elements coming from outside; you are awakening your intelligence as you go along. Your intelligence becomes greater and greater, more and more powerful. It begins to eat through the skins of ego, the layers and layers of ego-manufactured walls and barriers. That's why the idea of *awake* rather that *saved* is important in the bodhisattva approach.

Student: You have emphasized maintaining a cynical attitude. When we choose the bodhisattva path, do we give that up, or is giving that up blind faith?

Chögyam Trungpa Rinpoche: Giving up cynicism is blind faith. When you develop an intelligent attitude as to what you definitely need, the frivolity of what you may not need but you think you need could be stripped away by a cynical attitude. Once you identify with the teachings, you begin to know what would be best and what would be a frivolous thing to do. As you go along, there will be successive frivolous mentalities happening—and you could cut those down.

S: There seems to be a very strong desire to confirm the reality of the teachings, to have a glimpse that it actually happens. You want it to be true so much that the desire itself can become an obstacle. That desire could be an expression of the *lack* of faith in the teachings. So it could be an expression of faith in the teachings *not* to push on all the time.

CTR: Even if you decide not to push, you are still making a forward journey. It is like changing your car tire when you have a puncture.

That is also a part of the journey you are going along. So it's the same thing.

S: Rinpoche, what is the difference between the way the sangha, the people we are living with, become mirrors to us and the way you represent a mirror to us?

CTR: I don't see any difference, particularly. In the case of your own friends, even if something reflects back on you, you may not believe that it is the real mirror. However, when you work with the teacher, you feel that the mirror must be a more profound one. But in actual fact, it is the same thing. It is a question of how much you are open to it.

S: When you are dealing with your friends, the question arises of your trips and their trips. It is different than with the spiritual friend, where you have the confidence to say, "It's *your* trip." You don't have to try to sort out this trip and that trip.

CTR: I think that's a matter of opinion, actually. It's like going to a surgeon who is your relative or going to a surgeon who has nothing to do with you. The surgeon who is your relative might have a personal concern about you, so he might make a mistake. So you go to somebody who is impersonal to you instead.

S: In dealing with our friends, it seems necessary to consider their trips in terms of the mirror reflection.

CTR: I suppose it's a question of what part is your version of them bouncing back on you and what part is really their true nature.

S: Rinpoche, what do you mean by their true nature?

CTR: Their true nature is different from your version of them. The true nature of the other person may be an act of neurosis, of frivolousness, or whatever.

S: When you are relating to another person, is their true nature their buddha nature, or is their true nature the way they manifest themselves? Is their true nature what is there beyond their hostilities and aggression, or is their true nature just their trips? Is it the way they are, their style, their buddha nature, everything?

CTR: I think of true nature in terms of their neurosis as well as their insight. It's their basic being. In other words, you don't lay preconceptions on them. Therefore you could see their neurosis coming out of them as well as insight coming out of them—which is very hard to do.

S: So their true nature is where they are at the time, which you can't possibly understand?

CTR: Quite possibly you can't—but there is a possibility that you might be able to do so.

S: I feel that I need awareness in order to keep the refuge and bodhisattva vows, but I see that I'm not aware. There's always this haunting feeling that I'm not keeping the vows because I don't have the necessary awareness. Are you saying that I should have faith that this awareness will come?

CTR: You don't have to develop awareness, particularly. As long as you see that you are *not* aware, that in itself is awareness.

S: But that doesn't help me work with the bodhisattva path. There isn't any discrimination. I'm not aware enough to deal with situations.

CTR: If you realize that you aren't aware, that's the whole point. You don't have to catch yourself being aware all the time. You do not have to feel good or to feel that you are always a solid, balanced person—the idea is to catch yourself. You see that you are not aware, then you create a gap. That gap doesn't necessarily have to be a good one; it could be a quite horrific one. Nevertheless, that gap in itself becomes very helpful because you begin to see that you are not aware of it.

S: How does that help?

CTR: It begins to break the chain reaction of speed.

S: Does it let you become more aware after that?

CTR: That is awareness.

S: Rinpoche, you said that as you go along the bodhisattva path, you feel a real need for certain practices, like the paramita practices; so nothing is imposed on you. There seems to be a very fuzzy line in my head between an intellectual approach and the way needs appear in my mind. Things seem to be coming out of my mind, but I am not sure whether they are thoughts or the gap.

CTR: Once you begin to analyze the nature of need, you are treating yourself and the teachings impersonally. I mean, we don't have intellectual hunger when we want to eat food; we have real hunger. We actually, physically need food. So there is no room for analyzing. The whole thing has to be very straightforward and very direct. It has to be abrupt.

S: Rinpoche, is recognizing the gap, the gap, or not recognizing it? Are you aware when it is taking place?

CTR: You do have some awareness when it is taking place. It is like when you suddenly fall down: you have some sense that you fell down. But then there is another kind of awareness, which is confirming that gap. That comes much later.

S: Rinpoche, where does hunger for the dharma come from? Does it come from something that happened in previous lives?

CTR: It is a very real thing. You feel that you are inadequate and you need further strength at that given moment—and you pick up on it. It's a very natural thing. Something is missing, and you want to fill the gap.

S: Rinpoche, could you talk a bit more about complete identification with the teachings?

CTR: Identifying with the teachings means that the teachings are not regarded as belonging to the teacher alone, but they are also a part of you. That is precisely what is meant by the teachings being true. If they are true, basically, they should apply to you as well to the teacher. When there is a fire, the fire maker gets burned as well as the person watching the fire. So there is no *belonging*, as far as the teachings are concerned. They are not purely information, they exist as a living situation. So the teachings transcend doctrine. In this sense, the teachings have nothing to do with the technical aspects of the dharma—they are just reality.

S: Could the same thing be said for the teacher?

CTR: Yes. That seems to be the meaning of spiritual friend. The spiritual friend is a friend for all, rather than a friend for one particular situation or one particular person.

S: You said something about not trusting your body. I'm not sure what you mean by that.

CTR: It's a question of feeling that there is a natural organic situation happening. If you don't relate with that, then your ground is lost, and you have no way of developing clarity. Body, in this case, is a sense of experience, real experience.

S: You said we should pretend as if we can practice in this way, but in trying to practice generosity, patience, or meditation, what happens is that you see your lack, that you are *not* really generous, patient, and so forth. You have this feeling of always being less than the teachings, rather than feeling you are up to it, or you can master it, or it is coming through you.

CTR: As long as you begin to make everything solid and sure,

I don't think you can get anywhere. As you begin to realize your deception, that is another deception. So you have to trust your first perception of being a fool. You start by being a fool. You are giving away security, being a fool.

S: Rinpoche, among the contradictions to the paramita of morality is not committing evil acts for the sake of compassion. Another contradiction to the paramita of morality is rejecting immoral people. Those seem to be extraordinary reversals of ordinary emotions and morality. Could you say something about that?

CTR: From the hinayana point of view, or a very traditional idea of evil, such actions are evil. However, in the mahayana, if somebody is so highly involved with food that they have stashes of food stuck in their room, it is your duty to steal it from them. That is an evil act according to hinayana—you should not steal—but in the mahayana you are *supposed* to do that! It is some kind of a joke!

S: If you are angry, should you just be aware of that and have faith that it is all going to work out okay? Suppose you think it is harmful and you want to stop doing it—do you have any advice on skillful means for dealing with that, or for imposing some kind of discipline on yourself?

CTR: If you have an impulse that you want to kill somebody, and you have faith that you are going to kill that person and it's going to be okay—somehow that doesn't work. The very act of killing somebody is a cowardly thing to do. You can have faith in your anger—but you don't have to kill somebody, particularly. That anger is a self-contained thing, so going as far as murdering somebody doesn't apply. The point is to have faith in the basic being of the anger, rather than having faith in the impulse.

S: Many times the action you do arises spontaneously out of the impulse.

CTR: Such actions could be regarded as needless.

S: When you feel an impulse, such as the impulse to have a cigarette, is it really important whether you act on it or not, if you are aware of both the impulse and the action? Maybe that is being too hard or strict on yourself.

CTR: I think there are degrees of actions, of how much rebounds from your actions, and how much your actions are free. If you have to go to the toilet, you don't say that is purely in the mind, or a frivolous thing, unless it is obviously psychosomatic. Some actions are not regarded as frivolous, but organic. Saying that going out and murdering someone is frivolous is another matter altogether. You don't have to go out and kill somebody in order to survive, like you need to go to the toilet. It's a different matter altogether. So there is a sense of fantasy and there is a sense of reality. The question is what your body needs in order to survive and what your emotion needs in order to survive.

S: What do you mean by rebound?

CTR: When things become heavy-handed, you get consequences. If an action is just simple and direct, then there are no consequences.

S: Rinpoche, can you give an example?

CTR: Smoking a cigarette and killing somebody are entirely different. Killing someone needs more emotional buildup; smoking a cigarette needs less. However, if you had planted a bomb in the cigarette or you had been told that smoking a cigarette is a terrible, sinful, destructive thing to do, it could become the same as murdering somebody because of your attitude.

S: In that situation, should one try to lose that attitude and make it a simple act, or realize that it is complicated?

CTR: It depends on how you approach it. It is possible that Hitler's attitude toward murdering Jews was to him like smoking another cigarette. It all depends on your attitude, how crazy you are.

S: Would it be true to say that if you act simply and directly, there are no consequences, but if you did the same thing calculating with your intellect or with your emotions, then you would create more karma for yourself? It isn't necessarily the type of act you do that matters?

CTR: It is your attitude *as well as* what type of act you do. Any action you do has all kinds of attitudes in it already. Whatever you do had different degrees of heaviness, so you can't just say everything is just attitude; action has something to do with it as well. I mean, breaking bottles is different from murdering somebody. Different attitudes go with different actions. So they are reciprocal.

S: In the case of the samurai warrior, their killing somebody may be a very simple and direct thing.

CTR: I wouldn't say the samurai warrior is acting within the attitude of the enlightenment approach. But their style, their philosophy, is fearlessness, which is good. The case of Buddha killing the bandit to save five hundred people's lives is another question. Five hundred people are more important than one person. So it is a matter of degree, a matter of how much consequences are involved with that act.

S: How can the Buddha be sure that one person would kill the five hundred people? He hadn't killed the five hundred people yet.

CTR: Maybe he had a record; we do not know.

S: If I know I don't need the cigarette, if I know it is frivolous, a fantasy, is it my duty as a bodhisattva not to have one?

CTR: It seems to be purely up to you whether you regard smoking cigarettes as frivolous or as just something that you do, a simple act.

S: Actions and impulses are very subtle. It is often difficult to determine whether acting is acting on impulse or acting spontaneously. How does one go about detecting the difference?

CTR: It depends. Certain actions mean a lot to you and certain actions are pure occupation; certain actions are harmful and certain actions are communication. When you are trying to destroy somebody or to create destruction, that action is not an expression of compassion; it is unaware and insensitive. Communication is connected with love and compassion. It says in the bodhisattva texts that passion is preferable to aggression because passion accepts the situation and aggression rejects the situation. That is one of the ideas of the bodhisattva path.

S: Is judging other people's actions a dangerous, self-defeating process?

CTR: It seems that way, unless there is some warmth in the judgment, in that you want to relate with those people and help them. Otherwise, it becomes very cold. You are just sharpening your sword.

S: Not expressing your emotions might be viewed as cutting off communication. That could be a problem.

CTR: The whole point is to start by communicating with yourself. Seventy-five percent of the world is you; after that, there is another world outside, the other twenty-five percent. If you don't cut communication with yourself, if you are completely in communication with yourself, then there is no problem. Expression comes out naturally.

Appendix

THE BODHISATTVA VOW

Just like the earth and space itself
And all the other mighty elements,
For boundless multitudes of beings
May I always be the ground of life, the source
    of varied sustenance.

Thus for everything that lives,
As far as are the limits of the sky,
May I be constantly their source of livelihood
Until they pass beyond all sorrow.

Just as all the Buddhas of the past
Have brought forth the awakened mind,
And in the precepts of the Bodhisattvas
Step-by-step abode and trained,

Likewise, for the benefit of beings,
I will bring to birth the awakened mind,
And in those precepts, step-by-step,
I will abide and train myself.

Those who thus with clear intelligence
Take hold of the awakened mind with bright and lucid joy,
That they may now increase what they have gained,
Should lift their hearts with praises such as these:

"Today my life has given fruit.
This human state has now been well assumed.
Today I take my birth in Buddha's line,
And have become the Buddha's child and heir.

"In every way, then, I will undertake
Activities befitting such a rank.
And I will do no act to mar
Or compromise this high and faultless lineage.

"For I am like a blind man who has found
A precious gem inside a heap of dust.
For so it is, by some strange chance,
That bodhichitta has been born in me.

"This is the supreme draft of immortality
That slays the Lord of Death, the slaughterer of beings,
The rich unfailing treasure-mine
To heal the poverty of wanderers.

"It is the sovereign remedy
That perfectly allays all maladies.
It is the tree that gives relief
To those who wander wearily the pathways of existence.

"It is the universal bridge that saves
All wandering beings from the states of loss,

The rising moon of the enlightened mind
That soothes the sorrows born of the afflictions.

"It is the mighty sun that utterly dispels
The misty ignorance of wandering beings,
The creamy butter, rich and full,
That's churned from milk of holy teaching.

"Living beings! Wayfarers upon life's paths,
Who wish to taste the riches of contentment,
Here before you is the supreme bliss.
Here, O ceaseless travelers, is your fulfillment!

"And so, today, within the sight of all protectors,
I summon beings, calling them to buddhahood.
And, till that state is reached, to every earthly joy!
May gods and demigods and all the rest rejoice!"

GLIMPSES OF SHUNYATA

1

Open Space of Shunyata

THIS SEMINAR IS ON shunyata, although we are quite uncertain what shunyata actually is. It seems that shunyata means not that, not this. So we shouldn't have a discussion at all. If it's not that, not this—what else? We could sit around and scrounge up something to discuss, but it seems to be insignificant, totally irrelevant.

The expectation to hear about shunyata is an obstacle; the shunyata principle does not lie in the expectation. We might get into the idea of what shunyata means: *shunya* means "empty," and *ta* means "ness," so *shunyata* means "emptiness." It is vaguely connected with the idea of the attainment of enlightenment. The idea of the attainment of enlightenment is based on ignorance, which is the opposite of enlightenment. So if you accept shunyata, you have to accept ignorance and enlightenment simultaneously. Therefore the shunyata principle is accepting the language of samsara as the language of enlightenment. When we talk about aggression, passion, and confusion, that automatically is the language of shunyata: Aggression as opposed to what? Passion as opposed to what? Ignorance as opposed to what? That kind of open space is related to the shunyata principle.

What we are trying to achieve with this particular seminar is to understand shunyata as such—that does not exist because of this, this does not exist because of that. We expect some concrete answer, something definite, something solid, but solidity itself depends on frivolousness, so to speak. Shunyata as opposed to the natural situation, or things as they are, seems to be a very important point to work with. The idea of shunyata depends on what is not shunyata—which is based on ego's manifestation.

We would like an ego manifestation of solidity: "I would like to understand that; I would like to comprehend that; I would like to attain enlightenment." So the idea of shunyata is based on the ambition to understand what shunyata is. If you are willing to give away that basic ambition, then shunyata seems to be there already. Therefore the shunyata principle is not dependent on that or this; it is based on transcending dualistic perceptions—and at the same time dwelling on dualistic ideas. The mantra of shunyata is OM GATE GATE PARAGATE PARASAMGATE BODHI SVAHA, which means "Gone, gone, gone beyond, that which is related to basic enlightenment mind is the essence of everything."

As far as shunyata goes, that you decided to come and take part in this particular seminar is futile. You might meet with disappointment in that this seminar does not say what is or what isn't. And you cannot get your money's worth. In other words, you can't get your money back. Oh, no! You expect too much. You're not going to be refunded. It' *your* hang-up, expecting too much out of shunyata, which means nothing! But it means everything at the same time.

We could have a discussion if you like. Please.

Student: You mean to say our money is gone, gone, gone—
[*Laughter*]
Chögyam Trungpa Rinpoche: Somewhat.

S: What's the relationship between shunyata and prajnaparamita?
CTR: Shunyata is the subject that prajnaparamita perceives.

S: Is it still a dual situation?

CTR: Shunyata? Sure.

S: I thought you said it transcended dualism.

CTR: Nonshunyata. Nonemptiness.

S: I'm not sure I quite understand how shunyata can now be dual, because I thought you said shunyata transcended dualism.

CTR: Shunyata is, in this case, nondwelling. But nondwelling in itself means dwelling on nondwelling. So we have to transcend shunyata from that point of view.

S: That's like saying not-two is one. But in previous seminars not-two is not-one, not-two—just the way things are. So nondwelling is not necessarily dwelling.

CTR: In previous seminars two is not one, in terms of meaning. But in this case, *one* is not one. [*Laughter*]

S: Well, why was the subject of shunyata ever brought up? [*Laughter*] Mentioning it seems to add something to the situation.

CTR: Because the subject of shunyata is there already.

S: I never thought of it! I never thought of shunyata. [*Laughter*]

CTR: Because of that, because you haven't thought of it, it is there already. It happens.

S: You mean the absence of that thought itself is emptiness?

CTR: Yeah, somewhat.

S: What do you think we should discuss tomorrow in our discussion period?

CTR: Shunyata. [*Laughter*]

S: Is it prajna that is negating? Is it prajna saying "not-this"?

CTR: Not necessarily. You see, the whole point is that there is something worth exploring—and having explored the whole thing, we discover nothing. But it's not worth it not to explore either, because things are so. [*Vidyadhara snaps fan shut.*] OM GATE GATE PARAGATE PARA-*SAM*-GATE BODHI SVAHA.

S: Gone *safely* beyond, right?

CTR: No!

S: In my translation of the *Heart Sutra* it says, "Gone, gone, gone safely beyond."

CTR: Safely?! [*Laughter*]

S: "Safely beyond," yeah.

CTR: Must have been translated on Madison Avenue. [*Laughter*]

S: I doubt it.

CTR: Possibly.

S: So how do you translate it?

CTR: "Gone, gone, gone beyond, no security saves you whatever." *Para* means "beyond," like the idea of parapsychology, it means "beyond concept"—"gone, gone, gone beyond the idea of gone beyond"—*sam* means "complete"; *gate* means "gone." Simple.

S: There's a translation that reads "gone *fully* beyond." Would you say that's a good one?

CTR: You don't need that kind of adjective [*laughter*]—because it is so! Black is black, white is white! So what, after that? It's as obvious as that.

S: If prajna cuts through duality, is that an action that evolves into shunyata? Does the operation itself still remain after that?

CTR: It seems that if you think it is involved, it is so; whereas if you don't think it is involved, it does not exist. It is purely up to your expectations. Quite simple. It is purely up to you. The teaching depends on you. In other words, samsara depends on nirvana and nirvana depends on samsara.

S: What I was trying to get at is that there seems to be something that remains after shunyata, because you said that after shunyata you get non-shunyata.

CTR: That's up to you.

S: Excuse me?

CTR: That's up to you.

S: That's just a view?

CTR: Up to you, up to you! It depends on you! It doesn't have to be that way. If you want some security, it always happens that way.

S: There's a statement that emptiness is form and form is emptiness. Is there a progressive relationship between the two?

CTR: I don't think so, because they are defeating each other. The statements defeat each other. Emptiness is form, therefore form is emptiness—they are defeating each other all the time, destroying the previous statement successively. So you have nothing to dwell on at all. Black is white, white is black. The statements defeat each other all the time, so you don't have anything to dwell on anymore at all. That's it.

S: But the dwelling still exists, although faintly.

CTR: Doesn't exist.

S: It doesn't exist?

CTR: Because you are already busted. [*Laughter*]

S: As well as absorbed into nirvana.

CTR: I don't know about nirvana.

S: Whatever, yeah.

S: Is there a relationship to skillful means?

CTR: That is skillful means!

S: Shunyata *is* skillful means?

CTR: Yes.

S: Then how come in the symbolism you have a symbol for each?

CTR: I've never seen a symbol for each.

S: I was under the impression that the *dorje,* or the thunderbolt, was symbolic of skillful means, and the bell was symbolic of shunyata, and that Dorje Chang holds both of them and that they're joined together.

CTR: So what?

S: That is why I was asking you, so what?

CTR: I don't know. I have no idea! [*Laughter*] I don't understand about that!

S: Neither do I.

CTR: I don't know!

S: What is the stage after shunyata?

CTR: I don't know! [*Laughter*]

S: Does anyone?

CTR: Your guess is as good as mine. I really don't know! [*Laughter*]

S: There are all sorts of practices, like mahamudra, that come after the shunyata experience.

CTR: I don't know.

S: Who knows?

CTR: Nobody! I really don't know!

S: Is it possible to be absorbed in shunyata materialistically, spiritually materialistically?

CTR: It is possible, definitely, yes. If you think you have grasped shunyata, you've been absorbed into it as a sedative, which is very dangerous. But beyond that there is no danger. So it is quite possible.

S: To be absorbed into it as a sedative?

CTR: Yes.

S: Could you explain what you mean by that?

CTR: Sedative! Quite simple.

S: To use it as a sedative you would have to *think* you've grasped shunyata.

CTR: Sure.

S: Which means you really haven't?

CTR: That's right. [*Laughter*] You are quite right. Well said!

S: Is the sedative quality related to the fact that shunyata experience accompanies the idea of giving up expectations, but that giving up expectations is a hang-up?

CTR: Yes.

S: So the sedative quality comes from the fact that you've given everything up—

CTR: That you have some technique to do it. Technique is a sedative, as it usually is.

S: Is it possible for the responses visualized through the tantras to be faster as a result of the breakthrough beyond duality?

CTR: It's possible, yes.

S: Is it spontaneity?

CTR: I think so. Spontaneity becomes hang-up.

S: Is the technique holding in or putting more out?

CTR: Both. It depends on the person.

S: Does shunyata mean not-hesitation, or is it just a concept?

CTR: It seems to be both. The idea of shunyata is a concept. You understand it to begin with, then you begin to dwell on it. That could be the cause of hang-ups or further concepts.

S: So it is a concept to begin with.

CTR: Yes.

S: So we don't exist without any hang-up.

CTR: It could be a hang-up, because there was a concept at the beginning that sent a message down to the underworld of security. It could become a hang-up, or problem, because you have something to hang on to as a handle.

S: Would you have thoughts?

CTR: Well, that's a problem—

S: But would you be one with the thoughts?

CTR: —because the whole thing is one with your thoughts. The concept of shunyata is involved with your thoughts; therefore the whole thing becomes a hang-up. Thoughts are usually concerned with what is not directed to you and what is directed to you; there is hope and fear as to what is for you, what is not for you. Constant fear or hope is involved.

S: Well, I meant thoughts in the sense that if you have a retinocyclograph machine, whenever a light flashes into your eyes, usually there is a corresponding thought, a certain kind of mental registration.

CTR: They're the same thing. That is thought.

S: Right. I'm just trying to think about if in shunyata you'd still have that kind of thought process.

CTR: I don't think so. In shunyata, these particular details are not involved—aggression or passion or accuracy or whatever. In shunyata, the whole idea of thought is things as they are, which is not dependent on logical proof. It transcends proof.

S: Is that a state of total awareness?

CTR: Somewhat.

S: You talked about the idea of shunyata as being a sedative, but could it be that shunyata is an antidote to suffering in the dark? Would it then be the same kind of sedative?

CTR: I don't think so. Shunyata looks at the definite quality of pain—pain as pain, pleasure as pleasure. It can be quite simple.

S: But if it's the actual empty nature of pain—I mean, isn't pain something that we think of as solid?

CTR: No, in shunyata experience you don't see the empty nature of pain at all. Pain is pain in its own existence because form is form and emptiness is emptiness. It sees its own identity as such a definite thing, constantly.

S: So it just acknowledges?

CTR: Feels it and acknowledges it as it is.

S: I was wondering, as a result of the relationship of subject and object, or observer and observed, you have a sort of duality set up. When duality is destroyed, does the observer become one with the observed, or do the observer and the observed both in a sense vanish?

CTR: That's right, yes.

S: Vanish into one.

CTR: Yes.

S: But it's not sequential, that the observed disappears and the observer doesn't, but the two simultaneously?

CTR: Neither would it be nonsequential, the observer and what is observed.

S: Yeah. In other words, discontinuity becomes continuous.

CTR: Yes.

S: Good.

CTR: Somewhat.

S: Why only somewhat?

CTR: Why not? [*Laughter*]

S: Every time you say "somewhat," there's the idea that we miss something.

CTR: Beyond doubt.

S: Beyond a doubt? Then you should not say "somewhat," you should say "precisely!"

CTR: No. You could say "somewhat." You have stretched over all areas, therefore you are imperial, you are the master of the whole situation. Therefore, *somewhat*! [*Laughter*] When you say "precise," you become a little businessman. *Somewhat.* If you say "something"— that's different. When you say "somewhat," you have preserved your whole thing.

S: You mean when you say "somewhat" it's more than just a little point but—

CTR: Precisely, yes. [*Much laughter*]

I think we should close this meeting tonight. We could have a discussion period tomorrow and some sitting practice as well. And we could discuss further what is known as shunyata—what *is* shunyata.

Thank you for coming.

2

Ground

I SUPPOSE we have to see the basic principle of shunyata in terms of practice and theory. In terms of theory, all kinds of philosophical speculations about shunyata could be discussed. But in terms of practice, how does a person perceive the shunyata principle in terms of the practical experience of daily living? The sense of shunyata is what we are discussing rather than the philosophy of shunyata. The sense of shunyata—what is it all about? Shunyata simply means emptiness, nothingness. But there is something more than that. When we talk about emptiness, that automatically means the absence of fullness. So we have to get into what is full and what makes it empty.

There are three principles of shunyata: emptiness as ground, emptiness as path, emptiness as fruition. As far as emptiness as ground is concerned, before we begin on the path, there is no beginning. So one doesn't begin on the path as a solid path, as one imagines, but by realizing and understanding that the basic ground is *so*—without searching particularly or trying to capture the experience of the ground as a starting point.

The starting point itself, the basic ground of shunyata or emptiness, is that one has to know a sense of no beginner. In other words, a complete understanding of egolessness is the starting point. Without that, there is no understanding of shunyata. So you have no solid ground to work with or to walk on. That is to say, you are not going to liberate yourself in order to attain enlightenment. You have to give up the notion of liberation at the beginning—and that also applies to the shunyata principle.

Shunyata, or emptiness, is empty of subject-object relationship. Nonexistent subject, nonexistent object. Perceiver and perceptions do not exist. As far as the groundwork is concerned, there is no definite ground. As long as there is definite ground on the spiritual quest, it becomes a struggle, a deliberate attitude of achievement. And once we begin to be aware of our process of searching as an ambitious struggle, that struggle automatically becomes a formulated struggle—a struggle with ideas, a struggle with theology, concept—which is perpetually creating samsaric mind rather than the spiritual path. The spiritual path becomes religion from that point of view, pejoratively speaking.

So the shunyata experience seems to be that which frees us from religiosity and leads us to true spirituality. Religion in this sense is dogma. You are already a bad person, a condemned person, you contain all kinds of wickedness and you should take those faults and problems seriously. You should try to get into a reformation process, or if you can't do that, you should take a vow and promise to somebody, "At whatever cost it might take, I won't do it again. It won't happen, I can assure you. I promise not to be naughty anymore. From today onward, I'll be good. I'm ashamed of what I was, but at the same time I am proud of what I might be in the future." Some kind of primitive positive thinking.

The shunyata principle has an entirely different perspective and feel to the whole thing. We do not think that we are naughty or being bad or that we are condemned. Instead we accept at the same time the destructive qualities in our basic mechanism as well as the positive qualities in our mechanism, so we have no ground to have a battle at all. In other words, the shunyata principle is a clear principle in which at the beginning, as far as the groundwork of shunyata is concerned, no battleground is provided—good fighting evil, evil fighting good, and so forth. It is free of all territories. Both good and bad could coexist. We are acknowledging that process but not regarding it as a defeat—or a promise, for that matter. In other words, dualistic mind has become confused. As soon as dualistic mind exists on the basic ground, it has to fight or to make love, it has to define enemy and friend. It cannot exist without all of those. So the shunyata perspective shows us a new dimension: in order to exist, we don't have to fight anymore and we don't have to grasp anymore at all.

It is a very powerful thing that we could *be* by doing nothing. In fact we be by not being. We could be by not being—that is the basic ground of shunyata. Struggle does not play an important part in order to exist. In other words, we could live without breathing. It sounds illogical: we can't live without breathing, can we? But somehow the definition of existence is that nonexistence could exist; therefore, it is existence. Nonexistence could exist; therefore, the samsaric process goes on and alogical things could happen; such eccentric ideas as shunyata could exist in the world. Absolutely nonsensical! Doesn't make any sense. How could I exist without fighting? How could I exist without grasping? Does that mean I should not eat food and I should not defend myself from dangers? One might ask that question. The answer is yes! You don't have to consume projections in order to exist, and you don't have to fight projections in order to exist either, metaphorically speaking.

There is a ground process in which we could accommodate everything that goes on without making a big deal out of it—the ground shunyata principle, the absence of hope and fear. We don't have to strategize further ways of maintaining ourselves or existing ourselves at all. This is negating the existence of that; having negated the existence of that, that automatically negates the existence of this at the same time. The ground shunyata principle. You could say that is the experience of freedom, being ultimately free. We do not have to associate ourselves with good or evil. It is true spirituality, positive thinking: good is good in its own way, unconditioned good; bad is bad in its own way, unconditioned bad; and both could coexist on the basic ground.

That ground shunyata principle starts the inspiration for the practice of meditation. Any formal practice of meditation could be said to be that nondualistic approach, equilibrium in its fullest sense. You provide ground, acknowledge the ground with certain techniques that have been presented to you. The techniques themselves are also expressions of that unbiased approach. They do not express or suggest struggle at all. The techniques are just existing, such as working with breathing, working with walking. Existing, working with existence, is the technique.

So the ground of the shunyata principle is basically uncolored by dogma or by concept. It is not philosophizing the whole thing but actually doing it, being involved in a process that is without dogma. The basic principle of shunyata, of seeing beyond dualistic process, goes on from that. One wonders what else is left with the path and the goal. That whole approach of the groundwork seems to be the path and the goal. But we will discuss them later. It is amazing that we can make something out of nothing!

Questions?

Student: There's an experience that people call a shunyata experience—that's a term—would you use that term yourself?

Chögyam Trungpa Rinpoche: Yes, somewhat.

S: Could you please explain how that is related to what you call clear light experience?

CTR: I think we are going to go through that in tonight's talk and tomorrow's talk.

S: Maybe I could ask you one more. The shunyata experience has a terrifying quality to it—

CTR: Definitely, yes.

S: —to people who are into their egos. [*Laughter*] As you are getting into that experience, it has a sort of stark, barren feeling to it. If you were prepared to get into that experience, would that feeling instead get into a singing, musical sort of quality? I don't know if that's right. In other words, where the familiar boundaries begin to dissolve, if you're prepared to accept that experience, it sort of goes into a dance or musical quality.

CTR: Well, it is obviously a terrifying prospect that you cannot have ground to struggle with, that all the ground is being taken away from you. The carpet is pulled out from under your feet. You are suspended in nowhere—which generally happens anyway, whether we acknowledge it as it actually happens or not. Once we begin to be involved with some understanding, or evolve ourselves toward understanding the meaning of life or of spirituality, we have no further reinforcement—nothing but just being captivated by the fact that something is not quite right, something is missing somewhere.

You have to give in somewhere, somewhat—unless you begin to physically maintain that particular religious trip by successive chantings, pujas, and ritual ceremonies. Or you may try to organize that spiritual scene administratively—answering telephones, writing letters, conducting tours of the community. Then you feel that you are doing something. Otherwise, there is no ground to relate with, none whatsoever—if you are really dealing with the naked body as an individuality, an individual person who is getting into the practice of a spiritual way. Even with a person's obligations, administrative work, or liturgical job within the spiritual scene, he or she has nothing left on the spiritual way.

You seem to regard your basic existence to be related with spirituality as a definite thing. By maintaining it through primitive language, you feel you have ground. But when the primitive language is removed from your relation to spirituality, you have nothing to relate with anymore at all. Terrifying! You have lost the whole ground. One is thrown back to the practice then, and the practice is very alien, spooky. "Does that mean that I cannot give a tour explaining to people the meaning behind this particular spiritual scene? Does that mean that I cannot conduct ceremonies, services, or perform holy sacraments?" There is the sense that your badges and your uniform have been taken away from you. It is not that this process could take place only if somebody took them away from you officially and formally. But halfway through, you begin to realize that your uniform does not really answer questions and it does not really mean anything as such at all. You are suspended in nowhere. That's the shunyata experience. No ground to walk on, no ground to work with. You have no function.

From that point of view, the idea of the bodhisattva's work, compassionate work, also could be regarded as an occupation. If you regard yourself as a professional bodhisattva, suddenly you realize that you can't be involved with the professionalism of a bodhisattva anymore. So the whole thing is completely wiped out. Your existence has no meaning because you want to be a bodhisattva, but you find that you can't be a bodhisattva. Your practice of the six paramitas is removed from your face, completely wiped out.

So what to do next—scream? Commit suicide? Attack what? Rage war? Once you begin to wage war against something, you know that the war will end one day. So that doesn't seem to be a permanent, secure occupation either. [Laughter] Somebody has to win or lose. Particularly if you don't want to win, you win. So the whole process is very scary. You could say that it is a dance, if you like. I'm afraid it is not a particularly musical one. [Laughter]

S: What is the relation of wanting to the ground, wanting in itself—not wanting any particular thing, but just wanting. You say that I don't have to fight, but I want to fight, *want*. And this obscures the ground. The wanting goes on, wanting in itself.

CTR: Well, the whole point is that if you want, that means that you are afraid of being without an occupation. You want something because you haven't got it.

S: I want!

CTR: Because you haven't got it.

S: I have wanted! I want!

CTR: Yes, but you can't want unless you don't have it.

S: Unless I don't have wanting.

CTR: Unless you don't have whatever you want, and therefore you want. That means you are standing on nothingness. Do you see what I mean? For instance, what if you say that I want to go to the moon?

S: I don't want any specific thing, I just want. I have wanting.

CTR: Well, that's the whole thing.

S: That attaches itself, the wanting attaches itself.

CTR: It means basically you haven't got it.

S: Right. Now, I don't want to want shunyata, because I won't have it if I want it. And I don't want the ground, because if I want it, I won't have the ground. I'm asking, how can I get rid of wanting without *wanting* to get rid of wanting?

CTR: Well, I suppose the whole point is that you have to acknowledge your double poverty. You are poor and you realize that because you are poor therefore you are poor. Because there is space, therefore you know there is space. *Realizing* space is another matter. But the realizer also realizes there is no space and there is also space. It is threatening, extremely threatening. In other words, you see something, but you are not really seeing. From this point of view, the shunyata principle is extraordinary. It sounds demonic or negative, extraordinarily negative. Unless we acknowledge that negativity of poverty and loss of ground, we cannot relate to the shunyata principle.

S: The problem is that wanting is incorporated into the emotional system. It's almost automatic. It's in the emotions! And it doesn't go away because I see all this.

CTR: No, but if you see that it is hopeless, then you don't try to strategize anymore. You give up the whole trip. It's not a question of realizing that you could stop wanting, which means you are still hanging on to something. You see what I mean?

S: Yeah, but the habit system is also built in there, the habit around the wanting. So if we let some stimulus appear, any kind, that emotion and habit will go right to work in the moment, right? So this is the problem, to dissolve that.

CTR: Well, you don't have to dissolve it. Just dwell on the problem and problem itself will begin to become hopelessness [laughter], which can't be saved. You can't be saved.

S: I'm not trying to be saved.

CTR: That's the whole problem. [Laughter] Unless you realize you can't be saved—

S: Oh, can't be saved. Different point.

CTR: —there's no other way. It is the hopelessness of the situation.

S: Is it possible to look at wanting as an expression of the ground?

CTR: It is the ground of something—it's more of a platform than the ground. [Laughter] It is something undoubtedly, but it's not the ground.

S: Rinpoche, saying that sounds very cold; is there any warmth at all?

CTR: Well—

S: Well? [Laughter]

CTR: Unless you experience the coldness, you can't experience warmth, can you?

S: True.

CTR: By logic.

S: Then the fact that you're cold indicates that there is warmth.

CTR: Your ability to experience warmth is heightened by experiencing cold, or the coolness. As far as the ground of shunyata is concerned, there is no warmth. It is an unkind world, uncompassionate, ruthless. I think you have to give up hope, it's a hopeless situation. When we discuss the path, that is the starting point of warmth, which we will get into next time. That's true. It's cold, it's not very kind. [*Vidyadhara snaps fan.*]

S: I just wondered if this is a process, if you have to keep going beyond this point over and over again, or if you just go beyond?

CTR: I think you have to go through it over and over again.

S: You go as far as you've gone before and then you can do so automatically, over and over.

CTR: Yes. And once you begin, you cannot help taking some steps.

S: When a person is having this experience, does he or she become really cold in his relationships? Would it be natural for a person having this experience to become cold in their relationships?

CTR: I wouldn't say so. That sounds like we are discussing the path. We are discussing the starting point.

S: Well, what would one's psychological state be?

CTR: One's psychological experience is that there is no room to maneuver about or to strategize anymore. It's a hard fact.

S: Sounds like a dank hole.

CTR: It is like a vajra. The vajra represents truth and shunyata at the same time. It is indestructible, a hard fact, indestructible fact. The sense should be harder than the words. It's the uncompassionate truth.

S: Then one would see one's environment as being uncompassionate also.

CTR: Well, the environment depends on you. It's your environment. There's no independent environment as such at all.

S: Well, this is true. But you come down to this coldness, which is internal, right?

CTR: Internal, yes, undoubtedly.

S: And yet the external situation remains. I mean there are people and communities and gurus and wives and the whole stuff. That doesn't go away. I mean there's still stuff to relate to and you're viewing it with this coldness inside.

CTR: Probably the communities and gurus will enforce that coldness. They might say to you that you have no hope. You're a hopeless case. "Much as I love you, I'm afraid you're a hopeless case." [*Laughter*] "Much as I'm your spiritual friend—" [*Laughter*]

S: With all this talking about hopelessness and giving up your uniform and not being able to conduct another tour, I keep going back to the experience of death. Is that at all comparable to shunyata in the sense that there's an equilibrium between life and death in which life is death?

CTR: That seems to be the whole process.

S: One which all of us will go through collectively.

CTR: Yes. The only security of any kind, if there is security, is discontinuity. It is the only security there is. In other words, hopelessness is the security. Hopelessness is the ground. Continual hopelessness is the ground; continual shunyata is the only ground. This could be said to be the hinayanist point of view of shunyata, but it is still valid at the beginning.

S: If total awareness of shunyata exists, can there still be action?

CTR: Shunyata exists on reaction, comparison. Shunyata is emptiness. Therefore it constantly exists on, thrives on, existence as opposed to nonexistence. Shunyata is still experience. It is not an absolute state at all.

S: What kind of experience?

CTR: Shunyata is an experience.

S: But can one act out of that experience?

CTR: One cannot help it.

S: Rinpoche, can you describe the inspiration to see what you see?

CTR: In what context?

S: Say in meditation, or just in general.

CTR: There's inspiration. At the same time, disappointment becomes inspiration. In that sense, that something is not seen is the beginning of seeing. For instance, if you are studying music, the starting point is to realize how unmusical you are. If you are studying art, the starting point is to realize how unartistic you are. That's a hopeful situation. That you have the intelligence to see how unartistic or how unmusical you are is the starting point. Hopelessness is the starting point. That is extremely powerful actually, and the most positive thought that you could have. It is an extraordinarily positive thing to discover how bad things are. [*Laughter*]

S: Why do you say that this would be great? What if after you actually discover how bad you are, you start deciding that you're not so great? Isn't there a danger of developing paranoia, becoming more and more paranoid about yourself?

CTR: I think that's the starting point. You can't be intelligent unless you are paranoid. I mean [the Buddha's teachings] begin with the four noble truths rather than the attainment of enlightenment. The first thing the Buddha said was that there is nothing but suffering, which could be said to be a slightly paranoid remark to make. [*Laughter*] Probably we would prefer enlightenment. He didn't say that it is a beautiful world, he said the world consists of pain, misery, and suffering. That's a very intelligent remark to make, extremely positive.

S: The first thing the Buddha said was, "Wonder of wonders, all beings are intended to be buddhas." If one had that experience, would one maintain faith in that?

CTR: I think so, yes.

S: So it's not totally hopeless.

CTR: But we have to be careful not to make a double twist.

S: Let's just take it as it is.

CTR: Yes, but let's not interpret.

S: Yeah, but nonetheless, even if the ground is gone, [*gong rings*] I am what I am and nothing can change that, right? That seems to be a basically stable—

CTR: No, I wouldn't say that, I would say the opposite: I am *not* what I am, and for that reason it can happen. [*Laughter*]

S: I can't be anything else.

CTR: Hmm?

S: I can't be anything other than I am.

CTR: You can. You could go through the impermanence of what you are.

S: Let's go back to the "Battle of Ego" seminar [*laughter*] where you described the basic ground that ego is built on as stable.

CTR: Somewhat.

S: In its stability is an all-righteous, is there not?

CTR: I think you are stretching too much. Elastic band.

S: It's a desperate situation. [*Laughter*]

CTR: I sympathize with you on that. [*Laughter*]

S: Considering the power of saying how bad things are, what kind of power could it be to use human good as an index?

CTR: How about goodness, do you mean?

S: In other words, you spoke of the power of feeling bad—not feeling bad but realizing how bad things are. Where is the index, which I often use, of feeling good? In other words, going in the direction that feels good, let's say, and using that as an index.

CTR: Well, to begin with, can you tell me what your idea of good is? A definition, so to speak?

S: It's when I feel loose and relaxed and not confused and clear.

CTR: Not confused and clear. That's reasonable. [*Laughter*] That's reasonable! But that's the whole starting point, you see. If you see how bad you are, you are not confused. You see *precisely* how bad you are! [*Laughter*]

S: I don't feel good.

CTR: Somewhat. [*Laughter*] You feel definitely, anyway.

S: Did you say that the advantage of hopelessness is to accelerate the receptivity? If I have nothing to hold on to, including hope, that might make me more receptive to what is going to happen. No attachment.

CTR: Can you restate that?

S: Yes. If I have a hope, that will blind me to what's happening around me.

CTR: Yes.

S: If I have no hope, that means I can react intuitively and completely to whatever happens.

CTR: Well, to reach the low point of hopelessness, you have to have hope and then it becomes hopelessness, rather than that you are completely wiped out at the beginning.

S: It's not a negative statement, the way I see it.

CTR: Well, you have to have a positive thing, to be hopeful, to begin with. Then you lose your hope. It's a question of nothingness and blankness—you see what I mean?

S: No.

CTR: Hope is based on hopelessness; hopelessness depends on hope. To begin with you have a drive to be hopeful, you struggle all the time. Then you lose that hope, you begin to come to the conclusion of hopelessness. Whereas if there is no hope at all in the beginning, there's no fertile ground.

S: So that's a condition?

CTR: Somewhat, yes. It's an interaction of some kind. If you say you have one eye, that automatically presumes that usually people have two eyes and you happen to have one eye. It is a logical process.

S: Or you have *at least* one eye—you may have another one I don't know about.

CTR: And so forth.

S: What's the difference between the hopelessness that people may feel before shunyata and the hopelessness that they feel after? There are a lot of people who feel very hopeless about their situation.

CTR: We could say that the hopelessness of their situation before shunyata, as you call it, is shunyata experience already. There is room to work with because we feel hopeless. That is shunyata experience already. It is giving up that and this. You are completely lost, you don't know how to fight or how to grasp. You feel completely hopeless, hopeless. That seems to be the starting point of shunyata experience. We could say that *is* shunyata experience, in fact.

S: What happens after that?

CTR: We experience the hopelessness of it and then we begin to experience warmth in that negativity. We are going to discuss that later on.

S: Is it that you start meditation with the hope that you are going to get somewhere or do something for yourself, and you realize on the way that there is no such thing. Is that the hopelessness?

CTR: Realizing that meditation is not going to save you, but you have to work on yourself. That is the idea of hopelessness.

S: How do you work on yourself other than by meditation?

CTR: Nothing.

S: Nothing.

S: [*Another student chimes in.*] Nothing.

CTR: That encompasses a lot of areas: meditation and meditation in action. But without that there is no other way.

S: Rinpoche, when you see the hopelessness and futility of the whole spiritual trip and of meditation, if you keep meditating anyway, wouldn't that indicate that you still have hope? I mean there's nothing out there, you know, it's futile, so why do it? If you see how futile it is and then you continue to do it, it's like beating your head against the wall.

CTR: In this case you appreciate doing nothing but just being, which is the epitome of hopelessness. [*Laughter*] That brings compassion and enlightenment.

S: I think I read it or you said it, but what we call meditation in the beginning isn't really meditation, it's just playing. After this hopelessness, we really start something with our meditation.

CTR: Yes. The whole idea of the mechanistic approach is "Before I do that, I'm going to get there." You have to give up that approach as well.

S: If the hopelessness comes out in the body, as a feeling of wanting to throw up and terrible anxiety and your stomach going wild and you feel like you might lose your mind—if the hopelessness comes out in that way, is that because we are doing something wrong, that we are taking the wrong approach?

CTR: Psychologically struggling too much.

S: Sometimes I feel the way he just described, maybe differently day by day, going too fast or feeling close to a certain kind of pain.

And it'll come time to meditate or I will be in my bed meditating and I'll notice that after I meditate for an hour I feel better. Out of that experience I can't help having some feeling about meditation, or attitude toward it, that it is salvation, or that it is at least a momentary release of something. Is that a good way to think about meditation or to connect those two? I don't know if I'm making that up or anything.

CTR: Well, in a primitive practice you might use meditation as a temporary service, temporary salvation, but in the absolute sense that doesn't apply anymore. Meditation means giving up hope altogether. You just sit and do it.

S: I don't enter it with the hope that I'll be released from some hangup I've been feeling, but it just so happens that I feel a lot better in terms of tiring and confusion and feeling my body much looser.

CTR: I think that is a misunderstanding. In terms of feeling that certain ways of doing things might help you, there's still a sense of therapeutic practice. Meditation is not therapeutic practice at all. We seem to have a problem in this country with the sense that meditation is included with psychotherapy or physiotherapy or whatever. A lot of Buddhists feel proud because meditation is accepted as part of the therapeutic system, a landmark of the Western world. But I think that pride is simpleminded pride. Buddhism should transcend the therapeutic practice of meditation. Relating with gurus is quite different from going to your psychiatrist.

S: But out of that experience I'm afraid of falling into the trap of getting too involved in the therapeutic aspect, because it does in fact dissolve pain. I mean, that is an experience that I have.

CTR: You shouldn't dissolve pain.

S: You shouldn't?

CTR: You should raise pain! [*Laughter*] Otherwise you don't know who you are or what you are. Meditation is a way of opening. In that particular process, under-hidden subconscious things come up, so you can view yourself as who you are. It is an unpeeling, unmasking process.

S: How is that related to freedom?

CTR: Because there is a sense not of collecting but of an undoing process. You don't collect further substances that bind you or further responsibilities. It is a freedom process.

S: There's a tendency for people to come forth with a specific psychological problem and to have somebody say, "Well, why don't you meditate?" But from the point of view you just expressed, that would be inappropriate and of no particular help.

CTR: It depends on how you meditate. It depends on your attitude to meditation.

S: For example, a meditation like Zen meditation or meditation as you've been describing it today has this quality of hopelessness. That seemed to teach me that it wouldn't be appropriate to tell somebody to do it in order to try to help them with their problem.

CTR: I think it would. To help with their problem is to bring the problem onto the surface.

S: Isn't that the same as therapy?

CTR: I don't think so. We don't talk about curing.

S: Therapy does make things surface.

CTR: No, it doesn't, actually. It is reputed to do so, but somehow you become a professional confessor so you know what language to use. In meditation there is no language involved at all. The whole practice is not involved with language, but just doing it.

S: But you do talk to yourself in meditation.

CTR: So what?

S: So it uses a language.

CTR: You don't try to get involved with proving yourself to somebody else, which is a much heavier trip. Moreover you don't pay yourself a salary or fees. [*Laughter*]

S: Does feeling pain have anything to do with feeling uncomfortable?

CTR: Comfortable is pain, yeah.

S: Comfortable is pain?

CTR: Comfort brings pain.

S: Comfort brings pain?

CTR: Mm hm.

S: Well, when you feel uncomfortable—

CTR: —that brings pleasure. [*Laughter*]

S: Sounds like masochists.

CTR: I wouldn't say that either; then you defeat your purpose.

S: Masochists find pleasure from pain, same thing.

CTR: I don't think so.

S: You mean they are different?

CTR: Because you are relating with what you are, premasochists.

S: Does this hopelessness rise out of seeing that you have never been able to establish anything in your mind or keep it there?

CTR: Hopelessness seems to come up because you can't cheat yourself anymore. You can't con yourself anymore. You can't con the situation, and you can't cheat anybody in that given situation anymore. Therefore you feel helpless and hopeless.

S: You are not consciously attempting to con somebody or other.

CTR: No. Psychologically, it's built in already. There's a tendency to provide as much personal comfort as possible.

S: What is your feeling about the original Sufi system, in the thirteenth century?

CTR: What system?

S: The Sufi mystical system of whirling dervishes, in which they use a process called *sama'* incorporating dance, music, and singing. They approach this tremendous despair and hopelessness and then gain some sort of enlightenment and become illuminated. What do you think about that?

CTR: Is that so? [*Laughter*]

S: I don't know. I'm just wondering if that kind of system might develop here in the Western world. It reduces your ego presumably, but it's accompanied by music and dancing.

CTR: It doesn't have to be the Sufi system, particularly.

S: Yeah, I know, that's what I mean.

CTR: They provide their own means once they are awakened, once they are opened. If you are trying to court certain practices of such a tradition, it is not particularly helpful. People could develop, and seemingly they are already developing, a way of communicating with themselves which leads to ways of loosening up. They provide all kinds of ways of loosening them up. It is already happening. So one doesn't have to produce or to present certain set patterns of how to loosen up—it seems to happen automatically.

S: Isn't one of the problems that one can invite hopelessness in order to find hope. Such hopelessness is really hopeful.

CTR: Well, that tends to happen automatically.

S: But if one knows this in advance?

CTR: I don't think so. You might know it intellectually, but when you actually experience hopelessness, it's quite different. We could talk about hunger in theory, but when we are actually hungry ourselves, it's quite different.

S: Is this hopelessness experienced as an emotional state?

CTR: It is an emotional state, yes, definitely.

S: Then what is the place of upaya?

CTR: To watch the hopelessness. Quite simple.

S: But it seems as if something more active is involved, at least in the way we were discussing it. The mind is doing something more active than merely watching.

CTR: Mind is acknowledging its hopelessness. And mind has to give up its trips. It happens naturally.

S: How is this arrived at? Is it arrived at by an active process of the mind?

CTR: No, it is arrived at by the actual process of the situation, seeing the hopelessness of the situation.

S: Is the hopelessness a projection? Is it some type of ground that is not empty yet?

CTR: That's right, yes.

S: When you reach this point of hopelessness you don't have to sit and meditate anymore. Do you see this process really without concept?

CTR: You see, the whole process does not look like the mechanistic approach of what we should do after that, but it evolves out of the whole situation. And maybe you will find yourself meditating *more* after that process.

S: Does the path toward the experience of hopelessness necessarily include pain and despair?

CTR: Definitely, yes. Because you have no ground to stand on.

S: Does that mean we should actively seek out and attract these situations? [*Laughter*]

CTR: Not necessarily. That's generally what we are doing, actually. [*Laughter*] We seek out our permanent answer, nest, home. That in itself is heading toward hopelessness. That happens spontaneously.

S: What positive thing can possibly come out of a truly hopeless situation such as the tragedy in Bangladesh, a place where people are actually starving, not just in their minds? I mean, they are not simply deprived of comforts that we take for granted; they are deprived of even having a meal. What positive thing can arise out of that for anyone who's involved in it?

CTR: I suppose you could say that it is beginning to realize that there's no ground, no psychological ground to stand on.

S: I can realize it, but do you think that those people can? As they are starving to death, do you think they realize that there's really no ground to stand on?

CTR: Much more so! It is physically obvious that you have no roof over your head.

S: But perhaps the despair leads right to death, so there's no beginning of hope at all.

S: Did you not say that mind watches the hopelessness?

CTR: Yes.

S: And doesn't that need some kind of training, say through meditation?

CTR: At this point it does not seem to be dependent on any particular training.

S: So the people in Bangladesh perhaps do not have the necessary training to realize their hopelessness.

CTR: No, but they begin to realize their solid idea of enemies and friends does not exist. The whole thing is purely a survival process, which is a very lucid situation. If an enemy comes and gives you food, you accept it gladly—as well as friends.

S: It destroys ideas.

CTR: There's no idea of politics at that level.

S: In actual fact, the process of experiencing this seems pretty complicated, though. One part of it is a growing sense of hopelessness and of the ground emptying out. But as you come up from there, the sun is very hot, babies are terrific, love is great from time to time, and work is good a lot. There is this counterpull. How does that not get broken? Or does this just deepen into an actual crisis in time? How to think about that?

CTR: I think the suggestion becomes deeper. Once you begin to realize that you can't control your physical situation, you begin to give up hope of strategizing. And the whole thing becomes a much more living process.

S: In this process, in regard to the bhumis of the last seminar, this seems to be "pre" any of them, is that right?

CTR: It is the first path, the path of accumulation.

We might have to stop at that point, friends, and have further discussion at the end of the next talk. Thank you.

3

Path

HAVING DISCUSSED the nonexistence of the basic ground already, we will discuss the nonexistence of the path. The basic principle of shunyata at this point, as far as the path is concerned, is a process in which the style of the path does not become a solid thing anymore. According to the shunyata principle, the style of the path is that it is an unconditioned path. It allows basic openness as well as basic confusion. Because of that particular nature, openness also could be regarded as confusion on the path.

Because of confusion on the path, because the whole path is confused, bewildered, one has to learn to relate with something. The way to relate with the path is by trying to relate with something that is there, which is the idea of compassion. The definition of compassion, or karuna, is basic warmth, the absence of duality, absence of comparison, clear and uncompassionate space. Because of that uncompassionate space, there is something basically healthy about that, solid about that. That is compassion. Something is actually happening, which is the idea of compassion.

The idea of compassion in this case is being basically open, willing to relate with what's happening in this given situation as it is. You don't expect reassurance and you don't expect threat. Once you are on the path it is definitely a solid thing already, and because of that there is warmth. You are finally willing to make a commitment to unknown territory. Unknown territory becomes known territory from that point of view, because it is unknown. You are taking a chance, you are willing to take a chance. That is the idea of compassion, being willing to take a chance as things develop in their own basic nature. You are willing to communicate. You are willing to take a chance.

Compassion is not being kind and loving necessarily; it is more openness. You are willing to relate with the whole process. Generally the experience of compassion is that somebody is rich and willing to give something away because of their charity. It is the idea of being charitable. You are healthy and you are going to save somebody else from an unhealthy situation. You know much more than other people do, you have more information, so you are trying to save those people from trouble. That is idiot compassion. Such compassion is based on levels: something is better than that, therefore I have the complete opportunity to do it.

The same thing could apply to dharma: somebody doesn't know about studying dharma and I do understand the dharma. Therefore I tell somebody about the dharma and I figure I'm saving them from their confusion and ignorance. Or I have lots of money and those people don't. Still they are good people, worth giving that money to, and because of their condition I give them money. That particular process of compassion is idiot compassion, as we mentioned. People who receive compassionate gestures from such one-sided compassionate persons should help them again in reverse because *they* are confused. They are distorted because their belief in one-sidedness is too strong, too overwhelming.

The idea of compassion in this case, on the path, is that you feel or see the situation directly, fundamentally, fully. Because of that you could help others. It is not that you want to see them be happy, good, or healthy, but that people need help in the sense of realizing healthiness within themselves. They are already healthy people, they are already wealthy people. The basic idea of compassion from that point of view is an open situation, which is based on the shunyata principle, not on comparison.

Once you begin to see the hopelessness of the whole thing, you give up any kind of expectations. Because you give up expectations, you become more generous. Therefore you are willing to relate with what is there without your expectations. And because of that nonexpectation, you are more equipped when you are relating with other situations. That is the path of compassion.

We could say that the path of shunyata consists of compassion and wisdom, or knowledge. The knowledge that things need to be done according to what things are, as well as things are so because you can't escape from that particular situation. That things are as they are is knowledge. That things are so in a given situation is skillful means, that we are going to work with that situation without any hesitation. So the path of compassion and shunyata consists of the union of compassion and knowledge, karuna and prajna. Because you see things as they are, you act accordingly, in accord with the given situation. Those two situations become prominent in terms of the path of compassion.

We could have a discussion.

Student: In the state of hopelessness, one has compassion, one reaches the state of the true path of compassion?

Chögyam Trungpa Rinpoche: Yes, precisely. Because you feel hopeless, therefore you feel compassion—because you don't feel better than anybody else. You are completely in contact with things as they are.

S: Where does skillful means enter into compassion?

CTR: If you are fully compassionate, you can't miss the point. If you don't miss the point, then you act accordingly. That is skillful means. Very simple.

S: If you become open and act compassionately, is that because by being open you experience the situation of the person who is before you in the same way as you experience yourself?

CTR: Not necessarily. There could be a person who is quite different, compared to your nature, but at the same time you see their basic qualities.

S: When you're at the beginning stage, obviously you can't be right on the point, since you are only beginning. So your openness and compassion, your actions, will be off the point slightly. Does that mean you should go back and meditate some more, or just keep on and take the risk of irritation or tension in the space? Should you allow yourself to go into it, with the risk that you might not be on or get on the point? In other words, I guess that space is a lot like a mirror and will tell you whether you are not doing it right. Then you go back and meditate, I suppose. Or is it the kind of thing where you just sort of stumble along for a while and your actions sort of get on the point at the various stages of the path?

CTR: The idea of compassion in this case is straightforward. You can't strategize, you can't steer around. Therefore I suppose what you say is true, that you just have to accept the given situation. You just have to get into it. Mistakes become part of the creative process automatically.

S: You mentioned "basic qualities" in the other person. Is that seeing the ground of the other person as being your own ground, that basic quality you see in the other person? What is that basic quality?

CTR: It is a mutual understanding in terms of projection and projector. That you don't see a distinction between what ought to be, or what should be, and what things are, as it is. That other person or other situation is unmistakable; it is so. It is like the sun shines tomorrow, maybe overcast, and sets tomorrow as well. One can't argue about that. That's the basic quality. The situation shows that as it is; you can't argue about that.

S: In other words, if we were free we would see that basic quality, if we were free in ourselves to see it.

CTR: If you are not free, you are going to be shaken by it. You are going to be awakened by it, reminded by it.

S: Do you think compassion is projection as well?

CTR: Both, theater and projector.

S: But that is something that is really not looking outward, there's no space—

CTR: That's right, yeah.

S: You talked about how compassion arises out of hopelessness. That has a very somber kind of feel to it. Somehow the whole seminar has a very somber feel to it, at least for me; whereas in the "Bodhisattva Path" seminar [March 1972 at Tail of the Tiger] you talked about compassion as arising out of generosity, in the sense of one's own richness and that the first stage of the bodhisattva path is called the joyful one. I'm a little confused as to why in that case it comes off sounding positive and in this case it comes off sounding so somber.

CTR: Well, if we are discussing the five paths, what we are discussing in this case is the first path, the layman's path, before you come to the bodhisattva's path. It is the path of accumulation. In terms of the path of accumulation, you must be concerned with the ten virtuous actions. There are three of the body (bodily skillful ways of dealing with situations), four of speech, and three of mind. So the whole process is a skillful one at this point.

When a layman begins on the path, he or she should relate with the path as choicelessness. There is no choice once you commit to the path. Laymen usually begin on the path by taking refuge. "I am part of the dharma. I take refuge in the dharma and the Buddha and the sangha. I have no choice." Because of its choicelessness, you have already escaped. Because you have already escaped, therefore the path presented to you is obvious. There is no way out, no way of giving in to dependencies of any kind at all. So it seems that we are discussing different levels.

S: Because of that, would you say it is important to have a rather clear idea of the levels on the path, without getting hung up on it, because of the confusion it will engender if you mistake the highlights of one level for something else on a different level? Or is that something that would happen anyway?

CTR: There are no levels. That is an important point. Absolutely no levels. That's what confuses us always. When spiritual teachings are presented to people, there are so many levels presented to you— etheric body, spiritual body, physical body, whatever. Those levels are nonsense, they don't happen that way.

S: No, by levels I meant the bhumis and the two—

CTR: They are not regarded as levels, they are regarded as steppingstones, a staircase.

S: That's what I meant.

CTR: I mean the bhumis are not really levels. They are staircases, so to speak. They are not regarded as levels as such. What we are discussing is body and mind, physical and mental, both situations. As far as the physical mind/body, psychophysical body, is concerned, there are no levels. It is a cooperating situation.

S: I'm not quite sure. Should you have a fair idea of the steps?

CTR: It's not particularly should you or shouldn't you, but it happens.

S: Mm-hmm.

CTR: For instance, should you be one or two years old? That is a matter of whether you *are* one year old or two years old. You are going to be two years or three years old and you are going to your own birthdays in any case. You can't escape that. It's not planned.

S: Just before my question, someone had asked something about generosity, confusing that level with the layman's level. That kind of thing could create certain confusions in whatever you are doing, perhaps.

CTR: I don't think so.

S: You don't think it would?

CTR: I don't think so at all. It has been said that laymen should not act like bodhisattvas and bodhisattvas should not act like yogins. Yogins should not act as buddhas. Buddhas should not act as herukas. It's quite definite.

S: Yeah, but do you have to know where the buddha is that you're not, that you shouldn't act as?

CTR: That doesn't apply, that's just a formula.

S: Just a formula?

CTR: It doesn't apply anymore—whether you are a yogin or yogini, whether you are a bodhisattva, you can't act like that. You'll be caught.

S: Are the refuges also supposed to be taken with hopelessness?

CTR: Definitely! [*Laughter*] That is a very good question, actually. You have no other alternatives, you give up hopes and sidetracks of any kind. Therefore you take refuge in the Buddha, dharma, and sangha. You are finally giving in to the main road, you give up sidetracks. It is a final gesture of hopelessness. That's why it is called taking refuge. You have no other resources. It is an extremely healthy thing to do and very sensible.

Generosity begins at the level when you give up hope. There is no other choice. Because there is no other choice, therefore you become more generous. You are willing to admit whatever. At that point, one also begins to realize that ego has no other choice but to give itself up. Discovering this is a further spiritual adventure involved in generosity.

S: I was wondering about attachment to compassion and if compassion is the product of greed. You said that the bodhisattva was attached to compassion—how is that possible?

CTR: Better make something up. [*Laughter*]

S: One time you said that you agreed that a bodhisattva does have an attachment to compassion and it seems to fit this basic description in any case. That's why he or she is not a buddha. But if compassion is not a projection, how is it possible to be attached to it? You can only be attached to a projection.

CTR: It is a projection; compassion is a projection. In many cases, it starts at the bodhisattva level of the different bhumis because of your objective of generosity, discipline, patience, energy, meditation, and prajna. Your object is to be related with all that. That is why they are called different levels, or bhumis. The bodhisattva path has levels to communicate, levels to be related with. It is levels automatically.

S: In this case then, is it an attachment to something that is both a projection and not a projection?

CTR: Whether it is a projection or not, bodhisattvas are concerned with their work. It is a question of their duty rather than convention or having to relate with their credentials. They just become serious, honest workers. That's what bodhisattvas are.

S: Then why aren't they buddhas?

CTR: Buddhas do not experience hopelessness. [*Laughter*] You might say they are *being,* they are not workers. The sun is not regarded as a worker. Although you could say that it fulfills the fertility of the earth, you can't say that the sun is working hard to fulfill the ground, to grow plants and produce light and things. That's why there is the analogy of one moon in thirteen hundred bowls of water. Buddhas don't work hard, they are just *being*. And by being, they work hard automatically. Their work fulfills for them.

S: In one of the sutras the Buddha said that for beings there is rest, but for me there is no rest. I forgot the sutra, but he said, "As for me there is no rest."

CTR: Precisely! The sun has no rest either.

S: It's not working either.

CTR: Not working. Being the sun is working hard—at the same time, it is resting.

S: And the bodhisattva is just a guy with—

CTR: A certain intention or direction is involved. It's more like a torch than the sun, as far as a bodhisattva is concerned. A torch has to survive on oil, but the buddha's standard does not need oil.

S: What is the oil, then?

CTR: For bodhisattvas? The energy is prajna, and shunyata is the oil. Shunyata is the oil on which they survive, and the flame is upaya, skillful means. So they work with the combination of shunyata and upaya.

S: But the historical Buddha was not buddha, because the historical Buddha was working—forty-nine years.

CTR: Well, he wasn't buddha until the end of his life; until he was twenty-nine he wasn't a buddha, he was a bodhisattva. But the historical Buddha was never buddha, because he was the historical one. [*Laughter*] If you say that, we will be regarded as renegades. But it is so.

S: At first we were talking about ground, which is everywhere. When we talk about path, it seems to set up a kind of narrowness or possibility of going off the path. And then there is the question of discipline. Is the analogy of the path kind of like computing, because either you are on it or off it? But if both are shunyata?

CTR: Well, when we talk about the shunyata path, in the beginning, we had a solid path, a narrow path, giving up hope and fear both. It is extremely austere, really. You have no way of venturing about at all; it is very austere. You only have one step to work with, which is without hope, without fear, just straight on the true path, absolute path. Beyond that, the path becomes an open path. It depends on how open you are. It is not a question of the nature of the path, but it is a question of how open you are. Depending on how open you are, that much freedom there is.

S: Rinpoche, I don't understand projection. Did you say that compassion is a projection?

CTR: Compassion is a *conditioned* projection. And projections are what exists between the chaos of that and this. In other words, we could say that projections are the chaos, and compassion is the intermediary between projection and projector.

S: You don't mean projection in the sense that psychology uses projection, as a fantasy, something you made up. You don't mean it like that?

CTR: Your enemy or your lover is a projection in this case.

S: Mm-hmm. Oh, I see.

S: Would the bodhisattva be in communication with emotions then?

CTR: What else? That is his path? That's the only path, that the bodhisattva can exist with his emotions.

S: How do you go about communicating with those noncommunicative things?

CTR: It has nothing to do with that, not communicating with the situation at all. Anything that exists beyond radiation communicates with the situation.

S: It seems they are pretty one-way. I mean, my emotions seem to be communicating with me, but I am not clear enough on whatever I've got to say to them.

CTR: Oy vey.

S: Yeah. I can be angry now or embarrassed now, but the emotion is coming toward me; whereas any communication coming to them is not—

CTR: I don't know what you are talking about, what you are asking.

S: Is the path out of hopelessness?

CTR: It is *within* hopelessness.

S: Why not just remain in the so-called hopelessness which is what *is*, completely true?

CTR: When you lose hope, you lose hope. Then true hope begins to arise, when you begin to realize hopelessness. It's the same thing when you begin to give up the clouds which cover the sun, which is the hopelessness of the sun. When there are no clouds, the hopelessness is gone—the sun is right there! I shouldn't have said that. [*Laughter*] Too much love and light. [*Laughter*] However—that is what we teach.

S: In the early stages of the path, when you're communicating, would there be a greater tendency for the communication to be energetic in the sense of surprise?

CTR: I think so, yes. There are constant surprises all the time, that you didn't believe it but it is so. What you thought turns out to be [*inaudible*]. All kinds of things go on outrageously. The confusion before the realization is regarded as the realization before the confusion. All kinds of confusion take place, which is realization and so forth.

We should stop at that point. I would like to have a good discussion, maybe tomorrow. The whole idea of the shunyata seminar is not to present further stuff so that you get more confused, but to find some way out of confusion because confusion does exist. So it would be good if you had a really solid, good discussion tomorrow. That would be good. And quite possibly we might have a discussion period before the talk, and then have the talk, and then have further discussion afterward. That would be good.

I feel personally responsible. Talking about shunyata is a very heavy subject. I might do a disservice to the audience by getting bogged down in the confusion of shunyata. And on the whole, this particular seminar does not provide promises of any kind of enlightenment— no promises, none whatsoever. You could say that it promises more confusion. However, that confusion could be intelligent confusion as opposed to confused confusion. [*Laughter*]

4

Fruition

HAVING DISCUSSED the path of shunyata, the path itself becomes
the goal in some sense. But at the same time, we realize that the
goal is not a place one finds permanency or permanent security to
dwell on or dwell in. The concept of shunyata is ceaseless space, like
the analogy of outer space which never ends. In some sense, the
shunyata principle could be called a goal: in the sense of going from
imperfection to perfection, it could be called a goal. But it is not
really a definite goal in the sense of achievement or a peak experience
in which the student stops. In other words, the all-pervading quality
of shunyata provides tremendous room to expand constantly. From
that point of view, achievement is the beginning point of another
odyssey. The energy of compassion and of prajna, or knowledge, constantly goes on. But metaphorically, if we discuss the idea of a goal,
then that goal is twofold kaya: the kaya of form and the kaya of formlessness. *Kaya* is a Sanskrit word meaning "form," "body." Twofold
kaya comes from the experience of transcending the twofold barriers
of ego: conflicting emotions and primitive beliefs about reality.

You might call conflicting emotions anti-shunyata, because they
do not allow or experience any space or lubrication to develop
things. They are solid and definite. It is like the analogy of the pig in
the symbol of ignorance which just follows its nose and never sees

directions of any kind at all. It just keeps following, constantly guided by impulse. And whatever comes in front of its nose, it just consumes it and looks for the next one. That is conflicted emotions. In this case we are talking about emotions as primitive emotions. Take the example of anger, for instance. There is the primitive, conflicted quality of anger and there is also the energetic quality of the anger, which is quite different. Conflicting emotions are those that are purely trying to secure ego's aim and object, trying to fulfill ego's demand. They are based on constantly looking for security, maintaining the identity of "I am." Conflicting emotions also contain energy, which is the compassionate nature, the basic warmth and basic creative process. But somehow in that situation of primitive emotions, there is very little generosity of letting energy function by itself.

Conflicting emotions try to hold on to emotions as obligatory emotions that should maintain some function, maintain ego. Of course there is constant conflict with that particular style. Such a one-sided point of view brings discomfort, dissatisfaction, frustration, and so forth. The operating style of conflicting emotions is that narrow-minded point of view. In some sense we could say it is a one-track-mind style. There is concern that there is a particular thing to fulfill, so the emotion goes directly to that peak point and never considers the situations around it. That is why we speak of conflicting emotions, or primitive emotions, as opposed to compassionate emotions.

We could say the compassionate aspect of emotions is quite different. It has more space and it has panoramic qualities. At the same time, the compassionate aspect of emotions still has a sense of duality, we might say, because compassion also contains prajna, or knowledge. In order to have a perception or knowledge, you have to have dualistic awareness, dualistic consciousness. But that is not particularly dualistic *fixation*, as in the primitive emotions. [Simply] seeing two situations is not regarded as dualistic fixation in the pejorative sense. But seeing two in terms of goal orientation or security orientation is primitive; there is no element of openness at all.

So the quality of primitive emotional conflict, conflicting emotions, is like color or paint. Primitive emotion is definite and solid—it can't be interpreted, can't be changed. Whether it is just blue, just green, or just yellow, it has to be a definite thing. [Primitive] emotions have different expectations to fulfill their desire, fulfill their function. But in order to be fulfilled, strangely enough, their particular color or paint has to have some medium, oil or water. And that oil or water is the sophisticated emotions of compassion, or the liberated emotions, whatever you would like to call them. In other words, the primitive quality of the emotions goes along with the advanced emotions of compassion or understanding. That is the only point where the conflicting emotions could be transformed into something else, for the very reason that conflicting emotions are dependent on that medium.

And quite possibly, the more concentrated the medium, the weaker the intensity of the colors. They would be just faint colors of blue, faint colors of yellow, in which the other colors could be introduced because basically that color is not a particularly solid color. The whole thing is that much more accommodating. So from that point of view conflicting emotions contain the weakness of maintaining their conflicted emotionness. They have the potential of changing and developing into something else. And the medium in which the color is carried could be said to be the shunyata experience. That is the fundamental lubrication in which emotions could be developed into a different style, could be made more transparent.

The other aspect, the second veil or bondage of ego, is primitive belief about reality. Primitive belief about reality is, again, not necessarily based on emotions as such, but on conflict. It is based on subconscious emotions rather than conscious emotions, that undercurrent which inclines toward goals, toward achieving, toward directions, toward security. It is more of a tendency rather than living emotions, as solid and powerful as the conflicting emotions were. But it also needs some lubrication in order to function. In other words, without oxygen we cannot breathe, we cannot function. So there is a basic environment or climate in which primitive belief about reality functions. The reason it is primitive is because it is dependent on something else; it is not a self-sufficient concept or idea.

Of the two veils of ego, conflicting emotions could be said to be that of psychological materialism, the literalness of it. The other veil, primitive belief about reality, is spiritual materialism. In some sense, it is highly sophisticated, but there is still belief in being saved or being helped. There is permanent promise. The achievement or attainment of enlightenment is regarded as one permanent situation in which you can function, you can relax. You can live in it, make a home of it too. And also, because it contains philosophical speculation in terms of a way to exist, there is a sense of survival. We are trying to survive, therefore we are searching for spiritual practice. But that spiritual practice is to attain immortality. The reason we search for a spiritual path is that we feel that we might not survive, might not be able to exist as an independent entity and being. So we have two kinds of misunderstandings. We have the childlike primitive mind, that you just want to get what you want, and if you don't get what you want you get frustrated. And we have the other one, that you think you could strategize the whole thing and then you will get what you want. Two types of struggle or bondage.

Those two types of bondage are related to the two-kaya principle, the two bodies or forms of buddha that we were talking about in terms of the goal of shunyata, the achievement of shunyata, metaphorically speaking. The body of form transcends conflicting emotions, and the body of formlessness transcends primitive belief about reality. The body of formlessness is the dharmakaya, and the body of form is the nirmanakaya and sambhogakaya. The body of form is based on a direct relationship with reality [nirmanakaya] and a direct relationship with energy [sambhogakaya], which is an earthy situation. Both are earthy situations. In other words, we could say that there is visual perception and there is audial perception. The visual perceptions could be said to be the nirmanakaya of the solid textures of life, and the audial perceptions to be the sambhogakaya of energy, vibrations, speech, and so on. And none of these final stages of buddha, the experience of buddhahood, can exist without the background of shunyata. You cannot perceive form and you cannot attain enlightenment unless you are able to see that form also contains space. And you cannot attain an ultimate understanding of energy or vibration or musical sound unless you begin to see that music also contains silence. Energy contains action as well as nonaction, both are energy levels. Otherwise there is a tendency to become self-destructive.

So in this case, the state of form in the final experience of shunyata is that of basic existence in which there is no distortion of any kind whatsoever. It is not influenced by primitive emotions or primitive belief. Everything is seen clearly, precisely, right to the point. Form is seen as form because we also see the formlessness of it. It is based on the form as well as the emptiness around the form. And sound is heard, energy is felt, because sound contains silence as well, and energy contains nonaction as well.

So shunyata in this case is panoramic vision in which things could be accommodated. At the same time, the accommodation itself becomes a perception of its own. In other words, the container and what is contained become one. They complement each other. Therefore there is no question about maintaining the container in order to contain what is contained. In terms of the dharmakaya principle, the formlessness of the second kaya, it is a state of complete openness because dharmakaya or formlessness is not dependent on any relative proof. It is completely free of comparison. For the very fact that it could exist by itself, therefore, this level of understanding of the shunyata principle is almost more at the level of what is called *jnana*, which means "wisdom."

The difference between jnana, or wisdom, and prajna, or knowledge, is that in the case of knowledge you still need relationship. It is still *experience* as far as the popular idea of shunyata is concerned. There is still play, interchange, interaction, at the level of form and energy. In the case of dharmakaya, there is no relationship, there is no interaction or interchange. But it seems to be rather difficult explaining that particular state, because in fact we cannot say that there is *not* interchange, there is *not* relationship. But quite much more to the point is that interchange or relationship is not valid anymore. It is already related, it is already interchanged. Therefore the question of being in that state of dharmakaya shunyata experience is futile. We can't say that we have achieved dharmakaya or that we have achieved that particular state of wisdom, or jnana, at all. In other words, we could say that jnana cannot be achieved. Jnana consumes one, rather than one relating to jnana.

So the last part of shunyata's achievement is the experience of ultimate non-ego. You could have the experience of ego to begin with as a hang-up, problematic, irritating. Then you have the transcending of that ego and you feel the absence of ego, the nondualistic qualities of ego; you feel a sense of emptiness, a sense of absence. In the end, at the dharmakaya level, even the absence of ego is not felt, because the whole thing is not seen as an attainment in any way at all. It is not regarded as attainment or nonattainment. In other words, the ultimate understanding of shunyata—or the attainment of shunyatahood, so to speak—is impossible from that point of view. If there are any possibilities, that in itself is self-defeating. "Impossible" in this sense does not necessarily mean that you can't have it, you can't get to it. But the question of getting it does not apply anymore. The question of having it does not apply anymore. It is the complete destruction of ego, completely dissolving the state of ego. So we cannot celebrate that we have attained enlightenment because there is no one to take part in the celebration.

We could have a discussion.

Student: Is there anything positive you can say about ego? Is there anything beneficial about ego? Do you know what I mean?

Chögyam Trungpa Rinpoche: Well, I suppose the spiritual search altogether is due to ego. Without ego, we wouldn't be studying. So ego is the instigator of the whole thing.

S: I have some difficulty with the idea of containment—for instance, that sound contains silence. I can understand that sound *implies* silence, that form *implies* space, or maybe sound *arose out of* silence, but the idea that sound *contains* silence is something I don't grasp.

CTR: You see, that is basically the point of view in which you don't regard yourself as the listener to the sound. The sound or music plays by itself and does not have a player or a listener. Then sound is contained by itself. It's a question of mostly using the language of evaluation, that there is an audience to judge it. So you hear the sound according to the audience, rather than the sound being heard by itself. [*Snaps fan*]

S: Would the formulation that sound *implies* silence and silence *implies* sound be consistent with that?

CTR: That's right, yes. They are complementary to one another.

S: One can't exist without the other.

CTR: That's right. Sound can exist without an audience, without a listener, but sound cannot exist without silence. The idea of shunyata that we have been talking about all this time is not shunyata as we see it, but shunyata as it is—from the point of view of its own dimension.

S: And it's always the ego that evaluates.

CTR: That's right, it is ego that evaluates. And it is also because of ego that we find enormous distortion.

S: But once you rid yourself of the ego, you merge with the total situation.

CTR: That only could happen through ego.

S: You have to pass through that door.

CTR: You have to have ego—somewhat. [*Laughter*]

S: But it isn't necessarily that we should all like it though? [*Partially inaudible*]

CTR: At that point, evaluation doesn't apply. Liking or disliking is arbitrary, because ego is also arbitrary.

S: What would be intelligent discrimination, as in the buddha family wisdom of discrimination, discriminating wisdom?

CTR: That is nonwatcher, from the point of view of ego. You don't have to watch, you don't have to experience, in other words. The experience is there already; therefore the situation becomes discriminating awareness rather than that you are discriminating. Therefore the whole idea of skillful means is that you work according to the situation rather than your view of the situation. You work accordingly, which is still very slow.

S: You said that at first shunyata has a very cold quality, and then you said that after you lose your fears, shunyata develops a warm quality. Could you comment on that?

CTR: To begin with, when we realize that the primitive idea of security does not apply anymore, it is very terrifying, threatening. That comes from the idea of looking for a secure home, to begin with, that you regard spiritual practice as something that secures you. But you come to the understanding that that is not so, that you have to give up the security and give up hope and everything. That gives new perspective to the whole practice. You tend to try to struggle with that, trying to interpret and to reinterpret—that giving up hope is the ultimate hope, giving up security is the ultimate security, and so forth. And we can go on like that, trying to find a way of twisting it around. But we realize that there is no hope, there is no way of finding a new strategy because shunyata is a hard fact. There is nothing you can con about it.

Then, having accepted the whole thing, you can begin to relax. You begin to let things fall through because you realize you have nothing really to lose. If you have anything happen, there is something to gain. So that is the starting point where warmth begins to happen, generosity begins to develop. You have nothing to lose, therefore you have nothing to secure about anything at all. And the spontaneous quality of warmth and compassion is the expression of generosity. You become generous to yourself to begin with; therefore the expression of being generous to others becomes a natural situation.

S: Would you say something about the primitive energy of anger?

CTR: Anger seems to be the same as any of the other emotions. You decide to develop repelling vibrations as a way of proving that you don't need anything. You have everything, therefore you can afford to lose, you can afford to crush down and destroy. It is based on passion, fundamentally speaking. You are so passionately involved in trying to prove something. And the way of demonstrating that passion is rejection, pressing down, destroying.

S: The liberation of it, being prepared for that through the tradition, would create security?

CTR: It creates apprehension. You find that you have to stick to the dogma as something to hang on to, otherwise you could lose everything—which actually doesn't mean that you won't begin to do that. So the aftereffect [of any of those] is to explode, destroy, crush down, and then stick to your own logic, your own dogma, your own philosophy, which secures you and makes you have the right to be angry.

S: Could you just think about the death of shunyata?

CTR: I suppose you could say that the death of shunyata is that when the first two kayas have been passed beyond, prajna becomes jnana. That is the death of shunyata, because shunyata means that you are being aware of emptiness, being aware of formlessness, of the nondualistic state. And that negativity becomes part of the learning process, part of one's experience. So finally, experience begins to merge into nonexperience, nonattainment. That is the experience of dharmakaya, that prajna becomes jnana. Thank you.

S: Do you mean that which is aware of space actually becomes space itself? So there is no, there is not—

CTR: That's right, yes. I know what you mean. [*Laughter*]

S: What is the difference between evaluation and discrimination?

CTR: You could say that evaluation is primitive discrimination. You don't see things as they are, but you need some help to see things as they are, which is putting value on it. But in true discrimination, particularly in terms of discriminating awareness wisdom, you don't need the help of evaluation anymore because you just see things simply as they are without reinforcement. In other words, evaluation seems to have a sense of uncertainty. You need somebody else, somebody else's help to make sure that your experience is the safe one, the right one, the good one or the bad one, whatever. In the case of discriminating, you are not dependent on anything at all. It's just firsthand experience, one blow.

S: Rinpoche, why does Buddhist literature sometimes say to stop discriminating and other times says discriminating mind is the mind of wisdom? Yesterday you mentioned something about discrimination and projection, that you discriminate that it's four o'clock or you discriminate that this is an enemy and that is a lover, that kind of stuff. That is a kind of discrimination, but I have a feeling that there is also a bad kind. Do you know what that is?

CTR: Well, as I said already, discriminating in terms of evaluation is primitive discrimination. Once you have perceived things, I don't think you need to evaluate them or that you need confirmation. In the case of discriminating awareness wisdom, evaluation doesn't apply anymore because evaluation confuses you further as to what you are discriminating.

S: Is it more direct?

CTR: Yes. We could say that it is your flash of experience.

S: What?

CTR: The spontaneity.

S: Rinpoche, I've been trying to figure out what you mean by discipline. I'm not exactly sure.

CTR: Again, there seem to be different levels of discipline: disciplining in order to achieve something, and disciplining because things are as they are. The first one, disciplining because of something, is not really discipline but looking for an alternative situation to occupy your renunciation by accepting something new into it. There's the story of King Prithika, who dreamt elephants went out of the house through the window but their tails could not get out of the window. He thought that was a bad omen for his kingdom, his future. So he asked the Buddha. And the Buddha said: That is a prophetic dream for my followers. They leave home and renounce their homes and sense pleasures, but their viharas, or monasteries, become secondary homes. So they can't get out of that; their tails get stuck.

Then there is another kind of discipline, which is just reducing unnecessary things. It is not necessarily giving up or renouncing, but simplifying, not producing new stuff or further confusions to occupy yourself. It is like the practice of meditation, for instance.

It is a simple technique, a simple practice, and you just work with that. You are not regarded as following a course, but you regard your practice as purely relating with your basic innate nature. No further stuff has been introduced at all. The same thing applies in your living situation. You live a disciplined life by not introducing further chaos. That chaos might take the form of seduction or the form of destroying seduction, whatever it may be. Both seem to be sidetracks. So discipline is being true, to the right point, not introducing further stuff, not giving yourself further toys.

S: You spoke of the obligatory emotions of the ego, the repertory of emotions driving the ego. I wonder if you mean that they are obligatory in the sense that in the state one is in—and the ego is the result of that state—those emotions are also necessary, that they are both necessary and convincing to this state. You also said that the ego is distorting something in the process. Is it the material of the higher emotions that is being distorted? Is that material always there, but in wrong function in the state where we are within the sleep of ego? And then one's recognition begins to awaken about how lost one is in this state and that recognition begins to free that material back into the place in you where it can function with its right normality. That is, you might mature emotions or develop emotions through freeing yourself from using the material of emotions.

CTR: Obligatory is simply from ego's point of view. It is obligatory because we have to maintain ourselves by presenting all kinds of occupations. We reject that which is about to attack our territory and we invite that which secures our territory. That seems to be the obligatory ape-instinct ego, animal instinct of ego.

S: To maintain its state?

CTR: To maintain itself, yes. But at the same time, the validity of ego is the question. Actually, there is no such thing as ego as a solid thing at all. Should we regard ego as a substantial entity? According to ego's appearance in the past, the meditative path as well as our own experience shows that ego is not founded on solid ground, but ego is founded on playing with interactions. Ego is founded on relative situations. Unless there is the logic of relativity, ego cannot exist; it cannot exist independent of relative law. So ego becomes irrelevant from that point of view for the very reason that there is no such thing as ultimate ego. If there is going to be an ultimate one then it has to be free from relative notions. So ego is not relevant. Therefore its obligatory actions are also not relevant.

S: If it's a false state, or a relative state, still it malfunctions possibly higher energy processes and it maintains the reduction, a pathological reduction of the energies of consciousness.

CTR: It's hard to maintain oneself. You'd rather stick to your whatever, your lie or your confusion.

S: Without knowing?

CTR: Without knowing. Even though you might know that it is a possible failure of establishing firm ground, still you may feel you should try to set up some kind of security, so you do it.

S: You like the mistake, you like it.

CTR: Try to like it.

S: Rinpoche, would spiritual materialism permeate as long as one has an ego? I guess it could be equated to that idea of gaining something spiritual.

CTR: I suppose in the subtle sense, as long as there is ego there would be spiritual materialism, definitely, as a faint subconscious desire. But the crude quality of spiritual materialism could be understood, including ego. While you are not free from ego, you still can understand spiritual materialism and take certain solid and crude measures to avoid spiritual materialism. It is not really a refined thing, to the point of dissolving ego. One can do something about it. At the same time, that doesn't mean there is no tendency of spiritual materialism at all. As long as there is ego, there will be some tendency of achievement, of getting somewhere, becoming a better person, whatever. There are always those tendencies there.

S: I was wondering also why there seems to be such an overabundance of spiritual materialism in the West.

CTR: Well, the Western mind operates in terms of achievement. If you are a climber of mountains, a mountaineer, you don't just climb, you climb in order to get some reward, break a record, make world history, or whatever. So even if the search is supposedly a pleasurable one, still there is meaning behind it. You must be doing something always. You must be. You must not be idle. The same thing applies even if we are meditating. We try to prove to ourselves that we are not being idle, but we are productive people whether we meditate [or not]. We meditate in order to be more productive! [*Laughter*] That kind of relation goes on always. So it's a natural tendency—losing grip is socially, economically, something that we don't want to face.

S: Is it ego, or ego image, that represses that? Because all these examples seem to be identical to the image we have of ourselves, in other words, ego image. Can't ego exist without the image?

CTR: That seems to be saying the same thing. Ego is built out of image, so if you don't have image you don't have ego either, because ego thrives on image. It's saying the same thing. There is no such thing as a subtle ego. Ego is always based on some form, some particular energy which is obvious.

S: You mean that without image there is no ego?

CTR: There is no ego, that's right.

S: Rinpoche, sometimes I just like to sit and do nothing, not even meditate, but just maybe feel my mouth get dry or my little finger hurt or something like that. But after a very short while I get panicky because so little happens. And yet I would like to be able to do that. It is like I'm enjoying that somehow, and then I'm not able to.

CTR: You are enjoying that?

S: Well, I think it's only pleasure, I don't know. The moment I'm doing it I'm enjoying it, but after a short while I feel panicky, like nothing is happening here at all. I can't explain why I get panicky.

CTR: I suppose we could say that when you lose your grip on something when you are alarmed; that always tends to happen. It's a question of meditation being especially presented so that you lose your grip on ego. So it's very frightening at the beginning. You begin to realize that you are losing something, but at the same time you don't know what that something is. But something is leaving you.

S: So should I forget about being panicky and just continue?

CTR: Even if you try to forget the panicking, it will be there always anyway.

S: Or should I accept the panicking and just go on?

CTR: Rather.

S: What?

CTR: Rather.

S: Rather? [*Laughter*]

CTR: Mm-hmm. [*Laughter*]

S: Rinpoche, in terms of the image, the ego being in the image, when you look at us, do you see the image before our expression of ego distorting something very high?

CTR: Hmmm! [*Laughter*]

S: How can you make me see that?

CTR: Well, if you were willing to see it, you could see it.

S: I like my expressions, you mean.

CTR: That's what I mean.

S: The momentum and the action of it is monumentally gripping!

CTR: Yes. [*Laughter*] There is no question of how to do it, but if you are willing to do it, it's there. That's very difficult to accept because we want to know *how* to do it, which means another kind of security. You simply refuse: you can't just do it, you have to be told how to do it. That is one of the biggest problems that a lot of my students have, it seems.

S: Sir, do various amounts of hopelessness develop along with the development of certain psychological states along the path?

CTR: Well, it depends.

S: But if it happens, it doesn't happen all at once but different amounts of it tend to go along—

CTR: Not necessarily. Depending on how much you give in to losing grip, that much development takes place.

S: What if a mountain becomes like a volcano?

CTR: Then it is so. What about it?

S: It's pretty frightening!

CTR: Delightful [*inaudible*] too.

S: But is there a good way to pacify a mountain?

CTR: No, it doesn't sound like a practical thing to do.

S: What about surrendering?

CTR: Even if you try to surrender in order to pacify, that in itself becomes a game. You are thrown back. You see, what we are doing in this case is dealing with natural forces. You can't strategize and you can't manipulate them because they are natural forces. You can think of different ways of touching fire—think this is not fire, think this is water, think it is going to be nice and warm—but nonetheless your hands are going to get burned whatever you try. [*Laughter*] There's no way of fooling the elements. What we are dealing with is the most powerful element of all, which is called mind.

S: But didn't you sort of guarantee that the operation would be a slow, surgical thing, that the operation would be very slow—not like the Naropa thing.

CTR: Well, there have to be some dramatic operations sometimes, as you say.

S: Rinpoche, Milarepa described his mind as residing in dharmakaya. I know he just said it, but nonetheless it seemed somewhat strange. And in the *Diamond Sutra*, Subhuti describes his enlightenment. The context there was "I think indeed that I don't, so I am." But he's saying that he is! You'd think that a person in the dharmakaya would not care about that. Why would he say, "My mind resides in the dharmakaya?"

CTR: The whole point is that you are not reduced to deaf and dumb.

S: I was afraid of that answer.

CTR: You become more intelligent.

S: Is it the dharmakaya itself speaking at that point?

CTR: Dharmakaya, yes. Dharmakaya is dharma body, the body which is the dharma itself. It has developed all kinds of skillful ways of presenting the teachings, so it could speak for itself.

S: And it is aware of itself enough to.

CTR: I wouldn't say aware of itself, but it happens that way. [*Laughter*]

S: There is no way you could compare that mind to our own as we experience it now?

CTR: Well, I suppose we could try very hard to compare, but it wouldn't be accurate to do that. You have to speak through the language of metaphor. Then the metaphor itself becomes a hang-up. It's like the old story of the person who points out the moon to his child.

When the child asks, "What is the moon?" he points and says, "That is the moon." And the child says, "Oh I never realized that the moon was oblong." [*Laughter*]

S: Is the light inside the mind part of shunyata, or is it a sidetrack, some kind of diversion?

CTR: The light?

S: The light, the clear light.

CTR: It depends on what you refer to as light. Obviously it is not just a visual matter.

S: When you go inside your mind, it's like there's a bright light, and if you keep meditating it gets brighter and brighter.

CTR: Does it?

S: I think so. They say there are seven steps on the way to the third eye.

CTR: Um—no! [*Laughter*]

S: I was wondering what that had to do with shunyata?

CTR: Doesn't sound like it, particularly. [*Laughter*] Shunyata is very simple. That's why it is called shunyata, empty. There's nothing, absolutely nothing.

S: But what is the light, what is that?

CTR: Reflections, I suppose. [Injuries?] tend to make, create a spark.

S: When you talk about surrendering ego, at least to me, it is a very fearful thing. Without the fear though, could the surrender of ego be the first act of generosity from your point of view?

CTR: But that seems to be what we have to start with. There's no other way, you see. There's no way of getting sedatives so that you won't be afraid of surrendering and *then* surrendering. That's not possible at all. We have to use the fear itself as a stepping-stone. That's the style of practice that is always presented—using whatever is there as an obstacle, as a ladder, as a stepping-stone. That seems to be the only way that we can do it. We can't start perfectly, but we have to start in a clumsy way. Finally, that clumsiness becomes perfection because we are willing to relate with it. It wears itself out. That seems to be the only way that we can do it—whatever we do.

S: By attrition it wears itself out, by doing it?

CTR: By actually pushing it, doing it—*as though* you are doing it, rather.

S: Does that happen only through meditation, or are these things that you can consciously have in your life?

CTR: Anything in your life. If your life is regarded as a learning process, there will be all kinds of opportunities to do that.

S: Rinpoche, is it possible that people who haven't lost their ego yet will sometimes act in an egoless way?

CTR: There are always possibilities. Glimpses of egolessness happen quite frequently. I wouldn't say that you have to get to a definite state, necessarily. There are always possibilities of doing something by chance—apparently by chance.

Well, we might have to close our sermon on shunyata.

S: I have sort of a ragged question—in the *Jewel Ornament of Liberation*, Gampopa described a whole series of hells, eighteen hells, and I don't know how many heavens. He also talks very definitely, that if you do this, the fate of that will naturally be that. How literally is all that supposed to be taken or what? [*Laughter*]

CTR: Well, the thing is that it is possible. It is possible and it might be literal.

S: You mean those hells actually exist in so many miles down in the depths of the earth? And you have beings boiling you in hot copper and putting things into your mouth and—

CTR: Possible. [*Laughter*] I think saying it is not literal, that it is purely symbolic, has a different tone to it. Somehow it is not wise to say that it is purely symbolic. But on the whole, what is the difference between symbol and reality, anyway?

S: We use the symbol as an expression of something which cannot be—

CTR: Precisely, yes. So the intensity of the result of aggression can only be described by hell, descriptions of how grotesquely you could be boiled or punished or tortured.

S: What marks the karmic sequences he lays out there?

CTR: Well, nobody has done any research work on that particularly, [*laughter*] like the study of physics and chemistry. But it is based on, or depends on, the level of absent-mindedness, of not being on the spot. There are all kinds of sidetracks that you suffer, anyway.

S: But he gives specific instances: if you do this, that happens.

CTR: That's right. Yes.

S: That's very precise speaking. How precise is it supposed to be?

CTR: Up to you.

S: I can't figure it out, that's why I am asking you.

CTR: Try to figure it out! [*Laughter*]

S: Well, . . . [*inaudible*].

CTR: Shunyata study seems to have evolved itself from the groundwork of shunyata, in which we discussed hopelessness and disappointment and so on—that you have no ground to work with. Then there's the path, in which giving up hope becomes connected with warmth and generosity. Finally one begins to realize that one can be generous, how to be generous. From that path, the final point of shunyata transcends, relating with shunyata as an experience. The question of goal and path does not exist. So it seems that the shunyata principle altogether is the ground in which everything functions, everything happens—it is the space that accommodates everything.

There are books on the *Prajnaparamita Hridaya* and *Prajna-*

paramita Alankara, translated by Dr. Conze,* which would probably be helpful if you want to follow up and study further the principle of shunyata. It seems that shunyata is, on the whole, one of the very important points of Buddhist teaching. The ideas of impermanence, suffering, and selflessness, or egolessness, are founded in the basic environment, basic idea of shunyata.

And quite possibly we could have longer seminars at some stage. This particular seminar seems to be just purely an appetizer. [*Laughter*] Thank you for being very patient.

Buddhist Wisdom Books (London: George Allen & Unwin, 1958) and *The Perfection of Wisdom in Eight Thousand Lines and Its Verse Summary* (San Francisco: Four Seasons Foundation, 1973).

GLIMPSES OF SPACE

PART ONE

The Feminine Principle

1

The Mother Principle

WHAT WE ARE planning to discuss here is the Buddhist approach to basic principles in feminine reality. So this particular seminar, I would like to point out quite boldly and specifically, is not a politics or sociology course, but is connected with the practice of meditation and phenomenal reality, and the feminine aspects as well as the masculine aspects connected with that.

We could approach the basic question from the beginning, in terms of the categories or principles known in the Buddhist tradition as the three jewels: the buddha, or teacher; the dharma, or the teachings; and the sangha, or group of followers, students. We are starting from the question of whether the chicken is first or the egg is first—that is to say, whether Buddha is first or dharma is first, in this particular case. We are not yet going to discuss if eggs should be utilized as further chickens or as part of a meal.

This question of whether buddha is first or dharma is first is a very interesting one. If there were no buddha, it would not be possible to have dharma; but in order for there to be a buddha, there would have to be dharma. A lot of teachers in the past have spent their lifetimes studying which comes first—as much as people spend time trying to figure out which came first, the egg or the chicken. It seems that both are related to the feminine principle. If there is an egg, then the feminine principle had to be involved; even if there is a chicken, the feminine principle had to be involved. That same principle implies that the originator of dharma, the originator of buddha, had to come first. At this level, we are talking about the question of the mother principle, the level of totality and background.

In the Buddhist tradition somehow—as a result of people's experience, their research work, so to speak, and from the example of the Buddha's life—it is quite clear that the dharma came first: the dharma of reality. That is to say, pain and pleasure, the conflicts of life, the idea of falsity and the idea of truth. Following the principle of the four noble truths, Buddha's first reaction to the world was the discovery that there is unspeakable, unnameable, fundamental pain, which produces the reality of the confused realm. Because of that, he also realized that there is a realm of nonexistence—no ego, no basic being, no substance. But at the same time, there had to be some intelligent mind to experience that realm. That intelligence is called prajna. Consequently, prajna is referred to as the mother of all the buddhas. So as far as basic reality is concerned, there is nothing but space, unconditional space, space that is not defined or labeled as product or producer. That is the mother of all the buddhas.

The question is, "How will we be able to experience that space, to understand it?" According to the teachings, the answer seems to be that we cannot understand that space, we cannot perceive it. There is no way to find out even whether that space does exist or does not. At the same time, we question ourselves. "Who said that?"—but if you ask somebody, nobody said it. But it still hums in the background. Such primordial gossip is all-pervasive and one can't ignore it. And having heard that gossip, if you try to find the source, you cannot trace it back.

That space is called, in the traditional terminology, dharmadhatu: *dharma* meaning, in this case, "basic norm," and *dhatu* meaning "atmosphere." Such a basic norm is created by this atmosphere. Not "created," that is a wrong term, but it actually exists like that. There is a basic atmosphere of openness and all-pervasiveness involved, so in this case we cannot talk about the mother principle as being one or many, but in some sense, the mother principle came first.

Prajnaparamita is actually *not* the name of the mother principle. The word *prajnaparamita* means "transcendental knowledge." The mother of all the buddhas is in some sense an incorrect term, in fact. When we talk about the mother of all the buddhas, we are talking in terms of its *function:* somebody produced a child, therefore she should be called "mother." That is still a conditional definition. If we look back, we cannot even call it mother. We cannot even define this particular relative norm as a masculine or feminine principle—we can only talk in terms of the basic atmosphere. The only way or reason we can refer to it as feminine principle is that it has the sense of accommodation and the potentiality of giving birth. Prajnaparamita, transcendental knowledge, is an *expression* of that feminine principle, called "mother." Mother is one of its attributes. Maybe that attribute is just a cliché; maybe it is purely a concept. But beyond that, there is nothing actually nameable, nothing actually workable.

Supposing one of its attributes is being a mother, then we could say, "Who is the father?" We generally automatically assume that if we call somebody mother, it means that somebody has a child and a husband, or father of the child. But in this case that doesn't seem to work. In some sense, the whole thing seems to be a dead end. Not dead end in the sense of being blocked or not having any further to go back, but dead end in the sense that we find that the child is born from this mother without a father. We do not know whether this mother is masculine or feminine. Something happened in the realm of the primeval state. Something funny has happened. Something has come about without any reason, without any causal characteristics. According to the descriptions of the Buddha, prajnaparamita is referred to as unborn, unceasing; its nature is like that of the sky. That is only understandable to the wisdom of discriminating awareness. Therefore, discriminating awareness is referred to as the mother of all the buddhas.

If this basic whatever is unborn, unoriginated, and unceasing, how can it exist, how can we talk about it? Well, we cannot talk about it. But we can—and actually, we are doing so at this very moment. Impossibilities are possible, un-talk-aboutness can be talked. One of the definitions of *dharmadhatu* is that which possesses basic norm, that which possesses basic intelligence. But again, we have to be very careful: we are not talking about the alayavijnana principle of storehouse consciousness in this case; we are talking about something beyond that. We are not talking of something that contains something within it.

It seems that this fundamental mother principle—feminine principle, if you could call it that, or "it," if you like—it has become feminine principle and it has become mother because it became expressive. It could manifest itself into various attributes: it became angry, seductive, yielding, accepting, shy, and beautiful. It became feminine principle, and then it became mother principle. And it made love to its own expressions. Therefore, it produced a buddha—as well as samsara, of course, and all the rest of it.

We could have a discussion on that, if you like.

Student: This thing being referred to as "it," or the feminine principle, which is somewhat beyond samsaric mind or even the alaya consciousness, seems to be very far away. And it is definitely "it," and it definitely exists, and it definitely creates or gives expression to buddhas and samsara. It expresses itself in wrathful ways and seductive ways, et cetera. What is the difference between this definite thing that exists and the common notion of theism or God?

Chögyam Trungpa Rinpoche: God is not referred to as she, usually.

[*Laughter*] I think also, one point is that God had a definite intention to do something about it and produced the world; whereas, as far as this is concerned, it is just accidental, purely accidental. It begins to put on makeup and so it becomes feminine. This is much more passive and realistic. God seems to be very dreamy and impractical—and very dramatic, unnecessarily so. Moreover, there is a much stronger sense of "I." God is supposed to have already separated himself from the rest of his creation—before he created anything, he had become himself already. As you know, the utterance of God is, "I am that which I am." So he is what he is, therefore he produced the others. In this case, that is not necessary—its beauty and its makeup are not apart from itself. Therefore, it becomes feminine, which is very passive. We could almost say the whole thing is accidental. And in terms of God principle, it has more substance.

S: It sounded very much like the description of the immaculate conception when you were saying, "This is the mother that gives birth to buddha, but in this case there's no father." What's the difference between saying that and saying there was an immaculate conception?

CTR: I think the question of purity doesn't enter here particularly at all. This does not concern conception. In fact, nobody got pregnant—you just produced buddha on the spot. So we are not talking about the womb, particularly, and we are not talking about an embryo in this case. We are saying that this has produced buddha on the spot, at the drop of a hat.

S: I wanted to ask one more thing. When you said that it could be called feminine or masculine, that it was almost accidental that it was called feminine, were you saying that it was sort of cultural that it was called feminine principle?

CTR: Well, I think it was a practical thing. If anybody has borne a child, you wouldn't call them a masculine person; obviously it is a feminine one. And if you have borne a child, even if you are a masculine person, you are called mother.

S: The feeling I get of this expression of space is that it could be something like a rock, that a rock could be an expression of space.

CTR: Why did you say that?

S: Because it seems like your idea of space is something more than our conventional view, in the sense that there is nothing there. It seems that space can have attributes and qualities that could be an expression of it, and even a rock could be an expression of space. Is that wrong?

CTR: Well, the only problem is that a rock is different from space—unless you are inside the rock.

S: What is rockness, as opposed to space?

CTR: A rock is a rock, you know. [*Laughter*]

S: As *opposed* to space? So it is something *outside* of space, then?

CTR: Well, a rock is sitting there, and rain falls on it and snow falls on it. You build a house with it and you walk over it, but you can't do that with space.

S: So then there is a duality, with dharmadhatu as all-encompassing space, and then things or rocks or various materials that are hanging out in that?

CTR: Well, everything seems to be, anything you can think of—or you can't think of.

S: Anything you can or cannot think of?

CTR: Yes.

S: What I'm trying to get to is that your idea of space is more than the conventional idea, such as air or something like that.

CTR: We are not talking about outer space. We are talking about that which is—that which *isn't*, at the same time.

S: Well, what are the attributes of dharmadhatu that you said it expressed? ("It put on makeup," "it took on attributes.")

CTR: Yes, which is a part of itself. Space is usually adorned or embellished with its outlines, which is part of the expression of space.

S: Could those outlines be a rock or something like that?

CTR: Yes. They could be anything.

S: Isn't there something unaccommodating about a specific attribute?

CTR: Anything other, anything conventionally not known as space, is part of space's attributes.

S: Okay. But that seems to have some lack of accommodation in it, doesn't it.

CTR: It is very accommodating.

S: What did you mean by *basic norm*? I did not understand that word at all.

CTR: Well, it's some sort of law that is not particularly created by a lawmaker. It is just characteristics of whatever it may be.

S: Just what is.

CTR: Yeah.

S: What are dakinis?

CTR: One never knows. [*Scattered laughter*] One never knows!

S: Rinpoche, could you please explain what attribute would accommodate the manifestation of prajna, the mother aspect?

CTR: I think it's like when you throw a stone in a very still pond: there are ripples that express that you have thrown a stone into the pond. You have thrown a stone in this water, which is called a pond, and the ripples begin to expand and dissolve at the edges of the pond. It's something like that. It is expressing its own existence through demonstrating, exhibiting, some form of glamour—in the form of passion, aggression, being seductive, whatever it may be.

S: It think one other time you said it was something like pollution, that would manifest into a form. Is that right?

CTR: That's an interesting metaphor. I suppose it could be pollution if somebody got an experience out of it. It's anything you can think of: lighting a match in the dark, somebody tripping over dog shit, anything.

S: You said that it just happened accidentally. Did you mean that the Buddha was an accident?

CTR: Mm-hmm. A big accident. A catastrophe!

S: Is prajnaparamita the intelligence that knows dharmadhatu?

CTR: Yes. It knows its mother.

S: But is prajnaparamita called mother too?

CTR: Yes.

S: So there's a mother that knows the mother?

CTR: Yes. The makeup knows what it belongs to. The makeup knows its source, its background.

S: Could it be said that prajna is the self-consciousness of dharmadhatu?

CTR: Not very much self there, but you could call it that way if you like. That would be some kind of Jewish logic.

S: Before, you said that whatever wasn't space was the attributes of space. What would be the substance of an attribute?

CTR: Well, that's a question: there doesn't seem to be anything—it seems to be everything. We do not know. We only know the gossip.

S: We seem to be able to know something is unknowable, though, as dharmadhatu?

CTR: Because it's unknowable, therefore we know it.

S: Why? The same thing doesn't apply with the attributes, though—because *that's* unknowable we *don't* know it.

CTR: Attributes are easy to know. They are prajnaparamita and everything.

S: Oh, I see. You mean we can know what we don't know, but we can't know what we know?

CTR: Sure. [*Laughter*]

S: Perfectly clear. I should have known!

Well, maybe we should stop here tonight so we have a chance to sleep and rest. Although this is a short seminar, still I would like to encourage people to try as much as they can to take part in the practice of meditation. We feel it is important that you do not become too heady through the seminar, and that we are not transplanting further samsara in your head and in our scene. In order to keep everything unpolluted, the best way to do something about that, or at least attempt to do something about it, is the practice of meditation. That is very important, needless to say. Basically it is part of the seminar intention that you should get enough chance to sit, as well as to think and listen. Unless everything is on an equal basis, you become too much of something or other, so that you are lopsided. In order to make this particular experience experiential, it is necessary to relate to the whole seminar. That is a very important point.

Once again, thank you for being patient. And welcome to Karmê Chöling.

2

Unborn, Unceasing

CONTINUING WHAT WE discussed yesterday, the manifestation from the unknown and its process to reality, so to speak, is quite an involved one. I suppose you want to get into this.

UNBORN

That principle is identified as a principle, or substance, with particular qualifications. It is threefold, as we discussed yesterday: unborn, unceasing, and its nature is like that of space or sky. So the question of unborn, in this case, is that the basic ground has manifested itself. It is taking a direction toward reality, through a sense of love, compassion, and warmth. The three qualities of love, compassion, and warmth are synonymous with the desire to manifest at all. The desire to manifest is that the basic space has been qualified, or become a personality. When that space has a tinge of something or other, then that is called manifestation—or love, compassion, and warmth.

At that point the process is still very undefined, in some sense; but at the same time it has the qualities of unborn. For one thing, there is no one to give birth. Another part is the rejection of a particular birth, a particular channel for birth, a channel to be born as reality, which is known as *dharmata* in Buddhist terminology. *Dharma* is "basic norm"; *ta* is "ness"; so *dharmata* is a sense of "isness," or "nowness." In other words, it's a question of living reality rather than preconceived, or uncertainty, or yielding toward a certain particular direction of giving birth to reality.

Unborn is also qualified as "unborn and not having the desire to be born." It is not willing to play with sophistries or garbage of all kinds. So the only basic area or basic feeling that we can come across is a sense of self-existing, transcendental arrogance. There is an unyielding quality, and there is a sense of complete certainty, at this point, which makes birth possible, unborn birth possible. Such confidence comes from having no characteristics, no background. Therefore we could say quite plainly that you have nothing to lose. So you can afford to be arrogant and proud and chauvinistic, in some sense, at that point. But some basic depth and basic texture that is fertility oriented takes place. Such fertility orientation is only manifested at the level of its fickleness, in the form of exchange back and forth: you are willing to play with phenomena, willing to give birth to phenomena at all. Therefore there is a sense of journeying, which is made out of energy. And the basic characteristic of energy there is its fickleness, its vibrating quality—the fickle quality of being willing to *associate* itself with something or other.

This approach may be quite similar to that of Nagarjuna's, when he talks about the Madhyamaka philosophy and his points of view to it. He said, "Since I do not stand for any opposite arguments; therefore, I cannot be challenged." It is that kind of fertility of really raving on some kind of egoless trip: you have nothing to lose; therefore you begin to gain the whole cosmos or universe. In that kind of chauvinistic approach, you are dying to give birth at the same time, because you have nothing to lose. The conventional idea of giving birth is that you are stuck with your kid or whatever. You have to feed the kid and change the kid's diapers, you have to give some energy—you can't have free time to go to theaters and go to the cinema and have dinner dates with friends. You are stuck with this particular kid, and you are imprisoned in some sense. But in this case, it's not so much details but the general creativity that takes place within the base of the unborn level. At the unborn level giving birth is not particularly accented as a reproduction of your image to someone else's, but it is a process of embellishment that takes place. That is regarded as giving birth—rather than producing a child who is separate from you, and you have to cut the umbilical cord, so you are producing another little monster outside of you.

I'm afraid the whole thing seems to be quite abstract at this level. I appreciate this very much as I haven't had a chance to speak this way for a long time. The question of unborn could be said to be an unoriginated one, I suppose. It is not production of some kind—but the question of unbornness is putting further embellishment on unborn.

[*Long pause*] What were we talking about? [*Laughter*]

Unbornness becomes *more* unborn if you begin to embellish it with its attributes. Obviously you accept that logic, that's the usual situation—that you could become more of you if you adorn yourself with all kinds of things; that adorning yourself makes more of you. Embellishment, in this case, is nothing, not very much. It is simply a sense of arrogance and a sense of fearlessness that whatever it is, it is presentable and powerful. It is more a taking pride in nonexistent achievement—which is in *itself* an achievement. Very abstract.

Saraha and other siddhas talk about this as being the imprint of a bird in the sky, which is the basic metaphor, the closest to it that one can use. In this case it is an embellishment of the sky and the bird at the same time. We are uncertain as to which one we are trying to embellish, the bird or the sky. But something is embellished by both; they are complementing each other. The sky is embellished by the bird, and the bird is embellished by the sky because a bird cannot leave any trace behind it. Naropa talks in terms of a snake uncoiling itself in midair: if you throw a coiled snake into midair, it uncoils itself and lands on the ground gracefully.

All of those metaphors and reference points begin to speak in terms of self-existing, self-doing, self-accomplishment of some kind. So we can say that reality can be realized only by realizing its unrealness. This is tantric jargon. [*Laughter*] It is not one of Rinzai's koans, particularly. It is not as subtle as Rinzai's approach. This is more bold and absurd, as you can see. But at the same time, we take pride in that. Maybe that has something to do with what we were talking about as arrogance—in this case, the basic principle of becoming, of femininity. That's what we are talking about at this point.

Becoming, or femininity, is very intangible. The feminine principle has become—for a long time in the history of the human race, from as soon as philosophy was set up—a debatable point. People try to create chauvinistic barriers of all kinds, a masculine *and* feminine approach. But none of them have become particularly good ones, or at least, enlightened ones. So if you resort back to tantric attitudes and ideas of feminine principle, you end up seeing everything as a real world that you cannot grasp. That seems to be the essence of the feminine principle—that real world that you cannot grasp.

You cannot actually capture that in the form of chauvinism. Why? Because the feminine principle is the mother of all principles. If you can catch the mother, then the mother ceases to be a mother—it becomes a lover. So the mother is regarded as something that is hierarchically above. Nobody will question the existence of the mother; the mother reigns on a high throne. She just behaves as a mother.

In order to experience that kind of situation, that kind of reality—however unrealistic it may be—one has to be willing to give in to it, to abandon trying to capture it philosophically, or by metaphysical concepts. You cannot put the mother principle in black-and-white written language. Although books on prajnaparamita are written, as the mother of all the buddhas, those books say that this book cannot be captured, cannot be put into a corner, cannot be cornered. This book cannot be realized. If you *have* realized the meaning of this book, you are regarded as a heretic! [*Long pause*]

UNCEASING

We can discuss unceasing here, which is our second topic tonight. Unceasing. Unceasing occurred because it is unborn, obviously. [*Laughs.*] You could say unborn is some kind of birth, *maybe so*, but on the other hand *absolutely not.* For the very fact that the idea of that becomes reality—that means that idea cannot be captured, which is the unceasing quality. You cannot grasp, you cannot hold, you cannot capture, anymore. The reason it is called unceasing is because out of that particular arrogance that we discussed, some kind of leak of secret information or of secret experience begins to take place. On the quiet, the unborn begins to manufacture a world, an under-world—in midair, the bottom of the ocean. And that is unceasing because it cannot be obstructed or prevented.

If the underground world is very active, the overground world of the established samsaric administration cannot see; it is not able to see that particular world. In other words, we are talking about the black market of the mother. That concept is extremely powerful, *extremely* powerful. That concept is some kind of spiritual atomic bomb—that has been manufactured in the basement. [*Laughter*]

The idea of unceasing is not so much unceasing as a resigned, passive thing—but it is unable to be controlled by any efficient organization of anything. The overlay of reality is unable to detect the underlayer of reality anymore. The surface may go quite nonchalantly, it usually does, but the undercurrent is extraordinarily powerful. It begins to manufacture a world of its own, in the feminine principle of potentiality, embryonic and resourceful and glamorous at the same time.

Well, I'm afraid that maybe you don't have any questions. [*Laughter*] I have completely cut its own throat—that is to say, the questions. However, I would like to make a gesture here, that we have space for that.

Student: Last night you talked about space expressing itself in attributes, and that was like space putting on makeup. Are we, as we generally see ourselves in this physical world of matter, that makeup? Or one aspect of that makeup?

Chögyam Trungpa Rinpoche: The physical world is not regarded as the makeup; it is the body. Within the physical world, the *expressions* of the physical world—that fire burns, water moistens, wind blows, space accommodates—that is the makeup. So the idea of makeup is expressing its own integrity.

S: You mean that the makeup is the qualities that the physical world has?

CTR: Yes.

S: If you took the qualities *away* from the physical world, what would you have left?

CTR: Basic minimum. [*Laughter*]

S: Well, considering that basic minimum, which doesn't have any qualities of its own—what's physical about it?

CTR: That's the biggest question of all! It doesn't have any, therefore it does. [*Laughter*]

S: It has the quality of having no qualities.

CTR: And all potentialities.

S: You mean the *potentiality* of having makeup is another of its qualities?

CTR: Yes, obviously. Space is not particularly castrated.

S: [*Pause*] Mm-hmm. [*Laughter*] It sounds like you're saying space is fertile in some sense.

CTR: That's one of the qualities.

S: Now we've got three qualities. Is space anything *more* than the potentiality for the makeup?

CTR: As well, space is that which accommodates *room* for the makeup.

S: Space is that which accommodates room for the makeup?

CTR: If you missed a part of your makeup on your face—that's space. [*Laughter*]

S: Wait, when you said *room* for the makeup—

CTR: I don't mean a room with windows and doors.

S: —you mean by *room* ability to accommodate?

CTR: Yes.

S: So space is that which accommodates the accommodation of makeup?

CTR: Yes.

S: Then what is the accommodation of makeup, if that is not space but something that is accommodated by space?

CTR: Well, that is the same thing.

S: So you have space accommodated by space, and that's space?

CTR: You got it! [*Uproarious laughter*] It is a question of making love to itself—but not quite at the level of masturbation.

S: What is the relationship between the black market of the mother and practice?

CTR: What is practice?

S: Meditation.

CTR: *The* practice.

S: *The* practice.

CTR: Mm-hmm. I think they are synonymous, as a matter of fact. Synonymous, yes. Meditation *is* the black market, from that point of view—it is a very powerful black market that could change a nation's economy.

S: What would you call the law enforcement officers trying to clean up that black market?

CTR: Well, I think law and order becomes, at that point, part of the black market. In the beginning they attempt to speak the language: the organization is trying to speak the language of the black market. And then, when they try to speak the language so that they can communicate with the black marketers, they find *themselves* in the black market.

S: The black market that you were just referring to, is that synonymous with sangha?

CTR: Not quite: it is the ghetto of the sangha. And actually, we have not gotten to that level yet, particularly. It is a very embryonic state we are talking about. We are not talking about anything that is actually applicable; we are talking about the metaphysics of the feminine principle at this point.

S: Also, could you explain the relationship between dharmadhatu as you spoke about it last night, dharmakaya, and dharmata? Mostly, how does the principle of dharmakaya relate to dharmadhatu? Is it some potential energy within that, or—

CTR: It seems that dharmakaya comes much later, actually. What we are talking about at this point is dharmadhatu, on a very primeval, embryonic level.

S: So dharmakaya would be . . . ?

CTR: Obsolete.

S: In the beginning you said that the substance of the feminine principle is threefold: unborn, unceasing, and like the sky. You described unborn and unceasing, but you forgot the sky.

CTR: Tomorrow. It's too many things to say at once.

S: Is space associated with both the underlay and overlay of reality?

CTR: I think so. You see, the underlay and overlay are interdependent, which is not a complete world. In order to have a unified world—in order to be under, in order to be over—there has to be some governing factor, which is space.

S: Is there anything you can say about the world that is revealed by participating in this black market?

CTR: What do you mean by this black market?

S: The black market that you spoke of.

CTR: You don't mean this or that—do you mean *it*?

S: It.

CTR: Yeah. Well, I think that you cannot get away from it, cannot not participate. You are participating in any case.

S: Yeah, but is there something you can say about the qualities of the alternative world that is sort of created on the quiet?

CTR: On the quiet is not regarded as an alternative—it is *necessary*. Among fires, they have their secret language, to be together as fire as much as possible—whether it is lit with flint or matches. Among waters, it is the same thing: they have their secret message all the time. It is a black market that doesn't have to be transmitted to each other or work out passwords. It is a self-existing black market that doesn't need a password anymore. It is a self-existing one already.

S: Are you saying that the black market is really the *only* market?

CTR: Well, that's just an expression. I'm not talking about marketing in terms of—what's the word?

S: Production? Commerce? Barter?

CTR: Commerce. I'm talking about black market in terms of purely the exchange of money and goods taking place that the rest of society doesn't know about. Basically what it does is use raw material.

S: What's happening with the masculine principle while all this is going on with the feminine principle?

CTR: That hasn't arrived yet, at this point.

S: You mean it hasn't manifested?

CTR: Well, as it goes on it *does* manifest, but somehow it is not quite visible yet.

S: Is the feminine principle manifest before the masculine principle?

CTR: Seemingly so.

S: Would understanding the white reality, the white market, as ego be in some way correct? That the world being created, the black market of the mother, is happening beneath the surface of what the ego sees? And if so, then the ego's willingness to learn that language, to be interested in communication with the black marketers—is that another form of subtle ego game, hoping it can do commerce in that market in some way?

CTR: First, it wouldn't be all that serious about the whole thing. And another, the whole thing is not really divided, particularly; it is an organic process. If you have ups or if you have downs, they are both the same thing. The growth of trees and flowers is the expression of the depressions of the earth, otherwise you couldn't have trees and flowers growing. So it works both ways. You can see beautiful flowers, with honey and nectar and everything—that is an expression of the depressions, which is the black market. [*Laughs.*]

S: So then ego in some sense is an expression of the accommodation of space?

CTR: Well, supposedly. But at the same time, it doesn't manifest that way. The whole thing becomes very confused. But what we are talking about at this point is a very primordial level, an early stage. We have not gotten into the later stages yet. So I wouldn't take it too seriously, in terms of a pragmatic level.

Well, talking about pragmatism, people should be hungry. We should close.

3

Nature like Sky

GIVING BIRTH to reality. I think we should be very careful about what we mean by *reality*, at this point. We do not know exactly, but we have some vague concept of it. And probably it would be difficult for those who haven't followed the previous two talks on this particular content to follow completely what we are talking about tonight, tomorrow, and so on. Therefore, it may be worthwhile for newcomers to try to follow up on what has already been said yesterday and the day before.

The question of reality that we are going to discuss tonight contains the basic capacity to give birth to reality; and the second question is, what is reality? The first one, the basic capacity to give birth to reality, is based on the idea of a sense of space: traditionally it has been said that its nature is like the sky. The reason why its nature is like the sky is that tantric imagery speaks of a triangle, or cervix, which is the basis, background, in which birth takes place as you present yourself as the mother principle. The notion of triangle is an interesting point. The definition of triangle refers to the three principles: unborn as one corner, unceasing as another corner, and its nature is like sky as another corner. So there are three corners, three qualifications, three principles. That brings a sense of triangle, at this point.

That basic point is based on a sense of noncentralized space, in terms of one's awareness. It is purely that there is a sense of reminder, or boundary, which actually helps us relate with reality as we go about our daily experiences. The only reminder that takes place is the absence of our awareness; that is the actual reminder. Once that has taken place, then we begin to feel that we have reached a state in which we are not aware of things that are going on around our life.

That sense of reminder takes place on different levels of intensity in our life. Sometimes we crash into a wall as we drive our motorcar, and we are reminded that we should drive very carefully in the future. Sometimes we just burn our finger, or we just have a small scar on our hand or a little bruise on our body. We have gone slightly too far, but somewhat we are sensible enough to refrain from getting too much damage to our body. We get pushed back and we begin to think twice. That is usually the case that happens.

A lot of images could take place. Also, a lot of images are further food for losing one's awareness, because once you have been reminded you regard that as a very solid and extraordinary message. You get tripped up on that particular message; in turn, you go beyond that level, more than you came. You get in more accidents and you become more hurt, thinking that you can play with phenomena because you got the message and you made the connections already. This is one of the problems that usually takes place in our life, overconfidence, which makes things very chaotic and lethal, in some sense. That is the problem with that kind of reminder, that kind of framework. It is literally a framework; but in this case, the frame happens to be a triangle instead of a square. It is to frame a picture of our life in it.

That is the nature like sky, discussed in the traditional framework. The nature like that of the sky is governed by unborn, unceasing, and openness. At the same time, we could also correlate it with three principles that exist: impermanence, suffering, and egolessness, known as the three gates of liberation according to vajrayana discipline, or the three marks of existence according to the hinayana discipline. We could also include that as part of its expression of the spaciousness.

That spaciousness contains a sense of openness. Openness, in this case, is the level where you are not taking too much advantage of your freedom. You expand as much as you could, you can, and then you do not advance beyond that level. You keep your space intact and workable, as a basic principle. This is like the analogy of the cervix, in which a baby could be born up to a certain level of size. You cannot give birth to a gigantic monster and you cannot give birth to a too little one—it has to be somewhat human size, as far as baby size goes. The function of the cervix is to act as some kind of censor. It acts as a customs official at entrances or exits. Anyone who is going to be born in this world is being censored and checked, and if they are too big, they cannot come out—unless you have a cesarean or something of that nature, which is an extraordinary thing to do. And if you are too insignificant, you are not worth bothering with.

It is like entering another country. When you come to another country, you have to show your passport and declare to the customs officials how big, how famous, what kind of wealth you are going to bring into the country, and whether the country can afford to accept such wealth. If you are bringing too many heavy-handed things, the country ends up having economic problems, if you bring too much stuff that is worth a lot of money. Or if you yourself are a heavy-handed person, that might put the citizens of that country out of jobs, because you occupy a great deal of time and space. So usually the governmental and economic approach is very careful as to how much such a country can accept your entrance into that new country, in terms of how much goods you bring and how much knowledge you bring, and if that knowledge is useful or destructive or whatever it may be in this country that you are trying to come into.

The same kind of process takes place at the level of the mother principle's giving birth to reality. It is the same kind of process. The question there is that some kind of basic censorship takes place. Although when we talk about "its nature is like sky," it seems to be carefree and happy-go-lucky, kind of spacious, and everything is good; somehow, the more spaciousness there is, that much more there are restrictions to it. The space becomes very sensitive and very discriminating in some sense, but at the same time very open-minded equally. That seems to be the basic point of giving birth to reality from the notion of space.

I think we could discuss as far as that level today. We could discuss further details tomorrow, if space and time are available to us. You are welcome to ask any existing questions.

Student: I take your first example very personally. Once about three years ago when I was studying your teachings in writing, I burned my hand and that same day went on to destroy my car and drive it into a brick wall. Later on, in a seminar in New York, I asked you how this would resolve itself, as we are all supposed to remember the lion's roar and have courage. I don't. Since you say that it is inescapable that when we get the first warning we are so tripped out by it that we don't—I mean, it seems like you are saying that we will inevitably have the second accident. What is the solution to that?

Chögyam Trungpa Rinpoche: The point is that you are not trying to gain victory from this particular warfare. You do not regard the whole thing as warfare, you regard it as just another way of settling down in that particular country. It seems that your attitude is that when you come to a new country that accepted you as a resident, you get a visa as a resident, and once you are accepted as a resident you have the freedom to do anything, go everywhere. But at the same time, you are not allowed to bargain at the supermarket. You collect as much as you can collect in your cart and you say to the cashier, "Come here. Look, I bought a lot of stuff here. How much reduction could you give me?" And you cannot bargain them down. Everything has to be counted, and it depends on the price tag.

From that point of view, coming to the supermarket is very interesting symbolism. That place you accepted, the country you came to, is your country for the time being; therefore, you go to the supermarket and make yourself at home. Having gone to the supermarket, you cannot bargain; you have to accept the values that are set up already. You have to go along with the law and order that exists in that country. You cannot get reductions, and you can't bargain down at the supermarket. So you can't do anything. You can't get out of it; you have to go along with it.

S: And you get your freedom from going along with it?

CTR: Yes. You can buy anything you want, but you have to pay for it, as we know. But paying for it is also part of your expression of freedom.

S: Very often the symbol of the overlapping triangles appears. What is the meaning of that?

CTR: I think it is a question of the symbol of double vision, that you see reality and you also see the shadow of it. Therefore, reality and its shadow begin to form a pattern together, which is the experience of reality and also the experience of its spokesman at the same time. Nothing particularly Jewish.

S: In relation to what you just said, what is the significance of Buddha having been born out of his mother's side?

CTR: We do not know. Whether it was a cesarean or actually giving birth, we do not know. From a common-sense point of view, the side is a question of bypassing the ordinary exit. It wasn't regarded as a cesarean. It was a simple accident: his mother took a walk in the garden and he suddenly appeared. He stepped out of her side and spoke and walked and behaved as a little prince. So the whole thing is very mythical. But at the same time, the question of being free from any kind of conditions seems to be a very interesting point. Maybe he was the son of prajnaparamita, who doesn't have to go through the hassles and problems of conventionality. He did something very extraordinary and revolutionary—he stepped out of his mother's side and he began to speak and to walk.

S: You started out talking about the birth of reality from the mother principle, with the three qualities of the triangle being the cervix. And then you talked about awareness, being aware of the boundaries. I didn't get the transition to awareness, in the sense of awareness as I know it. I mean, the birth of reality from the mother principle seems very distant—but awareness of burning my fingers seems very close.

CTR: I think we are saying the same thing. That is giving birth.

S: Then it is not nearly as far away as I think.

CTR: We are not talking about the meaning of once upon a time you were born as a little kid, in this case. But we are saying that you are being born each time, all the time, and talking about how that works with our reality.

S: What does the word *boundary* mean in that?

CTR: Well, the boundary before you had the crash and after you had the crash.

S: Beyond the boundary lies reality, or within the boundary lies reality?

CTR: Both. Reality is reality. If reality is framed with unreality around it, then it must be false. If falsity is framed with the truth, there is something very suspicious about that. It sounds like a Watergate plot.

S: You talked about what seems to be a control factor, which you called a customs officer and a censor, that has some relationship to the nature of the birth of reality. I am wondering if you can say some more about what this quality is—who is the censor, or what is it?

CTR: I think if I said too much it would probably be unhelpful.

We have to find out. Things are not very easy. We cannot just study the whole thing so we are geared up for everything and we can deal with it. There are guidebooks, of course, but they are not completely do-it-yourself books. The teachings are not do-it-yourself guidelines. One has to experience them. Instead of the book, one has to experience reality. I think the less I say the better at this point. My role seems to be to give successive warnings and successive suggestions, possibilities, and potentialities—and then you go along and you make the journey yourself.

S: Is part of that journey dealing with, or having a relationship with, that censor in meditation?

CTR: As well as anything that you can think of in life. Things that are uncertain to you and things that seem very certain to you—everything is included.

S: The way you talk about the framework and the reminders to pay attention to the situation feels a little bit like the bodhisattva thing of paying attention to what sentient beings need. I am wondering if there is any relation there. Is it something like the bodhisattva attending for the sake of other beings, keeping you on track through the opening, or something like that?

CTR: We have to be very careful about what we mean by *bodhisattva.* We don't mean somebody who does good intentionally in order to achieve enlightenment. Remember that bodhisattvas have abandoned the notion of enlightenment already, so they are somewhat fundamentally wild people. They are also seemingly very reasonable, kind, and gentle people at the same time. But fundamentally, in the depth of their hearts, they are unpredictable people. They have abandoned the notion of enlightenment altogether. So from that point of view, we cannot regard the bodhisattva path as being very predictable, particularly. There is that element of craziness involved, even at the mahayana level.

From that point, we can say quite safely that from beginning to end, as far as Buddhism is concerned, it is an extraordinarily unconventional approach. The conventionalities, moralities, rules and regulations, sensibilities, logics, and everything concerned are rooted in the unconventional approach. Unconventionality is not so much a question of a particular society or culture, that Buddhism may be unconventional to Westerners because it came from the East, or anything of that nature. Buddhism basically seems to be unconventional according to traditional Hinduism, which exists in the East; traditional Bön, Shinto, Taoism, any of the traditional Eastern cultures; and to Judaism and Christianity in the West. Buddhism is seen by all these established religions that exist in the East and West—and they all find Buddhism extremely irritating.

Actually, if you look at the history of Buddhism coming to various countries, people have rejected Buddhism not because they are unaccepting of the truth—they understand the logic of it—but because they found that something is very irritating about Buddhism, which is the unconventionality in accepting any common norm of traditional establishments of any kind. That seems to be part of it. But at the same time, it is quite different from just the revolutionary, or unconventionality from the point of view of carefree hippiedom. It seems to be slightly different than that. Mahayana goes along with that actually, in some sense.

Well, thank you. Ready for the next happening? [Bodhisattva and Refuge vows]

4

Prajnaparamita

HOPEFULLY WE COULD sum up roughly, which is rather hard to do as we have already laid a great deal of groundwork. Maybe we will have to continue to discuss this further, at some other time.

The basic idea, in terms of the space that we discussed yesterday, is how that materialized in the living world, so to speak. One particular point I would like to make very clearly is that when we talk about experiencing the world, we are talking only in terms of the world of mind.

It is very hard to discuss the so-called real world. There doesn't seem to be one. And even if there is, discussing it would bring all kinds of false notions of it and tend to give unnecessary security for people to hang on to. So the world we are going to discuss, that we are talking about, is the world of mind. It is our perception of the world, our version of the world, which is in some sense a true world, and on the other hand, is in some sense a relative world. We do not have to make up our mind which is which, particularly. If we try to do so, again, then at that point we begin to find ourselves with even further confusion or vague assumptions. We find ourselves more confused than actually experiencing.

So the point we are talking about here is the mind's world, the various perspectives and tones, the various emotions that take place—

which is actually the texture of the world, the kind of textures we have created around ourselves. The general assumptions of that particular texture are known, or categorized, into three principles in the Buddhist world. This is not particularly pejorative, necessarily, but in terms of pure energy it is known as the world of ignorance, the world of passion, and the world of aggression.

Those three worlds are somehow manifestations from space. Space in this case becomes more like sky, because very few of us have been to outer space, except one or two people. Our version of outer space is the sky. As we look up, we see the moon and the sun and stars. It is traditionally called sky, which sits on top of this earth. Mistakenly, we begin to see a blue color, and there is the rising and falling of the sun and moon. You can fly closest to it in an airplane, or if you are a bird, but you cannot cover it completely. You have to land again because of the problem of a shortage of fuel and energy—and food, if you are a bird.

So our notion of space is the sky, as far as we know, except what is theoretically written in books or what we might see through a telescope. But even then, if we are looking at the sky from a telescope, that is our version of the world of space. Traditionally space is known as like the sky, therefore; and it is the counterpart of the earth, needless to say. That particular space tends to bring some sense of sympathy, or a sympathetic atmosphere, to the earth. It encourages the earth to exist by providing all kinds of spacious activities—sponsoring rain and snow and the growth of plants. It sponsors all kinds of spaces: the potter's wheel and the pot on it. It sponsors pots to break and water to boil and it sponsors all the other elements to take place, which is very sympathetic. Similarly, we can say that is the feminine principle's compassion or love—which is, again, the same principle as the physical world of space.

That particular space, that particular compassion or love, has different functions. Sometimes its function is to create harmony and relationship; sometimes it creates destruction, which is another form of harmony, in some sense. The process is developed, and because the processes begin to relate with each other, the end product is destruction. Harmony, so called, is purely a conventional idea. If we look at general and basic energy activities, there is some kind of mutual basis of things working together in a particular situation. When energies occur, they begin to project onto situations, and situations begin to move through space and manufacture all kinds of events. That is the destructive one and the creative one together.

Similarly, the enlightenment level of compassion is described as that which contains shunyata, or emptiness, and maitri, a sympathetic attitude: together they become karuna, compassion. In other words, we could say that compassion is made out of the constituents of emptiness, or spaciousness, and at the same time an element of softness, or warmth. The spaciousness creates the destructive, the sort of vacant realm in which things cannot be latched on to and you cannot make a nest out of it. The element of maitri, or loving-kindness, begins to produce a sense of texture and solid reality. It seems that in some sense we all possess that kind of feminine principle in us, in all our states of being. We all have that feminine aspect. Whether we are men or women, we have that quality of basic accommodation without trying.

Out of that accommodation without trying, without effort, very deliberate effort begins to arise because we feel that we can make decisions. If no decision has been made, then it becomes easy to make decisions; or if decisions have been made and fall apart, we can remake decisions again. So we can execute activities in this particular world, which is the fertility aspect of the feminine principle. This encourages us to execute various activities—whether it's in the realm of confusion or in the realm of unconfusion, nonconfusion, whatever.

So the idea of the dakini principle is sometimes regarded as cunning and tricky and helpful and terrible. It also is a part of, or in fact represents in our state of being, the thought process, which acts in the midst of the process of nonthought—which is also another form of thought. So out of nonthinking, or the absence of thinking in which energy activity is building up like a vacuum—out of that, thought occurred. And thought begins to work itself out and begins to sprout arms and legs and to execute various decisions. In fact, it begins to be very fast and very speedy. And it begins to achieve some kind of purposes, whether they are absurd ones or absolutely good or solid ones—whatever—who cares at that point? Something is achieved. So that is the dakini principle, or the feminine active principle that exists in our state of being: the nonthinking process has produced a seed, and the seed sprouts arms and legs and begins to make a cup of tea.

It seems that the practice of meditation in this whole connection is developing another form of intelligence, or prajna as it is traditionally known. Prajna is another form of feminine principle, which is a very specific one, an acquisition of sharp perception. That can be achieved through the practice of meditation. Popularly, meditation is known as purely the development of steadiness and openness and intuition, the level of intuitiveness. But if you relate with the practice of meditation in connection with the feminine principle, the practice of meditation is somehow also regarded as, and becomes, an acquisition of intelligent perception. The reason is that in the practice of meditation, when a person first begins to sit and meditate, you don't get into the stream of activities, speed, business, or whatever. Somewhat you learn to step back and view it again: it is as if instead of being in the movie, you see the footage of it.

The difference is that meditation allows you to step back and watch what is going on in the world. You do not particularly try to cultivate a learning, analytical mind; but at the same time, you learn to see how things work, without a particular analytical way but purely from perception. Then you gain some logic. You begin to get some logic and a sense of understanding how things work, the way things work. You also are able to see through the play of that particular feminine principle that exists; you begin to see through the jokes that have been played on you. You also could see that it has been helpful to you and destructive to you, and everything.

You begin to see through that by stepping back and looking at it. That is another method of the feminine principle, which is known as "she who gives birth to all the buddhas," the prajnaparamita. That is how she gave birth to all the buddhas, to the attainment of enlightenment. In this case, it is quite simply keen perception. We will be able to see the world without misunderstanding, without confusion. We will see clearly and fully the apparent phenomena play of principles, the feminine principle in particular. That seems to be the basic point. So meditation is the only way of subjugating the uncontrollable energies of the feminine principle. Meditation in itself is an act of prajna, from that point of view. Therefore it is in itself the feminine principle. Therefore the whole process here is not so much that the masculine principle and the feminine principle are having a war, but it is the feminine principle seeing itself as it is. It is as if you are looking at your hand and reading your own palm: it is part of you, therefore you can see it.

It seems that the principle of the masculine side is quite an interesting one, again. It is the accommodation of everything that allows the feminine principle to act. This masculine principle is somewhat stubborn and solid and may be slow. It is not necessarily slow as such, but the feminine principle begins to create a contrast. When somebody is going faster, then there is somebody slower, so that kind of natural contrast takes place. It also lends another kind of energy, which is that of the earth rather than that of the sky. It has a journey-upward quality rather than a journey-downward quality. At the same time, instead of the sympathy and softness of the maitri principle that we discussed, the masculine principle seems to have a very angry state of being. It is highly complaining and resentful that you have to go through the space in order to achieve something. The masculine principle is somewhat resentful. At the same time, it gives in and accepts orders from the space—from the mother, so to speak.

In some sense the feminine principle cannot survive if, in fact, there's no one to play with—therefore, both processes are interchangeable in some sense and complementary to each other. We don't have much time to discuss the masculine principle, since we seem to be particularly highly interested in the feminine principle these days. We could discuss the details some other time. There is more to come, obviously. I would like to open this to questions.

Student: Before we were talking about the nature of the attributes of the mother principle. Does that come into the category of the masculine principle? Is that what you were referring to—is that what it is playing with?

Chögyam Trungpa Rinpoche: The attributes? No, I think that has been happening with some purpose, obviously. Embellishment cannot take place without purpose, and the purpose is to subjugate or seduce the critical energy, which is the masculine energy, to seduce that. In fact, the makeup is more likely the way to intimidate the masculine principle. It is like Africans painting their faces before they have a fight, or something.

S: So the embellishment is in some way relating to the masculine principle?

CTR: Yes, it has been instigated through that principle.

S: But originally when you were talking about the mother principle, it seemed like that was alone, that was first, or that was it—that there was nothing else around to be related to.

CTR: Sure, if you look at it from that point of view, as being alone.

But you have to be alone somewhere. You cannot just be alone; otherwise you wouldn't be alone.

S: That just seems to go to the same old question: the feminine principle is not alone because it is somewhere, which is the masculine principle—so then what's the masculine principle?

CTR: No, that is not the point. The feminine principle is alone.

S: In other words, what serves as its contrast to being alone is the masculine principle?

CTR: Yes. Very much so.

S: Could you say something about the relationship between dharmadhatu and shunyata? They are obviously not the same thing, and it doesn't seem like shunyata is an embellishment or a manifestation of dharmadhatu. I find that a little bit confusing.

CTR: Dharmadhatu is space free from relative reference point. It's just space. Shunyata is the study of things from the point of view of overcrowdedness. Consequently, the discovery is that you find everything apparently empty, because things are very crowded—which is the somewhat acute perception of contrast transcending contrast itself. You see through the trips of the contrast, therefore you see the reference points and contrast filling the whole universe, and you begin to see through that. You don't try to get rid of that particularly; you take the whole thing in. The result is that you find your mind is empty, which is the shunyata principle. Whereas in the case of dharmadhatu, there is no journey involved, no collecting of information, no studies—it is just a state.

S: Is there a relationship between the buddha families mandala and both masculine and feminine energies?

CTR: Well, the mandala is built on a ground, which is provided by both feminine and masculine principles. The ground is partially masculine and partially feminine. The activities of the buddha families are also masculine and feminine equally, at the same time.

S: Does that mean that each family has both masculine and feminine aspects?

CTR: Naturally, yes. I think that any kind of rules like that we might have—understanding the five buddha principles, understanding compassion, understanding shunyata, and all these big steps that one makes to discover further things, further subtleties through the inspiration of enlightenment and enlightened mind—all contain two parts within themselves. There is nothing isolated from each other particularly at all.

S: When we were talking about dharmadhatu as the feminine principle, everything was sort of lovely and alone. It was just the mother who cannot ever be had or be a lover—but by the time we get to the dakini principle, the attributes are disease, war, famine, good, birth, and death. Were these the embellishments of dharmadhatu, or something further down the line? At one point it is just pie in the sky, and the next point it's tricky.

CTR: I think it depends on how you take it—whether you regard the embellishment or makeup as a threat or an invitation. It depends on how you take the whole thing. I mean, things do exist that way, and it depends on how we take it. It's up to you, from that point of view.

S: I have a question about the unborn and bornness. Would that be anything like: if there is always now, is now always in motion? If we are always in the now, is now somehow always moving? If that is so, now is always the unbornness of the next movement of now. I can't say it—do you know what I mean?

CTR: Yes.

S: Is that so?

CTR: Well, I think that's a very tricky one, actually. Now has actually happened—or is happening, whatever. Now is happening; it is there. It is more than embryonic; it is complete—from the point of view of the first flash of perception of now. Then you begin to dwell on it, and it becomes embryonic. So we cannot really pinpoint what is now—it's both. Now is like you caught the train—and at the same time you missed the train.

S: Yeah. And for that reason it is just unbornness. Thank you.

Well, friends, maybe we should tentatively end here. I would like to link this study with further exploration that should take place, in terms of what we discussed becoming more experiential instead of purely metaphysical speculation. As I have already mentioned in my talk, the realization of the feminine principle can take place only through prajna and the sitting practice of meditation, which is what everything seems to boil down to.

Think very seriously about that and try to do your best. There doesn't seem to be a particularly complete discovery, complete mastery—of mistressing, or whatever—of the feminine principle. Nothing will be complete, in any case—but something might be complete. Thank you. [*Laughter*]

PART TWO

EVAM

EVAM.
*From the personal seal of Chögyam Trungpa
and the Trungpa tulkus. Design by Molly K. Nudell.*

1

Generations of Astronauts

WELCOME, ladies and gentlemen, fellow students. First of all, I would like to find out how many students did not have a chance to read or study the literature that was put out.* Anybody? Does that mean that everybody has done the preliminary study group? Okay.

This is an unusual situation, in that we provided some vanguard study before the seminar itself began. I am glad you had a chance to study and work with the material. That will certainly provide some kind of base, or footing—a great deal. However, what we are going to discuss is not all that esoteric and all that extraordinary, far-out, mind-blowing, and so forth. It is somewhat ordinary, to your disappointment. However, maybe you could pick up some highlights throughout the few days we have together. You might be able to find something particularly personal and real.

I would like to get to the topic right away, at this point. What we are going to study, what we are going to discuss, is the EVAM principle, as you know already. Do I have that right? Yes? EVAM? [*Laughter*] I will be working with Khyentse Rinpoche, who is my personal teacher and a friend of my root guru. Khyentse Rinpoche is in town,

---

*A sourcebook containing lightly edited transcripts of the seminar "The Feminine Principle" (reprinted here as part 1 of *Glimpses of Space*) was provided to "EVAM" seminar participants.

so I would like to also ask him for a few suggestions. We would like to work together on this topic, so that this seminar could become more potent, so to speak.

We often ignore the sense of general ground. Instead we usually try to pick out the highlights. We do that all the time in our life, and that has become problematic. We have no idea of the general perspective. We say, "Oh, those general perspectives, let us leave that to the learned or the technicians." We fight constantly, stitch by stitch, inch by inch, all along. By trying to have little goodies and words of wisdom here and there, consequently we become completely ignorant and stupid. We lost track of our sky, in trying to fight for a grain of sesame seed each day.

The vision of EVAM, basically speaking, is much larger than talking about the marriage counselor's level, or the relationship between two people, or simply the relationship between sky and earth. The interesting point is that whenever we talk about relationship, we manage to reduce ourselves into just simply one louse trying to fight another louse in the crack of a seam in our shirt, which we call our home. Psychiatrists do that, marriage counselors do that, physicians do that, local gurus do that. Usually we have a problem there: whether somebody can make glamour and glory out of how to get from here to the next stitch of thread going through that seam. As one louse, could we walk over to the next louse and make friends with it? Our vision is generally absolutely cramped and so poor, so little, so small, depressingly small.

Sometimes being small could be large at the same time, of course— if you are small enough. But you are not small enough. You are not so small that you become gigantic and fantastically spacious. In this case, we are neither absolutely small nor absolutely big enough— we hold ourselves between the two. So we find ourselves being just simply lice, trying to fight. A very small-minded level. That goes on with some encounter groups, some kinds of counseling, and in inviting troubleshooters to shoot your personal problems. We missed altogether—completely!—the notion of basic vision. With the EVAM principle, we are not talking about how you can comb your husband's hair in the most Buddhistic beautiful way, so that he wouldn't complain—or, for that matter, how you can tell your wife not to cash too many checks from your mutual bank account. This vision is much bigger, greater. It is enormous, very vast, gigantic.

There are two principles, of course, E and VAM. E represents basic accommodation, basic atmosphere, which could be said to be empty or full—it doesn't really matter, that's purely a linguistic problem. Then we have VAM, which is what is contained within that vastness, whether it is full or empty. What is contained, if it's full, is emptiness; what is contained, if it's empty, is fullness. Those little logics are no longer problematic. We usually start out by saying, "What do you mean to say—is there something or not?" But we are not talking in those terms. When we talk about empty here, we are not talking about the emptiness in our wallet. That kind of emptiness is slightly different than basic emptiness, which has nothing to do with poverty or mismanagement. [*Laughs.*] We are talking about basic adventure, if we could talk actively; or if we talk passively, we could call it our basic being. It depends on what way you want to look at it, the basicness of it.

That basic vastness, E, seems to be unconditioned. That is to say, unconditioned by love and hate, this and that. It is also unconditioned by good or bad, of course; that's one of the most basic things of all. You have a logical problem there. You could say, "If everything is completely unconditioned, then how could it exist as E, as basic space? How can you even say it's basic space?" True, you can't. Maybe that's it. Not even maybe—that is it. That is that, whatever.

The unconditioned also could create further conditions, unconditioned-conditions, naturally. If that happens, we have no end. We have unconditioned, unconditioned, unconditioned, unconditioned,

unconditioned, unconditioned, unconditioned, unconditioned of unconditions. We go back and forth, back and forth. We are completely lost, at a loss completely. However, in this case we are not purely talking in terms of conditions being metaphysical speculation, but about the unconditioned simply as something viewed, looked at, by bottomless mind, mind that doesn't have a bottom. There is no problem of full or empty. It is obviously some state of meditation, state of awake. In other words, when we are awake, we do not have to refer to ourselves every minute, every second, or every half an hour, saying, "Now, I'm awake," anymore. We are just awake throughout the whole day. Therefore, unconditioned means not putting things into categories, but simply being and not possessing.

The metaphor is being in outer space. If you are an astronaut, for instance, and you decide to step out of the ship, you find that you are neither pulled nor pushed in midair. If you are high enough for planets, you are not falling down and you are not falling up. You are just swimming, floating in the space. You are not going to hit anywhere; you are not going to be in any particular danger. Nevertheless, there is the biggest danger of all, which is the danger that you want to hang on to something while you are still floating. Sometimes you wish that you might have contact with the nearest planet so it could create a magnetic field for you—so you could commit suicide, crash onto that planet. At this point, we are not only talking about outer space as the greatest excitement of the Buddhist ultimate idea, particularly. We are talking about it as the closest analogy for the idea of the E principle, which is that you are suspended in air. It is extraordinarily basic.

We usually try to make sure that we do not end up in the loony bin, hopefully—or end up in something worse than that, whatever that may be. More courageous people are trying to make sure that they are getting somewhere beyond simply trying to prevent themselves from getting into the loony bin, making some kind of success beyond that level. "Now that these problems are solved, whew, I don't have to go to the loony bin anymore. That air is cleared at least, fantastic, bravo—and then I want to go further, progress further." Further what? [*Laughter*] What is going on there? It seems to be impossible. There's too much space. Fantastic space! Gaps of all kinds! If we want to get to the nearest planet, we can't even lay hands on it.

Further what? You are busy reading books, trying to get quotations. You have interviews with your teachers and meditation masters and whatnot, here and there. You take courses, of course, and you get busy, getting the whole thing rolling. But then, if you are intelligent enough and not caught up in spiritual materialism, the whole thing you have been doing—trying to hold on to something or other—just disappears. You just float along in space somewhere. You are not coming, you can't say that; you are not going, you can't say that. You are just somewhere there—you can't even say that! E! [*Laughter*] That's it.

It's very frightening. It is more frightening once you get hold of that particular understanding, so to speak—"hold," metaphorically speaking [*laughter*], just a linguistic problem we have here. But the more you see it—it is more dangerous, seemingly. And you find yourself being more frightened, absolutely frightened, petrified, terrified that there's so much space once we get into the path. And once we begin to explore ourselves, there is a lot of space, too much space. We try our best to create problems, of course. That happens in my experience working with most of you here, actually. You come to me to review your state of being and have interviews. We have done that with a lot of you people, and you are very eloquent, all of you. You begin to dig up little things here and there. But that is not what I particularly regard as a masterpiece—it's just occupational therapy, you want to have something.

The more students get into the practice, the more space that provides. It is very unfriendly to begin with, seemingly unfriendly. The reason is that you think you are not in the position to jump in, and you still regard outer space as foreign territory. That has become problematic. Other than that, there's no particular problem. It is a matter of your concept. If you begin to think, even in the conceptual mind, that that particular space is no longer frightening, you could dive right in and swim in the space. You could swim beautifully, if you were not afraid of your environment. [*Laughs.*]

You see, an interesting point is that once you begin to get into big mind—as the Yogacharins or Zen call it, the BIG mind [*laughter*]—it extends your vision. But then, once you begin to get into VAST mind, even BIG mind is so small. At this point of our work in this particular age, so to speak, this particular year, and in the growth and aging of Buddhism taking place in the United States of America and North America at large, so to speak, people are frightened a lot these days. It is not because they are doing something wrong, but they begin to panic that they are getting into something large, something vast. It is more than just big mind, it is something large. That largeness is what we are going to talk about, what we are talking about actually, at this point.

That principle in question—E—has a lot of attributes according to the scriptures. It has been said that E is supremely unchanging, that E is basically empty, that E possesses immense power. In this case, when we talk about power, we are not talking in terms of bang-bang-bang, or the level of fistfights, for that matter. We are talking of power in the sense of how much power there is in outer space if you are an astronaut floating around in that space. There's immense vision, immense power. Your little earth is over there in your vision, in the corner of your eye, and your little moon over there that you are trying to get to becomes irrelevant. You are just floating in this big space, which is deep blue and deep black, velvet black. You are floating in that space. Occasional sunlight glancing off your hand or your shoulder corners somehow makes a certain amount of confirmation that you are still seeing the same universe and the same sun.

Nevertheless, you have nowhere to relax or nowhere not to relax. You are just floating in outer space, being an astronaut.

It is interesting how the American culture of space research has provided us more evidence about big mind—or vast mind. That is magnificent, actually. That's precisely what they have been talking about for two thousand five hundred years. They didn't have space-crafts, they didn't have anything of that nature but they still knew how that experience would be, and they did experience that themselves. At this point, we have thirty-three astronauts in the Kagyü lineage. [*Laughter*] If that's the case, every one of them was successful; they never freaked out. They actually experienced vast mind, and they managed to transmit their experience to the next generation. So, in fact, we are generations of astronauts—very enlightened ones, of course.

Vastness is an interesting point. Even when we feel that we are so cramped in our own space, and we are spaceless, when we are so locked in our particular relationship, particular mind, body, what have you—nevertheless, that is part of the pressure coming from the space of E that is taking place all the time with us, which is a very interesting point. I don't think I should freak you out too much at this point, so to speak. Maybe we should have some discussion. I would like to answer your questions, if you have any questions.

Chögyam Trungpa Rinpoche: Don't be shy! You're in outer space. [*Siren howls.*] Young lady at the back over there.

Student: Did you say what I think you said, that people generally—that is, people in the world—are getting frightened because they are getting a sense of vastness? That something is permeating constantly?

CTR: Yes, indeed. Yes, indeed. So?

S: So—that's fantastic!

CTR: Well—

S: How do we as Buddhists deal with that? It's somehow a responsibility for us.

CTR: You might get frightened as Buddhists too—much more so than the others who are frightened by getting into vaster space.

S: That's true, but we have the teachings to guide us.

CTR: The teachings are no longer little planets; the teachings are the space itself that you are floating in! So the teachings no longer provide you with any kind of footing, except space itself.

S: Rinpoche, could you explain further how the sense of being locked into your own space is some kind of pressure from space?

CTR: That's it: its pressure is locked in. It is in your own body trying to survive independent of space. We tend to put hundreds of paintings on our walls, and we decorate our floors with multicolored carpets. We put all kinds of knickknacks, tchotchkes, on our mantelpiece, and we try to entertain ourselves. But if we have none of those things at all, then we have nothing; we feel we are barren—and better we feel barren than we have too many things. The problem begins at home, as they say. Home is your body, and you are afraid of the environment.

S: Thank you.

S: Rinpoche, you used the terms *big mind* and *vast mind*. We have been working with the notions of dharmadhatu and vajradhatu. I wonder if the term *big mind* and the term *vast mind*, for that matter, have some corollaries with that, in our language?

CTR: I am not completely concerned with our language. If I get trapped up in language, that's too bad. What are you trying to say anyway, my dear gentleman? Say it again.

S: Well, the term *big mind* is familiar from, for example, Suzuki Roshi's book.

CTR: Yes.

S: It's familiar to me.

CTR: Yes. Yes, indeed.

S: And the term *vast mind* is a new term to me.

CTR: New term to you. Yes, indeed. [*Laughter*] So?

S: And I've become familiar recently with the terms *vajradhatu* and *dharmadhatu*, and I have some sense of them. Maybe there's no correlation between big mind and some of these terms that we've been working with, but I was wondering if there is?

CTR: Well, big mind seems to be the notion of being brave—brave and very powerful, heroic. Fundamentally, being heroic is big mind, because you can sit a lot on your zafu and all the rest of it. You have a big lung.

S: A big what?

CTR: Lungs. [*Breathes hard in and out; laughter*] And you have a good backbone to sit up. Those are all big minds. It's somewhat good. Having a good vocation is big mind: Jesuits have good big mind; the pope has good big mind; maybe George Washington had big mind; maybe Lincoln had big mind. On the other hand, vast mind is somewhat questionable. Can you make something out of that? I hope you will. Just sleep on it. Thank you.

S: Thank you.

S: Suppose that together with the feeling of fear, at one point you begin to be attracted and almost court this feeling of being lost in space. Is that the usual thing?

CTR: You see, the interesting thing about fear—that you are going to lose your grasp, your magnetic field that comes from all kinds of planets—is that it is part of the entertainment, part of the passion. You don't want to be there in that particular vast space anymore, so you have suspicion and a sense of possible boredom. Although at that particular time you are occupied, you have possible boredom taking place.

S: But suppose you get attracted to the idea. Is it just entertainment?

CTR: Well, everything is idea, everything is ideal, at this point. You want to complain because you are delighted, actually. You are delighted to have something to complain about. You know, that kind of situation. There's nothing we can hang on to there, particularly. It's just that a little, little breeze comes along and tells you little whispering things in your ear, and you come up with all kinds of ideas. You are trying to execute them, and then they go away. So you feel, once more, vast. You have lost your space, your inner space, so you float along in outer space once more. It goes on all the time. [*Laughs.*] It's quite exciting, but nevertheless, it is disheartening. You thought you had found something, a little butterfly coming in the middle of space, outer space—ah!—but it turns out to be a reflection from the glass window you have—phew! [*Laughter*]

You cannot win over space; it is too vast. That's why you put little tchotchkes on the wall, on the mantelpiece, to protect yourself from being lost in space. But you are not ever actually lost; you gain space—actually, you gain a lot of things, but not particularly any space.

S: So is this E, this vast space, any different from the mind which perceives or experiences it?

CTR: Not different. It is mind. When you experience your own mind, it is vast. But when your mind has begun to be used as a tool to understand something else, then it's different—that is big mind, or maybe little mind. When you begin to understand, to realize your own mind, it is too vast. It is too close to home. That's why you might freak out: it's very close to home.

S: It seems that when it gets that close to home, being frightened is almost like a defensive unwillingness to make friends with the space?

CTR: Absolutely. Yes. Tell everybody about that. [*Laughter*]

S: But it doesn't—

CTR: They may not understand, but tell them.

S: It seems to be stuck.

CTR: No, lost in space. You can't get stuck in space. [*Laughter*]

S: Two questions, Rinpoche.

CTR: Yes, indeed.

S: First, did you say that VAM is contained by E?

CTR: What? "Bomb"? [*Laughter*]

S: VAM.

CTR: We are going to discuss that later, tomorrow maybe.

S: Okay. Then the other question: in vast mind, is there an experience, or an awareness of self, in vast mind?

CTR: That is part of the whole thing. If there is an experience of self as such, usually you create a little pouch like a kangaroo—you could put your little babies in your little pocket.

S: That wouldn't be vast mind.

CTR: Not having that—that is why the whole thing turns out to be so challenging and freaky and impossible. The personal experience of recording anything back is not happening, so you might think your system has broken down or something. Then you freak out. That's one of those things that happens. You see what I mean?

S: It sounds like a shame.

CTR: Shame? Well, of course. Then what do you want to do?

S: It is a shame that you would freak out at that point.

CTR: What's the opposite of shame? Please.

S: Joy.

CTR: Joy. Joy is the opposite of shame? [*Laughter*]

S: I don't know. What's the opposite of shame? Pride.

CTR: Yeah, more likely pride, actually.

S: Arrogance.

CTR: Arrogance. Yes. Absolutely. So you see, the opposite of shame is arrogance, which is equally shameful. [*Laughter*] Even joy is shameful. We do not actually want to relate with anything that's going on. We want to hang on to this, to that, that little trinket, this little tchotchke, this little image—which are called theistic problems, on the whole.

S: Hanging on like that, then there can't be the experience of vast space.

CTR: It is amazing that America was actually able to take the journey, that American astronauts were able to take a journey into outer space. It's quite magnificent, but they did. And the reason they did was because they regarded themselves as human beings rather than religious people. Because of that, they had some kind of buddha nature in them that could actually relate with that kind of space. I heard reports that afterward they became spiritual this and thats and all kinds of things happened. But there was some kind of sanity experience of the actual demonstration, or visualization, of outer space—how that could actually manifest your mind in real living, which is a very interesting point. Maybe we missed the point of your question. Have we? In outer space somewhere?

S: Thank you.

CTR: Would you like to say something more?

S: I was wondering, I wanted you to confirm my own idea [*laughter*] of whether there could be those two things at the same time: the hanging on and the experience of vast space. You say the result of that is freaking out, and I can understand that.

CTR: Well, let's sit and practice and find out that way, rather than me fortune-telling you at this point. Okay?

S: Thank you.

CTR: You're welcome.

Well, ladies and gentlemen, I think at this particular time and space [*laughs*] we should stop. It is getting earlier already, so we might be ahead of time tomorrow. Thank you.

And, once more, welcome to this particular seminar. I would like to encourage you people to sit a lot, practice a lot. Without that, we cannot actually communicate; we become foreigners to each other. So if you don't work with that basic discipline, there is nothing happening between us. Let us not regard this seminar as a circus scene but as a real working practice situation. I'm sure you can do that. Thank you very much for being very patient tonight.

2

Vajra Question Mark

GOOD EVENING. Where did we leave off last night? Somewhere. No reference point. You might find that it is very difficult to pick up—but somewhat, very interestingly, when you leave things without a reference point, that is much more precise. Because there is no reference point to pick up, the next situation is not conditioned by anything at all. You just come out and launch in, so to speak, which is tonight's issue. And that issue will go on during our entire seminar.

The interesting point about what happens in that particular type of outer space we were talking about last night is what? That seems to be it—it is what. There are a lot of different ways to say what. You could say it from the point of view of panic; you could say it from the point of view of satisfaction; you could also say it from the point of view of hunger or uncertainty. But with this kind of what, if there is no space, you cannot say what anymore. Once the space is provided to say what, what is that? Some kind of clear perception begins to dawn in the midst of that gigantic vast space. It becomes very real, very powerful and open, but at the same time, dynamic, equally. That is what we are talking about as the second principle, VAM.

Unconditional space gives birth to unconditional question— what? Somewhat you could say you couldn't care less what that is all about—but still you will say what. It is like the traditional idea of mantra—first utterance. There is a vajra carved out of a diamond floating in this gigantic space, outer space, glinting lights all over. Or, for that matter, you could say there is a question mark carved out of diamond floating in the midst of space. But whatever it is, it is made out of diamond, indestructible.

In order to cope and work with such situations as the vastness and openness of that particular space, one has to develop—one has to have rather than develop—a greater sense of indestructibility. The notion of indestructibility is not so much that you actually asked the question, "What?" It takes the form of a question, but it becomes a statement rather than a question. But it still has the essence of yearning, openness, possibilities—open possibilities of course—that which we call compassion. Indestructibility and a sense of softness, or warmth, put together is the essence of VAM. We have a sense of directness and indestructibility, and a sense of openness that doesn't stand for any kind of germs or dirt.

In that journey of E and VAM together, any element of native germs does not survive anymore. It is not necessarily that the atmosphere is too pure and clean, but the atmosphere is unyielding. The atmosphere developed in such a way that the situation doesn't accept any form of anything whatever: there is no room to be feared, no room for claustrophobia, no room for cowardice or localized pride. Any conventional approach is not applicable. You wouldn't take the journey at all, if you were in that particular condition, of course.

That notion of indestructibility also contains an immense sense of joy—bliss, if you would like to call it that. But in this case, we are not talking about a happy, yippee, kind of joy. That is localized joy, conventional joy, joy from the point of view of one planet's concept. In this case, we are talking about joy or bliss being beyond any context; therefore, it is completely total. For instance, if your car is partially damaged in an accident, you will still think in terms of getting it repaired. But if your car is totally wrecked, absolutely wrecked, you just give up, which is some sense of relief. It also contains a kind of joy, so it's not a terrible disaster, particularly; a sense of relief comes along with it. I hope you know what I mean. [*Laughter*] There's a sense of relief, a sense of freedom, free from a certain burden. Whereas if your car has a dent here and there, you have to take it to the body shop, you have to pay money and all the rest of it. That's more of a burden. But the whole thing is completely gone, completely wiped out, so it is a different experience. Totality of some kind is taking place there. That kind of joy, bliss. Such joy doesn't have to be maintained. You simply go to the insurance company and claim the money. It is as simple as that—if you have a good policy, of course. [*Laughs.*] That kind of relief is not particularly relief as such, but a sense of totality, of course.

The notion of totality is based on the idea of nonclinging. If there is a sense of space around you already, then the notion of totality is obviously there; whereas if there is no sense of space, lostness in space, there is not. If you are without an umbilical cord attached to your mother earth anymore, then a real sense of space begins to take place. We are talking in this case about journeying out into space, without telecommunication to relate back to mother earth, so to speak. You have freedom to do what you want, what you like—but you also have freedom to land, to come back to your world and work with your fellow people.

At a certain point, pain and pleasure become one. An immense dynamic situation takes place at that very point. That is what is known as the VAM principle, mahasukha, great bliss. This concept of great bliss does not mean that you are completely exasperated in tremendous fantastic joy—like a grain of popcorn in a little container that gets cracked dead, with its own grinning smile coming all over its body. You might think that is somewhat funny, but I'm afraid people think that way. People think that great joy means that you become completely dead and rigid and frigid with a gigantic smile—and you can do it eternally! [*Laughter*] That is a popular notion of spiritual bliss, actually, from the materialist's point of view, of course.

This VAM also contains the sense of essence, and possibilities of giving birth. It contains semen, egg, sperm, seed, what have you, yeast, whatever metaphors might be visible or appropriate. It is a tremendously dynamic situation where you are not afraid or hesitant to sow further seeds anymore. And once you begin to sow seeds, your seed becomes a dynamic one. It begins to present itself naturally, very simply. So you give further birth to space and the contents of space, simultaneously. You are giving birth to further solar systems, further planets of all kinds. You are not afraid of that at all.

In relating with this situation, if there is any localized notion, pressure does not come from inside, particularly, but from outside. You begin to create a big blast: keeoh! [*soft explosive sound*]. If you are not willing to accept the space, and instead hold on to your territory, then space will organize the ultimate blast to break those shells. Some people call that vajra hell, in the tantric tradition; others call it damnation, what have you. Nevertheless, holding on to something is being made into a mockery. You cannot hang on to anything, particularly. When you begin to do that, you are made into a fool, an absolute fool. So suicide is achieved by trying not to commit suicide. The sense of being suicidal is achieved by trying not to commit suicide but to preserve territory. That's the interesting point. It is a motto. Natural suicide takes place when you are not trying to do so. Very sad—very, very sad. Too bad.

I shouldn't say too much. I want you to think about what we have discussed. Maybe, at this point, we could have a discussion, if you would like to contribute with questions.

Student: Is this experience the vajra-like samadhi, or is it more like a nyam, a temporary experience?

Chögyam Trungpa Rinpoche: We are not talking about an experience; we are simply talking about what it is, at this point. We are not particularly talking about path. We are talking about what it actually is. We haven't discussed the path concept yet.

S: Is the vast space equivalent to nonduality?

CTR: Basically it is, but somehow I did not like the way you asked the question. [*Laughter*] Where are you? It sounds as if you are trying to put things into pigeonholes, if I may say so. We are not trying to create a dictionary here—though we would like to do so eventually. We are not trying to put things into neat compartments. Thank you, anyway. That's a very useful contribution.

S: When you mentioned that unconditional space gives birth to unconditional question, are you talking about question in the sense of total, unconditional confusion, or the issue of what? That question?

CTR: It is the nature of the question rather than the issue. Issue is just *poof!* It's very simple. You might have a very serious issue: "When do I see you again?" But the nature of the question is different than the issue, actually, if you can separate the two things. That is an interesting point. What we are talking about is the nature of the question from the point of view of how you actually ask your question rather than what you say. You may say, "Is there another cup of tea left for me?" or "Is somebody next door?" or "Is there going to be another sunrise tomorrow?"—anything. Here the point is the manner and style in which you do it.

S: I was wondering about a way of perceiving ourselves on the path. If we are involved, say, in Buddhism, there's a possibility of space there that can accommodate both our failures and our mistakes. I was contrasting that with the sense of paranoia—that we have to pay attention to detail—that you spoke about yesterday in the sense of the louse crossing the thread. I was wondering if that sense of space, of our perception of ourselves on the path, is what you are talking about in EVAM—or is that some sense of indulgence?

CTR: Anything you want to believe. [*Laughter*]

S: [*Laughs.*] Thank you.

CTR: At this point, everything's open. I want you to float, so to speak, and become real by floating, rather than become love-and-lighties. However, the choice is yours, sir. That's it. Anything you want to believe. Anything you want to do? It's yours! It's your seminar. I'm just a mere push button here. [*Laughter*] You get the picture. That's it! [*Laughter*]

S: [*Laughs.*] I got it.

S: Rinpoche, I was wondering if you would say a few more words about the VAM concept in relation to its indestructibility and unyielding quality, and then the softness or openness that it also seems to have—

CTR: —at the same time.

S: At the same time.

CTR: At the same time. Sweet and sour at the same time. It is like the question of space. You cannot destroy space, but at the same time, space is very accommodating, nevertheless. Space also kills you; it is very uncompassionate—but at the same time, it is very accommodating, nevertheless. The essence of space is the VAM principle, which is put together with the vastness of space, the E principle. So the VAM principle is nothing other than space. VAM is the particular attributes that exist within the E principle. VAM becomes the manifestation of the characteristics of space.

S: When you were talking about the VAM principle then, you were talking about both the E and the VAM together, the softness and the unyielding?

CTR: E's expression. E's manifestation is VAM. E is just the vastness of it, basically. That's it. Full stop. But beyond that, qualities exist.

We could talk about the light and brilliance of the sun, or about the destructive qualities of the sun. The sun also produces creative principles. You know, that's kind of saying the same thing. Nevertheless, that's an interesting twist in our state of mind. Usually we want to relate one situation with one thing, another situation with another thing, because we would like to split things, usually. But in this case, we cannot. We cannot at all. We have to relate with That, which is everywhere, so to speak—not to become too religious. [*Laughs.*] It is everywhere because it has its own expansion, everywhere because it is active everywhere at the same time.

S: Would that relate to compassion in any way, that softness?

CTR: Yes. Accommodation, of course—definitely so.

S: Thank you.

CTR: Ruth, are you still waiting?

S: Last night we were talking about space, this vast space which was filled with terror. And we made a great leap tonight into this combination of the journey of E and VAM coming to the point where pain and pleasure are one, into the great bliss. But it is not very clear how the terror turned into bliss.

CTR: Well, you see, what we are doing here is trying to point out the highlights. What could happen. What might happen. It is a question of presenting. I could come up with a piece of something with joints, and another piece with joints, which might not speak because it's been well oiled. It is your job to join those two pieces together. The puzzle-work is left to the students actually, at this point. I don't want to be mysterious about that, but I think you could give more thought to what's been said in connection with this idea of joints, joining things, putting it together. How we could make things work, and make a robot out of that—make a Buddha out of it, or a Christ out of it, whatever have you. So the subtleties seem to depend on you, actually. I don't want to go to great lengths, how you could be so subtle. That would be very dangerous, teaching you a new game, which would be fundamentally deceptive and destructive at the same time. So I would like to leave it up to you people here to at least figure out what's going on. [*Laughter*]

Well, friends, I think we are getting rather early already. Maybe unless there is some announcement—any announcements? Okay. Well, have a good sleep, and a good dinner if you haven't had one already. [*Laughter*] Thank you.

3

Missing the Boat

THANK YOU for being patient. I would like to continue with what we discussed previously. At this point, we are beginning to set out the basic pattern of the whole thing, the concept of E and VAM altogether. We have laid out the groundwork of the E principle and the VAM principle, somewhat, and how we can actually relate with such vast mind to begin with, once we begin to realize how vast, enormous, the basic area that style of thinking, known as Buddhism, covers. It covers an immense area altogether—vast.

The introduction to this particular issue has been somewhat vajrayana oriented over the past two days, of course. And now, hoping and thinking that you people have had some groundwork and that some understanding has taken place already, that you studied and so forth—in turn, I feel myself somewhat relaxed in presenting the material at this point. However, having presented the basic ground, basic map already, we must come back, so to speak, to reality. E is the accommodation, the container, and VAM is what is being contained in the situation—personal experiences, domestic, physical, psychological, metaphysical, what have you. So tonight I would like to backtrack, so to speak, from tantric "hoo-highs" of all kinds. The tantric presentation is interestingly inspiring; nevertheless, it is not all that practical, shall we say. [*Laughs.*]

Here we are, back to square one, in spite of glory possibilities, et cetera, et cetera, et cetera. However, the EVAM principle can be approached on several levels, so to speak: the foundation level, the level of activities, the level of greater magic and powerful subtleties. These levels are divided into the three principles of hinayana, mahayana, and vajrayana. These three sections are not actually divided, but they come along that way, like infanthood, teenagerhood, and adulthood. Those stages are not actually divided, although we decide to do so by labeling people in a certain way; nevertheless, it is a natural growth that takes place. From that point of view, there are no sharp points per se; nevertheless, there's a sense of a basic growing process taking place on this journey, the three-yana journey.

In this particular seminar, we are going to view things from the EVAM principle's point of view, which is exactly the same as what we have discussed before. I'm afraid we are not going to discuss anything particularly new or extraordinary. The magic has been told already in some sense: that we have to sit a lot, practice a lot, study a lot, develop devotion, develop a sense of humor, and all the rest of it. And over all, we have to overcome spiritual materialism! So that's it! [*Laughter*] I'm sorry to disappoint you; however, it's better to be good than worst. [*Laughter*] Better to be honest rather than hypocritical.

The hinayana level of the EVAM principle we could find in the hinayana sutras. There is a saying at the beginning of each of these sutras that is translated into the English language as, "Thus I have heard." That saying creates five types of situation: (1) "Thus" is the teachings; (2) "I" represents the student; (3–4) "have heard" is the proclamation of the dharma in a particular space and time: spring, summer, winter, autumn, or whatever; and (5) "Thus I have heard" is heard from the teacher, of course, which is another element, the teacher. So there is the teacher, the teaching, the time and place the teachings are being taught, and the student. That makes five situations. Those five—the nature of the teachings, teacher, time, place, and situation where the teachings are provided, that is to say, the student—are in the Sanskrit beginning of all the sutras, *Evam maya shrutam* [lit. Thus-by me-was heard], "Thus have I heard." The teachings cannot begin without mentioning the words E and EVAM. E is the situation where teachings are being taught; VAM is the teaching actually taking effect on individuals, personally. So it becomes a real thing: personal and absolutely real at the same time.

In the hinayana level of teaching, there are two levels of discipline taking place: renunciation and discipline. Renunciation and discipline are the two basic hinayana principles, renunciation being E and discipline being VAM, at that point. When we talk about renunciation, we are not particularly mommy and daddy behind, and you should rush into India or Thailand or the North Pole. And it doesn't necessarily mean that you should say, "Fuck America! I will find something better." [*Laughs.*] Renunciation is very subtle. To begin with, a lot of uncertainty, of course, and a lot of pain and dissatisfaction of all kinds takes place. But within that dissatisfaction, which is usually based on anger and resentment of all kinds, you are pissed off at the world that you were trained and brought up in. That is precisely the basis for the propagation of hippiedom that developed lately.

Until a few years ago, hippiedom was a very popular movement, of course, as a reaction against any kind of setup, a reaction against any kind of personal, business, economic, or social interaction with the world. A reaction against that general world that has been trying so hard to relate with the public, how we could live together in housing developments, city developments, social welfare developments, and what have you, public broadcasting systems, pension systems, all kinds of situations. You begin to feel all those programs are somewhat claustrophobic, so claustrophobic. The more pleasure is presented to you, the more painful it is. You prefer to wear rags rather than silk, prefer to wear dry twigs rather than gold and diamonds; as opposed to having a nice hairdo, you prefer to have shaggy, lice-infested, matted long hair. That's not particularly renunciation, that's reaction, that's aggression. That is protest rather than livelihood, actually. It is a temporary thing. I think so, actually, quite possibly. Of course, you have a better judgment of this, since you have had those reactions yourselves. I never grew matted hair myself; I'm just observing the whole thing, what's been happening, as a commentator. If you could excuse my saying so, I could actually comment on what's happened. I have great confidence! I think I'm right!—if I may say so. [*Laughter*]

From the hippie's point of view, we don't have to conform to anything. Hippies feel that if you join a particular tradition, they will tell you to work hard—so you should try to avoid that. That is, you could work spontaneously and get the same effect by doing something else. What is that? Doing something else—what is that? Of course, taking LSD, smoking pot, what have you. Sniffing cocaine is lower level somewhat, in terms of the drug world, but LSD is held in high esteem. There's a book written about the *Tibetan Book of the Dead* and that whole thing,* of course, that says that taking LSD is supreme, the buddha of drug power. It's interesting how renunciation can be built at the beginning, from that level.

All of those things are not regarded as a waste of time, of course. If that particular culture were not here, you wouldn't be here at all; otherwise, none of you would be here. I would be speaking to an empty hall at this very moment if none of those things had happened. I wouldn't be here and you wouldn't be here, for that matter. Nevertheless, the interesting point is that we begin to shed constantly, again and again, and again, and again. That shedding process takes place all the time. But we begin to realize that that occupation no longer has a sense of renunciation. Giving up your life is not renun-

---

*Timothy Leary, Ralph Metzner, and Richard Alpert, *The Psychedelic Experience: A Manual Based on the Tibetan Book of the Dead* (New York: Citadel Press, 1964).

ciation; abandoning your wife or husband, your kids and your house, selling your things, giving up and running off to somewhere else is not particularly renunciation. Real renunciation is to regard all those things that you have been doing as really bleak. Nothing will actually give you up, unless you give up altogether.

In your real life, you might have the same situations happening again and again. Relatives hover around you; your friends hover around you and offer drugs and all kinds of entertainments, all kinds of things, this and that. You could fill your schedule completely. But underneath all that, you might feel the whole thing is completely bleak, absolutely bleak—very bleak. The only thing that is vivid is the possibility of death and the real possibility of going crazy, losing track of things. Whew! Real bleak situations, real bleak situations in the real, real, real sense! [*Laughter*] If you know what I mean. [*Laughter*] It's not just that you are kidding with things—it is a really bleak situation. [*Vidyadhara smiles; laughter*] Nothing seems to work. All our gadgets, purchasing extraordinary motorcars, or trying to be rustic and rugged and buying a bicycle, beginning to wear overalls or dressing up in suits. You could try higher levels or lower levels of all kinds—nevertheless, the whole thing is completely bleak. The other day, when I spoke to quite a famous pop singer, she happened to say precisely that: she feels the whole thing is bleak, that she is kidding herself. That seems to be an interesting point, actually. Somehow, it tends to fit that particular pattern: that the more successful you become, the more bleak you feel—and also, the more unsuccessful you feel, that much further bleak! [*Laughter*]

It is interesting how bleak we feel, how we feel we are so minimum, absolute minimum. Nothing is happening, cosmic frigidity of some kind. We do not see the space that goes with that, actually. It seems that we are too concerned with bang-bang-bang, and this and that relationship alone, all the time. We forget the rest, beyond the eye level—the other hundred and fifty degrees, or whatever have you.

210 | GLIMPSES OF SPACE: EVAM

We forget that. If we watched that general degree, we would see that there is immense vast space there, in spite of our little bleak pinhole. But that's just symbolism: the rest, the whole thing, is empty. It is E, completely vast space. That's the notion of renunciation.

Renunciation is not so much that you should give up smoking cigarettes, stop wearing shoes, or try not to wear earrings or lipstick, or not say hello to anybody you don't know. Or, for that matter, not to put your finger in your nose. [*Laughter*] Renunciation is not so much just giving something up, like a New Year's resolution. It has nothing to do with New Year's resolutions. Renunciation is a total lack of possibilities, complete bleakness. We begin to feel that. If you were not a real believer in the buddhadharma, you would never feel that way. It's real, the real personal experience of actual bleakness. There are no possibilities of improvising anything at all from your own resources, your own hypocrisy, anymore at all—other than the dharma.

The dharma comes like a second layer, beyond bleakness. It is somewhat rich; nevertheless, it is not going to save you particularly, at all. It is an interesting point: life is completely empty, whether you live in the Orient or the Occident. Whatever life you lead, it is always bleak, always meaningless. It is always changing—constantly! You're about to get something together, or you are about to click into something—miss it! [*Laughter*] You missed the boat. All the time you missed the boat. All the time. Whew! Always miss the boat, always. Have you ever caught the boat? [*Laughter*] You might say, "I did for a moment, but then I missed it." [*Laughter*] Missed the boat, constantly.

That particular principle of E is very bleak—needless to say again and again. It's very personal, absolutely personal, very seriously personal. That personal bleakness brings individuals into buddhadharma. The basic point seems to be that there is nothing you can actually hang on to personally at all. Because of that, there is a problem usually created by the theistic Judeo-Christian tradition, of course, saying that if you are in bad shape somebody will come along to you and say, "Hello, how are you?" Somebody will come along, an agent of God, who will save you from that. The vicar's wife or the vicar himself or Christ himself or messengers of God, archangels of all kinds will come along to you and save you and encourage you, keep you company. They will keep you company, and they will be proud of being bedfellows. If you don't mind, they would like to sleep next to you, next to your bed, and they are willing to feed you with bottles and give you candies. They would be willing to turn on the television if necessary—the good channel with the good message, of course. Whew! That is an interesting point. I'm sure to a lot of people this is a sore point, of course, but I personally take delight in that particular sore point. I feel that we have nothing to lose and nothing to gain here, particularly. My concern is just purely to tell the truth. [*Laughter*]

The notion of loneliness, therefore, could not come from being babysat by different spiritual levels: the vicar's wife or the vicar himself, Christ himself, or God himself coming along to you and making you bedfellows. You still find the whole thing to be purely mind's duplication, nevertheless. So the Buddhist approach to loneliness and the E principle at this point is definitely the idea of the nonexistence of God. A lot of my Tibetan friends warned me, telling me I shouldn't say the whole thing: "You shouldn't talk about the whole thing. Why don't you just be nice to them and tell them half of the truth?" But I personally feel that that's not the way I should approach it, and now here we go. It is a very natural and ordinary situation, where you can tell the truth. And the truth only comes from the experience of reality, the absence of God, from personal experience, how we relate with reality. [*Siren blares.*] That's a good one! [*Laughter*] It's made by man. Personal experience makes it more bleak, more lonely.

Human beings usually feel much better if there is a conceptual, philosophical figurehead of some kind. With some kind of ghost worship, you feel much better. If I drop dead, my ghost will tell me what to do about it. If I'm about to drop dead, my ghost will tell me how to not drop dead. If I'm about to drop dead, my ghost will warn me so I can avoid the whole thing and lead my life. Believing in mysterious forces does not bring real bleakness at the hinayana level—that you have no place, no room, that you are in the vast charnel ground completely, altogether, and there's no place for a savior or the notion of being saved at all, absolutely not at all. [*Laughs.*] You feel delighted, because you don't have to relate with relatives anymore. [*Laughter*] There's a real sense of genuine freedom—and at the same time, genuine paranoia, of course. There is nobody to help you, which is terrible, absolutely ghastly, petrifying; nevertheless, it's delightful. For the first time, you realize nobody will mind your business. You can conduct your own business, whether it is ill or well, whatever. Hinayana's approach to E is that.

If you have any questions, you are welcome. Thank you.

Student: You were talking about bleakness and aloneness, and in one sentence you mentioned that we forget the space. Does that come later in the talks?

Chögyam Trungpa Rinpoche: You forget the space?

S: You said that we forget the space. We look through a pinhole rather than see all the degrees.

CTR: Well, usually we start by looking at a pinhole, then you come to it much later. So we can't switch those roles at all, at this point.

S: I don't understand what effect seeing the space has on the bleakness.

CTR: Emptiness?

S: On the bleakness.

CTR: Seeing the whole thing is very bleak. [*Laughter*] Yeah.

S: It's even worse than just seeing it through a pinhole?

CTR: Yes. [*Laughter*] You got it!

S: Today was the first day you talked about time, that time had an essential part in learning the dharma. And you also said that E was related to renunciation and VAM to discipline. How does time fit into that situation?

CTR: Take time with the renunciation, and also take time with discipline. What else? What do you mean by *time,* anyway?

S: Well, that's why I was . . . I found that there was a very conspicuous absence of you talking about how—

CTR: Are you talking about time as initials or time as a word?

S: Time as what?

CTR: Initials.

S: Initials?

CTR: Yes, which stand for something else, or else time as a word, vocabulary: T-I-M-E.

S: [*Groans; laughter*] I meant time . . .

CTR: As a word.

S: I guess as a word.

CTR: Rather than initials.

S: I was hoping that it would stand for something. You know, you talked about space. [*Laughter*]

CTR: Yeah.

S: You talked about space, and to me, space and time are very, very closely interrelated.

CTR: Space and time, sure. What's the problem? [*Laughter*] Is there any problem?

S: No. There isn't really a problem. I was just wondering why you avoided talking about time until today. You said that time was related to learning the dharma, but it didn't seem to relate at all to the previous principles you were talking about.

CTR: Well, time comes along if you have space. That's one of the interesting points about theism and nontheism. In the theistic approach to space and time, time comes first and space comes later.

But in a nontheistic approach, space comes first and time comes later, because we don't have to try to prove who did the labor or created this world anymore. The world is made by itself, naturally, very simply. That's it. That seems to be one of the basic differences, you know. Do you understand?

S: I think so. Thank you.

CTR: That's it.

S: Rinpoche.

CTR: Yip! [*Laughter*]

S: [*Laughs.*] Would you say that—

CTR: I wouldn't. [*Laughter*]

S: [*Laughs.*] How do you know? You haven't heard what I was going to say.

CTR: [*Laughs.*] That's why! [*Laughter*]

S: [*Laughs.*] Well, now I'll say it and we'll see. Would you say that some experience of the phenomenal world, or your experiences as your companion, is an experience of the bleakness?

CTR: What do you mean by *companion*?

S: Well, that's a direct experience. You just simply have a flash of your experiences as your companion. I mean, you have some kind of flash of that experience. Is that related, somehow or another, to that sense of bleakness?

CTR: I don't think so. You're creating and collecting more buddies if you do that. [*Laughter*] I'm afraid so, George. [*Laughter*] It will never work.

S: God, I thought I had it! [*Laughter*]

CTR: Never work. [*Laughs.*]

S: Well, I can't thank you for that. [*Laughs.*]

CTR: Condolences. [*Laughs.*]

S: I didn't hear you, I'm sorry.

CTR: Whatever. Good luck, George. Very sad. [*Laughter*]

S: In another way of talking about renunciation, you seemed to say that it was something that you do. And in the way that you're talking about it tonight, it's something that you discover. At least that's the way I understood it. That sort of means that it's always there, but you discover it at some point. Is that what you meant?

CTR: You do it and you discover it at the same time. It's like being pushed into a corner. Do you understand? You are pushed into a corner. So you are being pushed into a corner and you do it that way. And you are pushed into the corner at the same time by life.

S: By life, yeah.

CTR: It's very, very hard, but it's very spacious and very freaky at the same time. When people begin to realize possibilities of renunciation, it's very freaky, extraordinarily freaky. People begin to feel they lost their whole being, which is good. That's what it is all about, really. And they begin to feel they can't play the same games anymore; they can't create their same opulence or dictatorial conmanship of all kinds anymore, at all. You begin to face your real, good old life, whatever that may be. It is bad news; at the same time it is fantastic good news in the long run. That's how the whole thing goes. [*Laughs.*] It's somewhat depressing, but it's very exciting, nevertheless. Depressive-exciting. So at some point, depression becomes excitement, when you begin to wake.

S: Is there something that retards that process, or that has to do with the process of finding yourself in the corner?

CTR: I think I should leave it up to you. I can't tell you how to go about it. Everybody's experiences are different. Each time, it's absolutely different. Good luck, sir.

Thank you. Tonight you should get a good sleep. Thank you for being very patient, waiting. We were just trying to get away from this very magnificent banquet we had for Khyentse Rinpoche. We just came out of that and I'm full. And hopefully I will share with you—I did share with you this particular talk, however. Well, good night.

Tomorrow is to be a sitting practice time, right? I would like to push further the fullness that we have been talking about. If you personally want to understand and realize what we are doing, you will have no understanding at all if you don't sit! That's the flat truth, the real truth. You should be able to understand what we are doing and what you are doing with our relationship, particularly in terms of the teachings and the examples of the teachings that are transmitted through generations and generations. People have understood themselves, realized themselves, by the sitting practice of meditation.

So tomorrow we have a somewhat modified nyinthün taking place. If you would like to understand what we are discussing, it would be very useful to sit. And also, we would like to reduce the density of spiritual pollution, which is known as spiritual materialism. If there's no sitting practice involved, there's no real cleaning-up process taking place. So I would like to invite all of you, if I may say so, to take part in sitting practice—tomorrow's organized nyinthün practice especially. Please pay heed to this. I would be more than grateful if you would go along and do that. And we may have more things to discuss after that, in the three further talks that we have. So by sitting, you might have more understanding of what's been happening, and that will make our personal communication much more open. Thank you. Good sleep! Good nightmare! [*Laughter*]

4

The Chicken and the Egg

THE OTHER DAY we were talking about the E principle from the hinayana point of view, the first noble truth level of bleakness and so forth. Tonight we might discuss the VAM principle connected with the hinayana tradition, which is that out of the bleakness, some manifestation of reality begins to take place. That is equally bleak, confusing, and painful—in the same way as the E principle of hinayana. Confusion and pain begin from the point of view of the possibility of losing territory: usually unhappiness occurs because we begin to feel that we might lose our territory, we might lose our world, so to speak. Consequently, we are continuously trying to reestablish ourselves. We are trying to have a sense of the possession of ego constantly taking place. But when that is happening, then there will be further problems, of course—the potential death of ego, and so forth. The possibility of the death of ego, which causes a lot of pain and problems, is the E principle. E is the space that is created, potential death, so to speak. Beyond that level, what to do about that, is the VAM principle, what we are going to do about those things.

According to the tradition, and in the discipline and techniques that developed throughout the buddhadharma, there is a sense of utilizing that desolateness in terms of some concrete practice. Practice is trying to match that bleakness we experience at the potential loss of ego. Meditation practice seems to be the way, or the particular point, where energy and spaciousness could be put together. The sitting practice of meditation actually brings the E and the VAM principles together. So the EVAM principle goes on throughout all three yanas, each time the teaching is presented. It is not so much a complete E and a complete VAM; but EVAM becomes indivisible each time. That is why the techniques are bringing them together in the basic point.

In the sitting practice of meditation, we feel that there is a sense of simplicity. It is almost at the level of simpletons. The simple sitting practice of meditation, the very basic and very ordinary discipline of sitting on a meditation seat and doing nothing seems completely absurd—as if that's going to cure anything, as if that's going to do anything for you. It's very absurd. It's utterly absurd, as a matter of fact. Because of the absurdity, it has some wisdom—not even some, but lots of it. Immense wisdom goes along with that. It goes along with our general rhythm and style, how we operate, how we actually ego-center ourselves throughout the process. So that anti-ego [activity] is somewhat prescribed, that going against the ego.

In the sitting practice of meditation there is basic space, basic openness. Somehow, strangely, there is also basic uncertainty. If your discipline is completely certain and you know what you are doing, then there is no journey. The uncertainty that takes place in the sitting practice of meditation is the VAM principle. The E principle is the general attitude, the general atmosphere that is always there. Putting them together makes a complete work of art, so to speak. The desolate situation of life is brought together [with that uncertainty]. Together they present our work, our life, our existence, as being somewhat pushed into the teaching.

In the Buddhist tradition, the notion of renunciation means realizing the truth about suffering and understanding how much we have fooled ourselves. How we have been captivated by our own garbage, so to speak. Our own cobweb, our own thread, has imprisoned us constantly. And when we feel more imprisoned, helpless, chaotic, and terrible—that is the space, actually. Whether you like to believe that or not, it's a fact. The more we feel claustrophobia, the more we feel that we are completely cluttered with stuff, that we are caught in the middle of a traffic jam completely. Those kinds of little, or even big, things around us. We are being surrounded by that situation and we cannot get out of it at all. When we try to get out of such a situation, we have to produce or manufacture more stuff in order to get out of it. And that stuff in itself starts to get in the way all the time. All that is actually space, the E principle.

Because of that, we begin to look for something else, another space-type situation, other refreshing possibilities—and unable to find anything better at all, we begin to sit and practice, meditate. The practice of meditation begins to give us some perspective: that the claustrophobia is the space, or E; and the inspiration to work with the claustrophobia is the dynamic possibilities, or VAM; so E and VAM put together. The sitting practice of meditation is like that. It's seemingly quite simple, actually. It's very, very basic, extremely basic. The general principle is that there is always a container and what is contained. That is always taking place in practice of any kind, according to the buddhadharma.

Let us discuss the narrowness of the hinayana. The narrow and militant, so to speak, discipline of hinayana becomes very powerful and important. The more narrow and more disciplined you try to make things, the more you begin to have some sense of fresh air taking place simultaneously, all the time. One of the interesting points here is that contradictions make sense. Contradictions make sense unless you are telling a lie, then it doesn't make sense: you are telling a lie rather than contradictions. There's a difference between contradictions and lies. Contradictions could be facts and figures, realistic views of things as they are. Telling a lie is trying to cheat somebody, which has nothing to do with contradictions at all, actually. You are trying to go beyond contradictions, so that becomes a lie, untruth. The important point is that where there is a lot of space, that means there is a lot of claustrophobia. And a lot of energy means a lot of low energy. You can get high on the low energy, of course—in many cases, we have done that ourselves—nevertheless, it is energy, which we call depression, as a euphemism. When you are high on low energy, that is depression.

The Tibetan term for renunciation is *shenlok*, which literally means "nausea." You are completely nauseated with the claustrophobia that takes place in your life, in your ordinary basic life. Piles of dirty dishes in your kitchen sink, unmade beds, unpaid bills, unfriendly telephone calls, and friendly telephone calls. You begin to descend into dust and cobwebs completely—as if, or literally in some cases. You get phone calls or mail from people who say that they are going to kick you out of your apartment, and they are going to cut the telephone connection, and somebody is going to sue you. And if you had higher connections previously, when you felt frivolous in the early days, then one of those Mafiosi will come along and try to kill you on the spot; there's a price on your head. It's interesting, that point of view. There's a lot of claustrophobia, and there is immense space, and lots of energy taking place in ordinary situations, at the kitchen-sink level. It is very powerful, and makes us think twice, thrice.

The sitting practice of meditation seems to be the only way we can actually bring together the notion of pain and the notion of inspiration simultaneously—sweet and sour at once. That's been done in Chinese cooking, and people find it quite delicious, as a matter of fact. In this case, it is much more than sweet and sour, actually; it is hot and cold simultaneously, freezing and burning simultaneously. Particularly when students begin to get into the practice, they begin to get burnt—but simultaneously they are being frozen. You have the frigidity of being frozen, and you have at the same time the scorching qualities of being burnt. And that seems to be the general view or general experience.

I begin to feel that myself. And in my personal experience of watching our students, I begin to see that they have the facial expressions, physical behavior, and format of being burnt and frozen simultaneously. That brings some kind of massage system. They then begin to dance, to like it. However, they can't like it too much, because once they do so, they begin to take sides, either to the cold or the hot areas. But when they feel some healthy awareness or wakefulness taking place, the hot and cold are balanced completely. So they are cooled and warmed simultaneously. All this is taking place at the hinayana level, of course. E and VAM, E being the cold and VAM being the hot, take place together at that point.

If you have any questions, you are welcome.

Student: When we understand or accept these contradictions, is it a feeling of just accepting things the way they are, rather than coming to a greater logic?

Chögyam Trungpa Rinpoche: "Accepting things as they are"—what do you mean by that?

S: Just opening up to the situation and not taking sides, not trying to maintain a hold on it.

CTR: Sounds too naive for me. There's more energy than that.

S: Would you explain?

CTR: Accepting things as they are could be just leaving it up to the situation to work itself out. But that's not the case here. Accepting things as they are from one angle would be simply and directly experiencing without any fear. You see, you could be accepting things as they are with a sense of panic. You could say, "Now this is the folk wisdom. We should be accepting things as they are. Let's cool it, cool off, just sit back and smoke our pipes in our rocking chairs." That's not quite the case here. There has to be some kind of continual wakefulness rather than just sitting back and letting things happen on their own accord and everything is going to be hunky-dory. You see what I mean?

S: Yes.

CTR: It's very taut—chippy is the only word I can think of. [*Laughter*]

S: Thanks.

S: What's the relationship between EVAM and the feminine principle?

CTR: E is the feminine principle; VAM is the masculine principle.

S: But it sounds like one could see E as the mother aspect of the feminine principle and VAM as the dakini aspect?

CTR: Not necessarily. E is very tricky, it has everything. And VAM is just the mere occupants of the container, which is sometimes helpless. So the feminine principle has greater power from that point of view. In other words, we can't breathe without oxygen, and that oxygen is the feminine principle.

S: But that can involve energy too, or manifestations of energy.

CTR: Well, we have to use oxygen in order to function, so to speak. So the feminine principle is life strength, the strength of life. We can't function without space. That's it. And once we have space, once the feminine principle is graciously accepting the masculine principle, then you could do all kinds of things. In this case, we are not talking about a man and woman particularly at all; we are simply talking in terms of principles. And we are not saying that women are superior or men are superior. In this case we are just talking about how the cosmos works, the mechanics and chemistries. There are two elements—the container and the contained—that interact with each other. If there's nothing to be contained, the container becomes irrelevant; and if there's not enough container for what is being contained, then vice versa, so to speak. That's the idea we are talking about here, although we have to rush a lot.

S: I'm shocked at how familiar hinayana seems. That's where I seem to be. In any case, I have been thinking about how it is not only difficult to transcend misery, but it is difficult even to acknowledge it. There is even a sense of embarrassment about it, a sense of shame. Is there a kind of subterranean sense of responsibility, that we choose this kind of existence?

CTR: I think the notion is that you are still not willing to be public, so to speak. That's one of the biggest obstacles. Even at the vajrayana level, the yeshe chölwa principle of crazy wisdom is that willingness to be public. At the hinayana level, there also should be some notion of being willing to be public. We would like to keep some little privacy, so there is still the faintest of the faintest of the faintest—or maybe even a much thicker level—of deceptions taking place all the time. We really don't want to present ourselves as we are, but we would like to reinterpret ourselves in order to present ourselves to the public. Always there's that kind of translation of what you like to see yourself as, rather than what you are.

S: There's a kind of pride involved in that.

CTR: It is a neurotic pride of some kind, but I still think it is workable, actually. There's no particular problem; it had to break through. Obviously, there's always going to be some kind of stage fright taking place; nevertheless, you can overcome that. That's what it is all about. And actually, that idea of performance is getting into the vajrayana level, that you are performing onstage—everything is a dance on a stage. In hinayana, the point is to acknowledge that stage fright much more. Then you could overcome it.

S: Hopefully.

CTR: I'm sure you can do it. See what happens.

S: Rinpoche, you said EVAM is happening all the time throughout the three yanas, and then it becomes invisible. What do you mean by invisibility?

CTR: In-di-visibility! They become one. At each level, it is the indivisibility of E and VAM together. That happens through all the yanas.

S: And yet you can work with it, work with the EVAM principle?

CTR: Work with the EVAM principle? Well, hopefully. I hope so, otherwise there's nothing left. If you cannot work with your atmosphere and your body, there's nothing left for you to do, is there? No house, no body, no practice—*poof!* [*Laughter*] What is there left? I hope so. It has been promised in the scriptures and texts that it is workable, that the journey is the indivisibility of the accommodation and what is being contained in it working together—which we are trying to correlate with the E and VAM principles at this point. Good luck, sir.

S: I don't know about that.

CTR: I'm sure you can do it.

S: Rinpoche, at the end of your talk, you began to describe the experience in sitting practice of burning and freezing. I think I didn't quite get it. You said that after a while the student begins to like it?

CTR: Well, I don't mean "like it" in the sense of indulgence, but the student begins to feel familiar with it, that hot and cold are one.

S: Is that what produces the sensation, if I understood you correctly, of transmutation from burning and freezing to warming and cooling?

CTR: No, no! It is having two experiences at once, which makes the whole thing indivisible. You get completely exasperated: your dualistic mind can't jump back and forth anymore, so you begin to accept the whole thing. You begin to give in. Then hot and cold are "so what?" One thing, one taste. That's it.

S: And that presents the possibility of moving into—

CTR: It doesn't present even the impossibility of actually experiencing hot and cold at once.

S: Well, the balance sounds like something—

CTR: There's not even a notion of balance anymore.

S: Okay.

CTR: That's that! [*Laughter*] You see what I mean? If you begin to talk about balance, then you have presented that as like tuning your record player—which is bass and which is treble. But in this case, it is the whole thing. It's like a broken bottle, and the juice inside is running out completely, with both hot and cold at once. That's what we call a potential vajrayana mess. [*Laughter*]

S: Thank you.

CTR: It's quite delightful, actually. It happens at the hinayana level as well. When we begin to give in, not choosing the hot or the cold, both become one completely. That's possible. It's been done.

S: What is the relationship between hot and uncertain? You talked about VAM in terms of uncertainty and in terms of heat.

CTR: Inquisitiveness. Uncertainty. Not knowing exactly what's happening. For instance, if you moved into a house that was not particularly familiar to you and you had not been there before, you would like to look into every closet, what it's all about. Uncertainty. Occupation. Problem. So?

S: So . . . you also talked about VAM in terms of being hot, and the E cold.

CTR: Yeah. Hot, of course, yes. Hot cannot happen if there's no cold to begin with—but you can't work the other way around. In other words, without a mother, there cannot be a son. In this case, we are saying the chicken is first and the egg is last. Finally, Buddhist tantrikas worked out which comes first! [*Laughter*] That's what we are talking about: the chicken comes first, the egg comes after.

S: Rinpoche, in breaking through stage fright, it seems that even in that commitment there is still a sense of deception, of being onstage but still playacting. How do you get to that point where you are even beyond playacting on the stage?

CTR: If you regard that as life. If you regard it as a performance, that's a problem. That's a problem with a lot of performing people in the theater as well: if they don't regard that as purely demonstrating their life, they make a terribly bad performance; they begin to act. You see what I mean? It is the same thing. You are not performing for anybody's entertainment; you are performing as you are—including wiping your bottom on the toilet seat and everything. Whether you are performing in public or private, you are there. Jolly good job. [*Laughter*]

S: Rinpoche, would you say that our first glimpse of space is usually perceived as fright or boredom or depression because we tend to compare it with what we experienced before?

CTR: Absolutely. We don't take it seriously enough, but on the other hand, we take it too seriously—which are the E and VAM principles, hot and cold. The problem is that we don't relate with hot as actually hot; we think it might be cold. If we run our hot-water tap long enough, it might come out cold water afterward, and if we run enough hot, the cold tap might run hot. That is a kind of distrust in the chemistry that exists, simultaneously. You know, you expect the moon is going to turn into the sun, and the sun might turn into the moon if you sit long enough.

S: So it's kind of a baby's view of space?

CTR: Infantile—that's it, absolutely.

Well, friends, that seems to be a good way to end. I understand that tomorrow I will be here earlier, according to my friends in the administration. Good night. Thank you.

5

Small People with Vast Vision

I AM BEGINNING to feel that we don't have enough time to discuss the whole thing properly; however, we could do our best at this point. Today, I was hoping that we could go through the mahayana concepts connected with the EVAM principle. One of the interesting points there is that there is some notion of problem, we could say. At the level of vajrayana, it is very clear and precise. At the level of hinayana, it is equally precise and clear because of its simplicity, its connection with reality. But at the mahayana level, there seems to be some kind of obstacle or problem, which comes from the possibility of religiosity and benevolence. The popular mahayanist view of how to conduct one's life and to organize the whole thing is based on the idea of goodness of some kind. That sometimes becomes problematic. It has become a big problem. However, we could work on that, so it is no longer regarded as an obstacle at all, by any means. The idea of goodness becomes an obstacle in certain situations. If the practitioner begins to become too involved with religion or do-goodism, that could lead into a notion of love-and-light. That seems to be the epitome of the problems of mahayana buddhism. On the other hand, it is impossible just purely to put hinayana and vajrayana together without the transition of mahayana. It would make no sense, there would be no virtue of any kind at all.

The basic point of mahayana's view and concept of the E principle is the notion of commitment, extensive commitment, and vision. Commitment means taking the vow of doing a bodhisattva's work, and vision means that there is nothing in the way between you and practice anymore. Commitment means that you are willing to work with the rest of sentient beings, not only sentient beings who crawl and walk on this planet, particularly—your commitment is to work with the complete universe, including the billions of solar systems that exist. There is such vast vision of your being willing to work with anything there is: you are willing to work with the sun and the moon, the rest of the stars, and all the other planets that exist in the universe, beyond your imagination of vast. Those vast outer-space worlds, any kind, all kinds—you are willing to work with the whole thing completely. That particular vow and commitment tends to become very warm and very personal at some point; nevertheless, that personality is not in the way. It becomes real experience. It is complete experience when there are no limitations put on your vision, your expansion, anymore. It is large mind, gigantic, great, vast mind.

Mahayana is known for its big thinking, its larger scheme. Therefore, the scheme itself, the big thinking itself, and the commitment to that larger scheme, become real, realistic, powerful, and important. That actually tends to create a sense of feeling belittled. Sometimes you feel belittled—the vision is so big and you are so little. Your activities and your particular personal existence are so small. You might feel it is very little; you are very little. An interesting contrast takes place there. That conflict between the vast vision and the small person doing the vast vision sets off some kind of atomic bomb. Such a small person can think so big—that becomes gigantic and extremely beautiful. The little thing is the trigger, and vastness is the explosion, and that begins to work together. That's the E principle, in the mahayana tradition, basically, generally speaking. Of course, other things, such as the notion of shunyata, become important too. But there we are not talking in terms of action; we are purely talking in terms of a state of mind that exists when a person begins to realize no form, no boundary, yet completely form, completely full of boundaries. You begin to get confused again by the boundary, or the form, and the formlessness—form and boundarilessness altogether. So some kind of explosion also takes place there.

As far as the VAM principle in the mahayana is concerned, it seems to be the notion of practicality, which is also the notion of faith. Faith here means not willing to give up, and a sense of complete joy. We could use the word "romantic," which seems to be quite kosher here—romantic meaning how fantastic it would be, how fantastic it is, that I am a child of Buddha, and I can actually fulfill buddha activities by conducting myself in the way of the Buddha: generosity, discipline, patience, exertion, meditation, prajna, and so forth. You might have vast vision and commitment of some kind, which is the E principle, but if you don't have a personal filler, so to speak, a personal occupant of that particular vision, then that vision becomes just heroic hoo-hah that doesn't mean anything very much. It's just somebody thinking big who doesn't have any practicality—so what?

There's always a conflict with the domestic, so to speak, experience of the bodhisattva's work, which also contains the notion of great compassion. Actually, we could say the compassion aspect of the bodhisattva relates with both the E and VAM principles, simultaneously and together. The spaciousness of the compassion, the largest notion of limitless compassion, is connected with the E principle. Nevertheless, simultaneously, the VAM principle also contains a sense of softness and compassion. Compassion could be divided into two sections, as it is traditionally done: the E principle is karuna, basic compassion; and the VAM principle, we could say, is maitri, the warmth and loving, the domestic aspect of it. So you have two types of things working together, but they are indivisible, nevertheless. The mahayana principle of E and VAM put together is very pragmatic, very domestic. The hinayana principle of EVAM is very much educational. The difference between those two is like the difference between going to school, college, and having your degree already and actually working.

Vastness and potency put together again bring the notion of hot and cold together. We discussed that last night. The same thing begins again. Hot is the domestic approach of the bodhisattva's work: the paramitas, the dedication and awakening of bodhichitta in individuals. Cold is the vastness: how your world, how you, can actually radiate from this little fire to the rest of outer space with complete warmth—which is a symbol of coldness in some sense. What takes place is that when you want to radiate immense heat, you are challenged by the possibility of cold at the fringe, at the outer range of your territory, so to speak, which is an interesting point. The VAM principle becomes more and more dynamic as we go on to the vajrayana level, continuously. And the E principle becomes much more laid back, so to speak. Nevertheless, it is very important. It is of atmospheric importance to the situation, as we go through the three yanas.

Well, I don't think I should confuse you further by presenting too much stuff. Maybe we could stop here and direct questions, if you have any.

Student: The last few days you have given us a conducted tour of outer space (at least it seemed to me that way)—galaxies, solar systems, beyond, and on and on. And somehow you crept into it such concepts as maitri, karuna, love, compassion. Well, they seem to have—in my scheme, let's say—nothing to do with all that you have been talking about. Those are secondary or tertiary phenomena of the world or universe, many arising from socialization, et cetera. Now, where do karuna and outer space meet? Is that maybe some kind of a sop you throw at us and say, "Well, we like to be comfortable, that is compassion. Nice. And there's love, nice." But that's not how things really are! [*Laughter*] There is none of that! There are only these energies you have been talking about. How do you bring this together?

Chögyam Trungpa Rinpoche: You see, the interesting point is that you don't bring them together—it *is* together. We just have to click to the situation. We have been presented with all kinds of alternatives, seeming alternatives, and we have been presented with all kinds of variations of descriptions—nevertheless, they all become one. You don't try to bring them together as trying to mix two things, but they are already so. It is like the notion of the fluidity and wetness of water being one. So from that principle, you do not try to bring them together. Karuna is the largest sympathetic atmosphere that we have. Space accommodates crime and virtue, pain and pleasure. If there's no outer space, we wouldn't be here at all. Space is going along and just letting us do all these things. They are letting us build skyscrapers, build farms and wood cabins, what have you. They even let us go through that by rocket ship.

S: All manifestations of EVAM?

CTR: I wouldn't exactly say manifestations, but I would say it is it. That's it. That's it.

S: I wonder when you talk about extending our imaginations to include compassion for beings other than those that we can see on this earth, if that's an exercise in imagination or something that we should really expect to encounter?

CTR: What do you mean? You mean that we might get somebody in our backyard from the flying-saucer world? [*Laughter*]

S: No, I don't really think that it's going to enter our world. I just wonder if we're supposed to be willing to enter other worlds in any real sense.

CTR: Well, I have been thinking the whole thing is very basic and natural. We think that this world is gigantic, and if we buy a big property we say, "Wow, how many acres we bought!" You know, "We bought almost half the state!" Still, it is very little. The idea is that there are greater worlds that exist, and we shouldn't be too provincial, too earthly, whatever.

S: Well, when we do the chants and we talk about asuras and gandharvas and various other manifestations, are those real, or are those psychological states?

CTR: I would say both. The question "Is it real?" is very tricky. Actually, you know, it is even difficult to say whether you are real or I am real, whether what we are doing here is real. So the question of reality is just a matter of speculation. [*Laughter*]

S: Thank you.

S: Hello. You talked before about the hot and the cold—being in it, experiencing it, being able to be both hot and cold. Is one of the characteristic aspects of the mahayana, as opposed to the hinayana, not just being in composure in the middle of the hot and cold but also having compassion in your environment?

CTR: I think so. You see, we should definitely try to make a real statement about shunyata as well as compassion. When we talk about shunyata, we are talking about space, the basic atmosphere where things could be allowed to take place. And when we talk about karuna, compassion, it also goes into that particular area—karuna being a state of sympathetic atmosphere that you could generate, predominantly by attitude but fundamentally by real chemistry. It is an atmosphere that exists there, that we have to sort of tune in to. So the point of view of compassion in Buddhist terminology is not that we are feeling sorry for somebody because somebody is in bad shape and we feel, or try to feel, kindly to them, or that we are in the position to help them, particularly. That kind of one-upmanship or social worker's attitude—Peace Corps attitude, or what have you—is not the real compassion that we are talking about. Compassion in this case is an actual atmosphere of warmth and friendliness that can take place, which is not the state of mind of an ordinary person but the state of mind of everything—both the lowest of the low as well as the highest of the high at the same time.

S: So this is what starts to bring the joy out of that, out of your feeling of being so enclosed: the compassion.

CTR: You got it.

S: Okay.

CTR: The idea of joy here is not so much that you feel great that you managed to snatch somebody's cookie [*laughter*], but joy in the sense of, we could say, cosmic appreciation of some kind that everything is delightfully so.

S: I wondered how prajna fits into this, because I had seen shunyata as being like E and prajna as being like VAM.

CTR: Yes. That's very clever, actually. It's true. Prajna is very basic. It is the sensitivity that exists within the space. Again, prajna cannot survive without shunyata, or the space of anything. Prajna is the inquisitiveness. Fascination in the healthy sense takes place if there's enough room left, in larger thinking.

S: Rinpoche, would you say that the samsaric condition results from ignoring the E principle, the space, and in regard to the VAM, relating to it improperly?

CTR: Well, I think samsaric conditions are completely the opposite of EVAM. Instead of relating with vast space, you put in your own territory to begin with; instead of working with your own energy properly, you try to fight with the space. Trying to fight with space becomes an insult. So you have the complete reverse effect there: the actual area where it should be bigger, you try to be small; the area where you should be smaller, you try to be big. You are completely twisting the whole thing, which is known as neurosis. Yeah, that's a misunderstanding, of course. It is not necessarily permanent damage, or permanent punishment, or the fall of man, or anything like original sin. It is just a complete misunderstanding, completely missing the point. Where things should be looked at as gigantic and vast, you make territory out of that, make it smaller, put a fence around it. And the area where you should try to make things smaller and compact and energetic you try to push out, so you end up with some kind of cosmic constipation.

S: Thank you.

CTR: Which is samsara. Yes. [*Laughter*]

Well, friends, I think maybe time is getting younger again, so we should stop at this point. See you tomorrow. Thank you.

6

Wash Your Dishes
and Take Off Your Roof

QUITE SADLY, TONIGHT—this afternoon, rather—is the last chance we have to go through the EVAM principle generally; and, quite timely, today's topic is the vajrayana aspect of that. Throughout the Buddhist approach, the process is one of trying to develop basic sanity. Several of the hinayana schools would say that the sense of developing sanity is simply not to be attached to material things. It is to see everything as created out of atoms and fractions of time put together, so we have nothing to hang on to. The more advanced-level hinayana schools would say that it is just states of mind that we tend to cling to. The mahayana schools of Yogachara would say basic sanity is a state of mind, and that mind is continuously luminous: ever-glowing clarity and luminosity take place. The mahayana schools of Madhyamaka would say that state of mind is totally empty—but at the same time, conditioned mind is also buddha nature, nevertheless, so there is hope for you. That is the process that generally evolved, as sophistication developed through the hinayana, mahayana, and vajrayana levels. A lot of progress in states of further subtlety began to take place, of course.

At this point, as far as vajrayana discipline is concerned, that state of mind, basic sanity, has two constituents: mahasukha and jnana.

Mahasukha is a Sanskrit word that literally means "great joy," "great bliss." *Maha* means "big," "great," "giant," and *sukha* means "happiness," "joy," "pleasure," "bliss," whatever. *Jnana*, again, is a Sanskrit word that literally means "primordial insight." That is to say, it is insight, understanding, clarity, oneness. Jnana is a state of discriminating wisdom that always occurs rather than being produced by temporary experience of any kind. It is an inherent state of being. So jnana is like outer space, which is inherently outer space. In spite of stars, moons, galaxies, and planets of all kinds; nevertheless, it is basic space. Outer space is inherently empty and inherently rich at the same time, like jnana, wisdom.

In the vajrayana tradition, as far as the EVAM principle is concerned, it is the notion of wisdom and great joy put together. Wisdom is regarded as the E principle, fundamentally. That is to say, being. Every situation we experience in our ordinary life has its basic subtleties, embryonic basic subtleties, which help allow us to express. That basic tendency, that basic format, is always there. In the tantric tradition, of course, that is often referred to as the principle of vagina—or cervix, actually—where birth is taking place, the birth of the phenomenal world. It is like giving birth to a child in that it is coming out of that particular cosmic mouth. It is not even a mouth, it is more; it is more than a gate, it is cosmic space. In vajrayana teachings, you often find it said that the Lord is dwelling in the cosmic cervix of wisdom. Because he is dwelling in that cervix, therefore, he is able to teach and to proclaim the vajrayana discipline.

In this case, we are not purely talking about sexuality, or anything to do with sexuality, particularly. That is a very small portion of it. Instead we are talking about the general principle, the vastness of the whole thing. The basic mother principle is not even female or male; it is just a basic principle that exists, which accommodates, which allows the situation to become pregnant, to be born. And also, it gives birth. Nevertheless, it contains everything—which is a different, larger state of mind than we discussed in the mahayana discipline the other day. It is much bigger than the mahayana principle in this case, much greater, in some sense. It is no longer even vision, anymore, it is just a state of being. That vastness is so. So vast, therefore it is so. That might have some correlation with the concept of shunyata, but it is nothing like the shunyata mahayanists talk about as being not this, not that, therefore everything is nothing. You don't even have to borrow the terms "form is empty, emptiness is form" anymore. It is completely total, absolute, from that point of view.

From the vajrayana point of view, the E principle, therefore, is impregnated space. We could say that space, in terms of physical space, is also impregnated space, because it is sympathetic to everything that goes on in that space. It allows things to operate in its own space. From that point of view, we could also say it is somewhat kind space, compassionate and accommodating space, precisely. That's an interesting pun—it is accommodating space, space that accommodates everything—a vajrayana pun of some kind. Probably you don't think it's so funny, but it's so. [Laughter] Space is very accommodating—and often, of course, it is very frightening too. Things seem to be a larger size than you are, as we discussed the other night in a greater version.

Why, if space is just open and accommodating, should we call it wisdom? Why wisdom? What is there about being wise? What is the idea of being wise? The concept of wise, from that point of view, is what is traditionally known as "one flavor." The Tibetan term for "one flavor" is rochik. Ro means "flavor," "taste," chik means "one"; so "one-flavor" experience. If you have one-flavor experience, there are two choices: you don't experience at all because it is one-flavor, your own flavor; or else you become a monomaniac. If you become a monomaniac, you just like one thing at a time. But in this case, of course, we are not talking about that monomaniacal level of one flavor, that you like only one thing, the thing, that you become a maniac about something or other. Instead, one flavor means tasting your own tongue and seeing your own eyes with your own eyes. It is where the state of mind becomes not dependent on feedback from the phenomenal world, but it contains by itself. So it is self-contained experience, utterly self-contained experience.

I hope the dakinis and dharmapalas and all these people will allow us to talk about such a thing as this. If they wouldn't, may this building collapse on the spot! [*Nervous laughter*] We are taking a chance, you know. But I feel that you have been studying already. Every one of you has been studying and had study groups—every one of you except one or two people who just dropped by. But still, those people are very safe people—who may be deaf, and hopefully will be mute too.

Anyhow, the question of one flavor is that space makes love to itself, and space also produces children and grandchildren and great-great-great-great-great-great grandchildren—and great-great-great-great-great-great grandparents, of course. Nevertheless, space is not the origin of the feminine lineage, because it is always one thing. It is ever-present, ever-ready, ever-simple, which makes the whole thing very interesting, in some sense. Eventually the sitting practice of meditation, shamatha and vipashyana, or shi-ne and lhakthong experience, also could become like that: self-contained experience that doesn't need, or is not asking for, a reference point anymore.

One flavor also brings the next notion, the VAM principle, which is mahasukha, great joy. Because of its one-flavorness, because of its own self-existence, because of its own self-contained situation, therefore lots of play can take place in our life, our experiences, and everything. The phenomenal world is the guideline completely, it is absolutely the guideline. There is a fundamental sign, or symbol, taking place. That often could become superstitious, of course; nevertheless, it is true, in some sense. It is like the very simple, ordinary, regular things we talk about. For instance, if you get angry with somebody and decide to walk out, storm out of his room, you are so pissed off at that person—you slam the door and catch your finger in it. That kind of situation. Sometimes it is very dramatic and vivid, and sometimes it is very subtle and ordinary. Nevertheless, those situations always take place with our life.

There seem to be no actual accidents as such, at all. Everything seems to have its own messages taking place. Why today's weather is somewhat warm. Why tonight is going to be particularly cold. Why we actually managed to get hold of this particular place to give a talk on the EVAM principle at all. Why you managed to churn up time and money to come here and do this together. Why your particular hairstyle. Why you are bald, why you have lots of hair. Why you are wearing a shirt or why you are wearing a tie—or why you are not wearing a shirt, why you are not wearing a tie. All those little situations seem to be very superstitious, when we talk about those little things. Nevertheless, there is some deliberateness taking place always.

One of the exciting things about all that is that the world is filled with magic—not from the point of view of a conjurer's trip, but magic in the very ordinary and very basic sense. How we came to be here— that our physical setup is such, our state of mind is such, our clothes are such, our way of behaving is such—is interesting. That seems to be the VAM principle: everything that exists contains great joy. It is not so much that you are having twenty-four hours of orgasm simultaneously. We are not talking about that, particularly, but about great joy from the point of view that some state of mind is here, and it is contained, and it is also very sane and wholesome. What we are doing is absolutely wholesome, the most solid thing that we could ever have done in our life. Right now we are doing a great job, all of us. We are doing what we should be doing—and it feels togetherness, it feels awe-inspiring, and it also feels very sacred.

We have created some kind of atmosphere, quite rightly so. We decided to put our chemistry together, you and me, and this and that.

The joy, or bliss, principle is not so much that somebody is tickling you or that you are in a state of ecstasy from the effect of some chemical, or what have you. Here joy and togetherness and wholesomeness have to do with something that is naturally there, completely there, a sense of arrogance and pride without neurosis, a natural state of being, which is so.

The vajrayana principle, VAM, is often referred to as the "vajra principle." That particular vajra principle is based on the idea of indestructibility. Nothing can challenge it, nothing can actually destroy it or chip off that vajra being. It is a state of being, generally—a state of being, a state of existence, a state of reality, a state of straightforwardness, sharpness, toughness, gentleness and everything, brilliance and so forth. We begin to realize that we possess all those qualities, even though we are mere beginners in the practice. We are mere beginners, we are just mere. We can only spell—if we could read the alphabet, that would be the best. We are at that level at some point; however, we have some sense that we are associating ourselves with some basic sanity in any case.

That basic sanity is so complete. Bliss, joy, can only occur when there is a sense of complete circulation taking place, without any mishaps or outlets. In other words, nobody is stealing your energy. The energy is yours, and you are actually utilizing that particular energy in an appropriate way. You feel completely harmonious; you feel complete harmony with that particular situation, which is joy. It is quite magnificent and fantastic. Nevertheless, the E and VAM principles put together, that we would actually bring together, are not separate—they are interdependent and indivisible. Much more indivisible than your nation. [Laughter] Much more so, I'm afraid. It is very complete. It is one flavor, again, once more, in the indivisibility.

Three levels. The hinayana level stirs up pain and pleasure and complications. The mahayana level makes you more relaxed, more committed to what you are doing. In vajrayana, finally you are presented with the ultimate healthiness, ultimate wholesomeness, completely. It is that you are okay, so to speak, and everything is fine. If you worry, that's great; if you don't worry, that's fine too. All the sharp edges, the sharp corners of this and that which take place—you should let them take place in their own way. Razors have their own place, and sponges have their own place too. So whether it's floppy or sharp, it's fine—they are the same manifestation of it. What is it? It's nothing, it's everything, it's everywhere. It is us. It is nobody. It is everywhere and it is so joyous—joyous and powerful. And also, we mustn't forget, it is very liberating. The highest mind that has ever occurred in this age and space and planet is vajrayana intelligence, which is so gentle and handsome [*laughter*], and so dignified, beautiful. That is why it is called vajra-yana, the "vehicle of the vajra."

Often this yana is referred to as the imperial yana; however, in this case, we are not particularly talking about politics, but we are purely talking about its all-encompassingness, overwhelmingness, expansiveness. Usually nobody is actually able to identify themselves with space, because we are hassled with our life. We have too many dirty dishes to wash, so we have never had a chance to look out the window even, let alone take our roof off. But in this case, the vajrayana principle is to wash up your dishes, make your bed, clean your room—and then take off your roof. [*Laughter*] That is the imperial yana. Thank you. If you have any questions, you are welcome.

Student: Could you say anything about the EVAM principle in relation to the context of devotion?

Chögyam Trungpa Rinpoche: Well, I think devotion is also a love affair at the same time, which is a very important point. The indivisible experience of taking off your roof and cleaning up your dirty dishes and everything could not occur at all if there were no basic devotion. Devotion is somewhat claustrophobic at the beginning;

nevertheless, you begin to become one with space. The object of devotion is the force that comes out of the space that we have been talking about. Without that, we can't do anything at all. Thank you.

S: Thank you.

S: A friend of mine told me that before she went to India to practice Buddhism, she spoke to you. You had just come to this country and she asked if you had any advice—and you said to follow the pretense of accident. [*Laughter*]

CTR: So?

S: Is that anything like what you were talking about, the magical quality of the details of your life?

CTR: Your guess is as good as mine. [*Laughter*]

S: I have two questions, Rinpoche. One, when you were talking about the one-flavorness of things, did you mean that there isn't an experience and an experiencer but that we *are* the experience?

CTR: Can you run down your logic?

S: Does that limited point of view ever disappear in the vajrayana, or does it just appear that whatever is viewed, or whatever is experienced, is all there is?

CTR: I don't think anything in particular will disappear or reappear. Instead, it is a state of being where we could actually make a further statement of things as they are much more clearly. You see, the idea of attainment is not so much getting to a new field, or a new experience, particularly, but refining what we have already. Otherwise we are completely helpless—if we have to reform ourselves, if we have to change everything, make green into yellow, yellow into black, or whatever have you. That whole thing doesn't work, because if you have to make rocks out of flowers, flowers out of rocks, and daytime into nighttime, nighttime into daytime, it doesn't work. The idea is very basically, simply, that we have every possibility already in us. That is our inheritance as sentient beings. What we have to do is refine whatever is there—refine and refine and refine, completely refine.

S: The other question I had was about the idea of space. In *The Tao of Physics,* Fritjof Capra talks about there being particles, or very basic constituents of the inner nucleus, that sort of support one another. He says that they are part of a ring and that you can't destroy them, because one just turns into another one of the constituents of what makes it up. So it is never really destroyed; it just turns into something else, and it can turn into things continually.

CTR: Well, that seems to be an interesting point; that actually fits. That particular particle has to have its own thing to begin with; otherwise it couldn't turn into anything else. And because of its existence, it has sympathetic qualities to relate with the rest of it. That seems to be what we were talking about. One-flavor, one-taste, is precisely that: it is one taste; therefore, all the tastes and flavors can be included in the whole thing.

S: Gotcha. Thank you.

CTR: You're welcome .

S: You have talked about the EVAM principle in terms of a lot of other terms that we have some familiarity with in other contexts: renunciation, discipline, commitment, faith, vast space, and now jnana and mahasukha. Is there anything actually new in EVAM, or is this just a superjargon that helps us understand the rest of the stuff?

CTR: What do you think? [*Laughter*]

S: Well, I think the second one.

CTR: I think so. You see, it's too bad. I'm afraid this whole thing is too bad—it's too bad that we didn't come up with a new gadget. That's one of the beauties of Buddhism: that new jargon could develop, or seemingly could develop, but it is based on old hat; therefore, it is new jargon. Old hat could be sold as an antique.

S: What do you mean "identify with the space"?

CTR: Float, but not float. If you are space already, you cannot float. It is it. *Comme çi, comme ça.*

S: What about sickness and total pain? Is there such a state of complete total pain that there is no sukha and no way out but pain itself? Then what happens? Or does the pain become one taste too?

CTR: My dear sir, vajrayana is not Judaism.

S: Yeah, well, that's why I'm asking. [*Laughter*] That's why I'm asking.

CTR: Everything is sukha—in fact, mahasukha rather than just mere sukha. No circumcision is necessary.

S: Circumcision is necessary, or no circumcision?

CTR: No circumcision.

S: Yeah, well, sure.

CTR: No circumcision!

S: Yeah, sure. Oh sure. Yeah, on that.

CTR: Come as you are, as they say. [*Laughter*]

S: Would you say something about the dakini playful aspect of E?

CTR: Well, it's atmosphere. In terms of practice, theoretically what should happen to a student of vajrayana is that the minute you wake up you are supposed to be able to create a new pun. [*Laughter*] In spite of the fact that you might have a hangover or had a depressed night or didn't get any sleep—still you are able to join in along with the cosmos. That's it!

Well, friends I think it is getting already early. Sorry that you have more things that you wanted to discuss, but we could hold off until later on. I'm sure we will be together for a long time.

I would like to make some closing remarks on this particular seminar, which has happened very beautifully. Your existence and the particular studies that you have done actually helped me a lot, so that I could freely present what we were going to discuss, what we were going to talk about. At the same time, auspiciously, the whole thing coincided with the visit of Khyentse Rinpoche here, so the whole thing has been brought together much more powerfully and beautifully. And now we are faced with a new challenge, which is how to relate with the energy and wisdom that you have already taken part in. Sitting practice is obviously very important. I hope you will be able to work on these things. Maybe what we have discussed needs further digesting and further work. So please don't jump the gun immediately, but study and think and practice. And also, once more, I would like to thank all of you for being very patient and gentle, and creating a fantastic atmosphere here. Thank you.

GLIMPSES OF REALIZATION

1

Why We Are Here at All

THE TOPIC OF this book, the three bodies of enlightenment, is somewhat out of the ordinary. Without a background in Buddhist study and practice, it may be difficult for you to follow. However, I am going to try to present the feeling of it rather than the whole thing. As you read, I want you to be open and awake. You have to use your antennae rather than purely your brain. In that way, we could make our journey together.

The three bodies of enlightenment are three types of atmosphere, which are involved with ordinary everyday life as well as with enlightened mind. The first body, to start from the beginning, so to speak, is background or origin. It is why we are here, not why we are here in this particular hall or why we are studying Buddhism, but why we are here *at all*. Why are we here on this earth? Why is there earth at all? Why is there sun and why is there moon? Why all of this? The first body seems to be our basis, or starting point. We start from outer space, to begin with. Then we slowly get into inner space and earth.

We have metaphysical, conventional, mythological ideas about why we are here—but those theories could be regarded as a load of bullshit. They don't actually say anything at all, but are based on rereading old books and reducing ourselves into bookworms. There is a problem with space—literally—physically and psychologically.

The psychological aspect is the tail end of the question and the physical aspect is the forerunner. *Why* do we have a problem with our space? *Is* there any problem with space, for that matter? There may be or there may not be. Things are not going too well in my life or things are going fabulously in my life—whatever.

Three expressions from traditional Buddhist texts summarize this whole area: unborn, unceasing, unoriginated. Such a summary isn't particularly helpful, but it at least gives us some landmarks. Of those three terms—unborn, unceasing, and unoriginated—the first is unborn. What are we going to do with that? Basically speaking, we are not born, we don't exist. That's the truth. It is a very courageous truth, a truth spoken or expressed because we are not afraid to tell the truth. It is the utmost truth. If you are afraid of telling the truth, what you say becomes bent truth, or a lie—but when you relate with the actual truth, although it may not be convenient or an ideally good message for the listener, you still speak the truth. From that point of view, we are unborn, we don't exist.

If we are unborn, if we never give birth to ourselves, how is it possible that we are here? We might say, "Literally, I was born from my mother, and psychologically speaking, I seem to have preconceptions of things. Ideas are born in my head or my heart, and I'm executing those ideas in my life." But *who* said that? That is the point. Who is actually talking about those things? Who is questioning that whole idea? Who is asking the questions? The questioner, of course. But who is the questioner? *What* is the questioner, rather than *who* is the questioner.

If you look back and back and back, after and after and after, it is like overlapping onion skins—you approach outer space and you find that nobody actually said anything at all. It was just a little burp. Somebody burped, which was misunderstood as language. Then, after that, someone said, "I beg your pardon?" And somebody said, "Oh, of course, I'm sorry. I burped." That cosmic burp, or cosmic fart, was an accident—a complete accident, unintentional—and that is what's called the origin of karma. Everything started on an accidental level. Everything is an accident.

When we get to that level, we are looking into enormous space. We are discussing and thinking about enormous space. That particular enormous space—that inconceivable, enormous space—is the basis of the original unbornness. We could ask a subtle question about the unbornness of space: "How is it possible for space to exist eternally, if space doesn't give birth to itself constantly? Otherwise, space would be dead." That's true. If space didn't give birth eternally, space wouldn't exist. The reason space exists constantly, but still maintains its unborn nature, is that space *never* gives birth! That non-giving-birth seems to be giving birth to a larger extent than giving birth in the literal sense of having a father and a mother and cutting the umbilical cord. So birth does exist in the realm of space in the sense that space constantly gives birth by itself. An analysis of space is that it has both masculine and feminine principles, both together. Fathers and mothers are one in space; therefore, nobody gets pregnant—or everybody gets pregnant. Nobody gives birth; therefore, everybody gives birth simultaneously. Mother and father are in the process of making love all the time.

We have a unique process at this point: immense space, which exists eternally or noneternally, does not give birth and at the same time does give birth, immense birth. That is why it is called unborn. Unborn is the safest way to describe it. If you have to use a term, it is much better to say unborn than eternally born. If you say eternally born, there is a tendency to think that somebody is being nursed. We think that we are going through the process of bringing up a child from infancy to the level of teenager and young adult up to the level of old age and death. We think that we have a process to go through. However, with this particular notion of space, we have no process to go through. Unborn is already birth. Therefore, no infancy or teenagehood or youthfulness or middle-age or old age or death exists. They don't exist because nothing happened! That seems to be the basic point. That all took place at a nonexistence level. This is very hard to understand if you look at it from the perspective of trying to understand. Obviously, when we try to give birth, instead of being unborn, something begins to be born. But now what we are trying to get to, and to understand—or not understand—is the *unbornness* of the whole thing.

There is a pattern taking place, in any case; and that pattern is workable, understandable, and realizable. However, in talking about that, we always reduce everything to a very domestic level. Not only do we reduce everything to the household domestic level, but we reduce everything to the bedroom level, saying, "If I did this, would that happen to me? If that took place, on the other hand, what would happen then?" and so forth. But in this case, the whole thing is beyond the domestic level, absolutely beyond the domestic level. Because of that, we can discuss it and we can question it. There's a lot of room for freedom, enormous room for freedom. It's not as if we are not allowed to talk about anything, or if we ask anything, we are dumb. Instead, *because* we are dumb; therefore, we are intelligent. There is a new opening of freedom, a level of freedom that we have never known in our life. That is why the whole process is very outrageous and quite incomprehensible, quite rightly so. Nevertheless it is understandable. It is feel-able, you can feel it.

On that basis, we do not discuss what section of that process belongs to samsara and what section belongs to nirvana. We do not even use those terms. The whole idea is that it does not belong to, for, or against. When we talk about nirvana and samsara, we take sides. We think of nirvana as our friend. We would like to associate with our friend, nirvana, and have enlightenment as our goal and aim. On the other side is samsara. Samsara means being imprisoned; samsara is confusion and pain. We do not want to relate with samsara or be a victim of that deadly area. That way of thinking has become the problem. Our conversations and our understanding of all this have been diverted to the level of what should be and what shouldn't be, rather than what is and what isn't. So we don't realize that, in fact, we are helpless. We don't realize that we cannot challenge this gigantic cosmic course that's taking place. We can't even sign our names to be in favor of it or against it. The whole thing is helpless.

We can reduce ourselves into a grain of sand; but, at the same time, we are part of outer space as a whole, cosmic space. So we need to have a certain amount of open mindedness, rather than always asking, "What does this mean to me at this point in my meditation practice? What does this mean to me in terms of my salvation? I have a problem with my husband, I have a problem with my wife. Is this particular argument, this idea or concept, going to save me from that problem?" We are not talking in those terms, at this point—we are talking BIG! We are actually tapping into an area that we have never touched, never looked at. Because we are so confused, we do not bother to look, apart from maybe the occasional glimpse. We think, "Who cares? This is not my cup of tea, my kettle of fish." We think that we were too poor, that it is too painful. We don't want to look at those areas that exist on a greater scale.

Ladies and gentlemen, it is about time for us to look! It is time to think bigger and open our minds to the possibility that nonduality does exist. You may not be philosophers or great meditators, but there is the possibility that greater areas could be opened to you if you bothered to look, if you bothered to open your minds. We are not talking about Tibetan Buddhism or Indian Buddhism at this point, or any other *ism*, but about how we could associate ourselves with a larger-scale world. To do so, we are using that mind in which we are not involved with *isms* of any sort.

A larger world exists, but we have never looked at it. We are too concerned with our microscopes or our magnifying glasses. We try to make things large by using magnifying glasses, but we have never looked at outer space with our naked eyes. If we looked into it, we could find it—but we don't have to use our binoculars and telescopes, we don't need them, they are false pretenses. We don't need any means to do this, we could just simply *look at it*, whatever it is, and enjoy it. An immensely larger version of thinking and of celebration is taking place. That seems to be the very important point.

Student: When you make a statement that something exists and at the same time it doesn't exist, does that mean that the entire question of what you're talking about just doesn't arise?

Chögyam Trungpa Rinpoche: You got it! It's the pre-question level. It is unconditional. Unfortunately, we don't have a term for that level. The closest is *state of being*, but that automatically implies existence, which is conditional. Unconditional being doesn't even rise to the level of question or the level of finding out.

S: Does unconditional being have qualities or characteristics?

CTR: Unconditional being does not have qualities, but, somehow, it has nonexistent qualities. However, saying that it has nonexistent qualities is entirely different from saying it does not have any qualities or that it is blank. Do you see the difference in saying no quality as opposed to nonexistent quality?

S: It's very easy for nonexistence to become just another thing—in my head, anyway.

CTR: That may be necessary, to begin with. We have to have something to work on. From that point of view, we are not being particularly dogmatic.

S: I really find it difficult to know how to use this material. If it's beyond experience, we can't say, "How can I have this understanding or this experience?" That would be beside the point.

CTR: That's right. That *is* beside the point, in fact.

S: But to go off and forget about it would also be beside the point.

CTR: You got it. That's right. In discussing this larger scale of thinking, novices at the beginning level might have difficulty understanding. In fact, they might find the whole thing extraordinarily claustrophobic. That's possible, because there's no room to move about—and there wasn't ever *meant* to be room to move about *at all*!

S: It seems that everything you're talking about—or not talking about—is pointing toward the play of energy. When you talk about space and unbornness and a nonexistent quality, it seems that you're talking about a dance, or the play of energy.

CTR: That's a bit of a tricky question, if I might say so. You are trying to get something out of that space, some kind of energy. But we haven't gotten to that level yet, we are still talking about space, rather than energy. At this point, as far as *this* level is concerned, we are not concerned with the idea of energy *at all*! We are simply concerned with understanding how the paradox can exist out of nowhere. We are not talking about energy.

Energy is very easy for people to understand, and if there is negative energy and positive energy, that is very graphic. But that is not quite what we mean here. In fact, that is the source of a big misunderstanding in mystical Hinduism, which has the idea of Brahman being all-pervasive, and in Christianity and Judaism, for that matter, which talk about the all-pervasiveness of God. In talking about all-pervasiveness, automatically the concept arises that if God is all-pervasive, there must be energy. The concept is that there should be the energy to be all-pervasive, rather than that nonexistent energy could *still* be all-pervasive. That possibility has never been looked at. So those cultures fail, from this point of view, and Buddhism wins. Rather than saying, "It's okay. If you find everything is nonexistent energy, that's fine," they have two levels: divinity and outer-space. That seems to be the difference.

S: Is there an openness to the *possibility* of energy, before talking about energy itself?

CTR: We are not talking about energy! It's just openness. Of course, some logic is involved. If it's openness, at the same time, that equally means utter claustrophobia. Space is not particularly good or bad. Claustrophobia is not regarded as negative nor is openness regarded as positive—they are equal. There is a parallel between the two; in other words, both are the same. Whenever you see light, in a dark or light form, it is the same—you are still seeing something.

S: Is there awareness at this point, or is that too dualistic?

CTR: Yes and no equally. Awareness is a very big topic, actually. When there is awareness, that automatically means categorizing and pinpointing something in particular or something in general—and that blows the whole thing. It begins to make everything extraordinarily chaotic and messed up. However, if there isn't awareness, then nothing is comprehensible or perceptible at all. You don't have anything to work on; you're just loose, in the realm of stupidity. So what we are talking about is *between the two*—not actually between the two, but it's *both at the same time*. It is intense awareness that sees all the details immaculately—simultaneously, this awareness does not exist, because of its so-aware quality. Because of its utterly awake quality, awareness is superfluous. We are still talking about parallels at this point. It is possible to perceive this; actually, it is very simple.

S: When you speak about the nonexistent quality, could a synonym be either *nonapparent* or *nonprojected*? Do those terms have something in common?

CTR: I wouldn't say so. Those terms are very tricky. *Nonexistence* is better. *Nonexistence* is a very simple term, which actually speaks of life and death. The other terms are somewhat manipulative business-deal terms: this happens, therefore that doesn't happen, which means everything happens at the same time. All things happen because things don't take place; therefore, they do take place at the same time. When you become bankrupt, you become rich, because you have become bankrupt. If you have a case history of becoming bankrupt, that means that you have big projects in your mind, so you still carry out that richness. Although your business failed, that is an incidental problem, it is not particularly a big deal. You had a bank account and it got corrupted.

S: Rinpoche, a term came to my mind, *unmoving awareness*, which is something that happens in zazen meditation—a state of unmoving awareness.

CTR: That's saying the same thing, I think, in that it is unconditional. When you begin to move, that is the same as conmanship, you are trying to con somebody. If awareness doesn't move, you don't con. Usually, in our ordinary behavior, movements are regarded as restless or as attempts to attract attention.

S: Does the openness occur at the point we are willing to accept chaos into our lives?

CTR: We are not talking about the *path*, at this point, or when openness *occurs*. Openness is there *already*, all the time! We are talking about what actually is there, rather than when something occurs as an *experience*. We are talking about the backbone of the whole thing. So the occurrence of opening, the moment when it happens, doesn't exist at this point. We are talking about outer space rather than inner space.

S: I guess I'm getting hung up in trying to relate it to myself.

CTR: That has become the problem. You try to relate with this as if you have a little lunch box and you can take it and eat it in the corner.

S: I don't see the difference between taking this big view and the power of positive thinking. The basic message seems to be that it is okay to think big—and somebody had to tell you it's okay.

CTR: I think that the power of positive thinking, conventionally, is trying to think everything is going to be okay, that there's nothing to worry about. But that is not enough, so the ordinary power of positive thinking is also thinking that somebody is going to help you or to save you from this problem. You think the divine is going to descend on you and save you; therefore, you have nothing to worry about. Humanistic, Buddhistic, nontheistic positive thinking is completely different. It is unknown. People have not been taught to look at things in that way. Generally, positive thinking is regarded as a cure, or medicine, rather than as a self-existing process. In the case of nontheistic positive thinking, however, nontheistic positive thinking is nondogmatic and not giving. In a sense, it is very mean, because you don't give a shit about anything, you just accept it as it is. You just let go and bulge out into outer space.

S: Is this space alive and existent in itself, or does it depend on the existence of paradox? Or should one give up any kind of effort or logic?

CTR: It is existent by itself. It doesn't depend on anything; therefore, it depends on everything—not helplessly.

S: In addition to unborn, you mentioned two other terms, unceasing and unoriginated. I was wondering whether there was any difference between those three terms, any kind of distinction, or whether they are synonymous.

CTR: I think they are the same: unborn, unceasing, and unoriginated. I was reading Longchen Rabjam's writings on this topic, and when I opened the book, the appropriate teaching came through. He said that the idea of openness and unbornness is a product of fearlessness. There is no fear to see. For instance, supposing you are an astronaut, and you are allowed to jump out of your rocket ship. There's fear, a sense of death, and a sense of enormous alienation, because you can't go back to your particular earth, where you came from. That is quite different from parachuting from airplanes, because airplanes are within the atmosphere or compass of this earth. However, if you are suspended in outer space, there is fantastic fear, transcendental fear that you have never known before. You do not want to die out in the open in that way.

If you jump out of an airplane, on this particular earth, you feel better—at least you are going downhill. You feel great, because compared with that, if you jump out of your rocket ship in outer space, you have nothing to hang on to, and nobody's going to receive you. Your body is not going to splash onto *anything*; it's just going to be recycling all the time, dragging through the whole of phenomena. That's the kind of situation we are talking about here. This particular teaching comes from the ati teachings of the tantric tradition. The ati tradition has an absolutely accurate concept of the outer-space journey from a meditative point of view. It's extremely accurate, as if the ati teachers had themselves been astronauts.

S: Rinpoche, is this any different from saying that if I die, awareness still goes on?

CTR: It is more than that: we are talking about the death of experience in *this* life, rather than what happens if we jump out of the Empire State Building. It's saying the same thing—it's just a much larger version of that whole thing.

S: It seems that what you are saying should give all of us extreme courage to try anything. Is there any limitation on that?

CTR: We are not talking about *trying*. That is a sign of cowardliness. Trying has a sense of desperation. Instead you have confidence in everything and try nothing. That seems to be the point. If you try everything, you begin to become a junkie—spiritually, physically, or whatever it may be. We are not talking about that level; we are talking about a larger version of thinking and opening.

S: How can you say that trying is nonexistent? Don't you have to try in order to see the trying?

CTR: When you begin to try properly, you find that you don't exist—you're simply trying. Your exertion is working very hard, but you don't actually exist. Your exertion begins to take you over. It's like an airplane flying by itself or a train running by itself.

S: Is it like tension that's just there, or trying that's just there?

CTR: It's something like that, but I think you have to experience it—you can't just talk in terms of hypothetical possibilities.

S: You started out by speaking about why are we here, and then you went on to discuss the unborn. I didn't quite get the connection.

CTR: Somehow, we find why we are *not* here. We *are* here, obviously, but we are *not* here. Nobody's here. This particular hall is vacant, nonexistent; therefore, there's a big crowd. Does that help?

2

Cosmic Disaster

EXTENDED VISION means that we have to step out completely from any concern and take an immense leap to a living experience of the perceptions of mind. That particular leap tends to be somewhat exaggerated or extreme because we do not allow any space or concepts to linger between perceiver and perception. Things become extraordinarily bigger in scale, so that we begin to lose track of who is actually perceiving and who is not perceiving at all—and that could be said to be the epitome of perception in the fundamental sense.

From that type of perception arises the notion of extreme extension—you are extended completely, extended extremely, extended as far as you can go. That is to say, if you have numeral figures, your figures begin to extend extremely until finally zero after zero after zero doesn't make any sense—and that whole experience begins to come back to square one, where you started. It comes back to the number one, or to zero, and that begins to dissolve along with the rest of the figures.

The whole thing, whether you put particular figures on it or not, becomes complete zero. There is a kind of recoiling process, as that infinite quality begins to come back. In fact, as that extension is closest to the infinite, it becomes number one or zero—and one or zero become infinite. So you begin to lose track. At the same time, you begin to gain a sense of perspective in which *you* do not exist, the *perceiver* does not exist—purely those phantoms of infiniteness exist.

In other words, nothing is lost. The infinite becomes your aspect of intelligence. You are only infinite; therefore, you have intelligence that can function and expand immensely. You can actually work with that infinite quality. Once your mind has expanded in such an outburst without any booster—that is to say, the reference point of "me here," or "I'm here"—starting with the number zero or one, that whole process becomes very fast, extremely fast. We have used this analogy before, and I would like to repeat it again: you run so fast, round and round and round, that finally the fastest way to run is to stay still. You run so fast that you begin to see your own back, and you begin to become still. At that point, the whole thing begins to become infinite. When you hold still, you supersede any kind of speed at all. You become the ultimate and utmost winner of that particular race.

From that point of view, being back to square one is one version of infinity. You are not back to square one in the sense of dragging yourself back or thinking that you have solved all your problems; and you are not back to square one in the sense that you went on and on and on, and finally you find yourself doing the same thing all over again. That's not the kind of square one we are talking about here. In this case, back to square one is the infiniteness of immense immeasurable space and expansion that you experience. Therefore, it is absolutely absurd to try to search further—and the only way *not* to search further is to *be*, to *stay*, to stand or sit still. That is the basic point.

However, we have a problem with that experience. We have the problem of retracing, or tracking back, what happens in our experience. By tracking back, we try to make some kind of *security* out of holding still. (I hope this makes sense for you, I sincerely hope.) We go through constant speed and constant stillness, constant death and constant birth. We go through all those processes simultaneously, at once, constantly. Each time we do this, a click takes place—and we expand into the infinite level. Some kind of click takes place, some kind of flash. That is quite unnecessary, as a matter of fact; nevertheless, it does happen.

It always happens that way, fortunately or unfortunately, and that is known as dharmakaya—unfortunately, actually. We do not need to have such principles, but they begin to arise—unnecessarily. Dharmakaya is called *dharma*-kaya, because it is the embodiment of all norms, all laws, all forms, all experiences, all dharmas. All existence is embodied in this particular *kaya*, which literally means "body." Kaya, or body, is not just the physical body, it is any tangible situation or tangible state, such as, for instance, the psychological body. So dharmakaya is a basic norm that exists unconditionally.

That basic state, dharmakaya, *does* exist because it does *not* exist. It is unnecessary, simply a matter of getting a new haircut. That particular experience is known as the beginning of the case history of the enlightenment principle. Earlier, when we talked about the infinite quality of the totality, the notion of enlightenment was superfluous. But somehow, some naughty child dropped a pebble in this particular pond and it began to create ripples. Therefore, we have the existence of dharmakaya in the form of a bubble. From this point of view, the notion of enlightenment is not ultimate liberation, final salvation, final transcendence, or emancipation. Instead, enlightenment is the realization of back to square one. It is understanding infiniteness, realizing that infinity creates a spark, somewhere along.

Such infinite simplicity is a tricky point. It is possible for the infinite simplicity of this click or flash to be extraordinarily simple or immensely complicated. It is possible that it is immensely complicated to figure out who actually pulled the trigger. Who did that? And who perceived the whole thing, and how and where? When you pulled the trigger, what kind of gunpowder did you use? What kind of bullet? What kind of gun did you use? Who had the motivation to pull the trigger at all? All those little details begin to become very complicated—and that is what is called the dharma. The simplicity cannot contain itself. It has to be explained by verbalizations of some kind—and the process of explaining and verbalizing the whole thing turns out to be absolutely complicated. In turn, there are what are known as the 80,000 dharmas. Those dharmas are absolutely unnecessary. However, because of their unnecessariness, they tend to become absolutely important.

Dharma is manifesting the truth. If we want to speak the truth, we have to *demonstrate* the truth. We have the truth, the truth is very simple—but truth can be attacked from all directions. Somebody may say, "If you're telling the truth, then this happens, but I find that does not quite correlate with what you have said. So how do you answer that question?" Then you have to answer back, saying, "Well, that is the case; nevertheless, this is what we are trying to explain." Then somebody else comes in from another corner of the universe saying, "That's okay, but on the other hand, something else pops up. How do you explain that?" So there are points of view or interpretations of truth based on confusion.

The truth is one, one dharma. The 80,000 expressions of dharma exist because there are 80,000 confusions, rather than because there are 80,000 dharmas, particularly. Each confusion can be worked with, explained verbally, and demonstrated in its appropriate way. Consequently there happen to be 80,000 dharmas. As I have said already, that is unnecessary. It shouldn't happen that way, it wasn't meant to. There was no particular plan *at all*, none whatsoever! However, things turned out to be that way, unfortunately.

We cannot apologize to anybody. It's just a cosmic disaster, and that cosmic disaster is called the dharmakaya. Basically, dharmakaya is a cosmic disaster. Dharma is truth, kaya is form. Truth is like water. If you speak truth, in order to taste the water, you have to put it in a container, you have to drink it, and you have to swallow it. However, as soon as that free water is consumed through our mouth into our throat, we find that unconditional water becomes conditional. Consequently it is turned into piss. That's true!

According to the mahamudra slogan, dharmakaya is "the indivisibility of samsara and nirvana." That does not mean that to be good guys or good girls, we need to say that we are all one. It does not mean that we are all on the level of sisterhood or brotherhood. That is a statement of resentment, in a sense. In fact, the euphemistic phrase used in the Buddhist scriptures—"the indivisibility of samsara and nirvana"—is not true. What it is meant to say is "the *unnecessariness* of samsara and nirvana," rather than "the *indivisibility* of samsara and nirvana." So indivisibility is a euphemism for unnecessariness.

That notion of indivisibility seems to be the seed of the love-and-light approach. In fact, that's where the problem started, right at the beginning. Everyone is looking for union. Everybody is looking for uniting you and me together so we could have domestic or cosmic union. Everybody's looking for pleasure and recommending worldwide peace. Everybody's tired of the pain and warfare, the neurosis and complaints, the millions of mosquitoes, the thousands of fleas, and all kinds of things that bother our lives. We are so tired of the whole thing. We are looking for uniting something together so that we don't have to fight, so we don't have to kill these mosquitoes or fleas or irritating friends, but instead make final friendship with somebody completely and properly. We would like to proclaim ourselves and make ourselves feel better. We would like to be great heroes. We would like to take the heroic approach that finally we are open-minded people. We do not accept any of the bullshit of separatism. Instead, we could be united, we could be happy. We could be one good, universal, cosmic family. In fact, that has been the problem, always. It is a problem rather than a promise or any kind of sanity.

The problem actually goes much deeper than that. Once you have made immense, beautiful unification and unitedness, you can fly the

266 | GLIMPSES OF REALIZATION

friendly skies where everything is completely hospitable, but you are not particularly hospitalized. Everything's fantastic! Fantastic service takes place all the time. At that level, that sense of unification and bringing things together as a happy family has created spiritual materialism. This is its long-term history. Its early history is that it is the *embryo* of spiritual materialism, as a matter of fact. We have that seed in our mind right at the beginning, before we begin to make sure that everything is going to work out. So everything begins to be a trick of some kind; and that trick functions in our life to provide all kinds of promises, kicks, and euphoric meditative states. That trick was begun right at the beginning, as early as that.

So the notion of the indivisibility of samsara and nirvana is not so much the indivisibility or *union* of samsara and nirvana—it is more the *unnecessariness* of it. That is an extraordinarily intelligent way of viewing the whole thing—as completely matter of fact, absolutely matter of fact. Things just happened that way. Therefore, as it *is* that way, let it *be* that way. The 80,000 separations of dharma are taught to people who do not understand that dharma is unnecessary. So, on one hand, prescribing particular ways to behave has become unnecessary. It *will* be necessary, on the other hand, if you begin to see the unnecessariness of it. If you see the unnecessariness, then it becomes necessary. That is a little twist—which has to be taken with a large dosage of leap—otherwise, the whole thing doesn't make any sense, it becomes pure riddles, and you can't live in a world of riddles. Although the Zen practitioners might say there's something to it; nonetheless, we find it difficult, sitting on our yellow and red zafus.

The unnecessariness of the whole thing tends to bring us the necessity of everything, at the same time. The concept of kaya is not needed; however, it happens to exist. In fact, the dharmakaya concept is somewhat of a nuisance. It actually provides a division between the enlightened and the unenlightened, the enlightened level as opposed to the unenlightened level. But maybe having another side of the coin, as opposed to this side of the coin, makes things more extraordinarily celebratory. We could celebrate and we could develop a sense of humor! I do not mean humor in terms of making fun of somebody else, as in, "Ha-ha, your neighbor's garden is so funny and yours is so straight." Instead, because you have a neighbor at all, it's very funny. It's ironical.

Student: Earlier you talked about the burp that was mistaken for speech, and you said it was all an accident; and now you are talking about the pebble dropped into the pool as dharmakaya. Are those two the same thing?

Chögyam Trungpa Rinpoche: The point of the burp is simply that we have to experience a larger version of the phenomenal world, which is bigger and tougher than we think, with lots of room all over the place. The burp is the pre-dharmakaya level, which is technically known as vajradhatu. The pebble in the pool is the sense of freedom, that you can do that. It comes out of that larger version of thinking.

S: The idea of unnecessariness is annoying, for some reason, in that it seems to be pointing at something else besides what's happening, something richer. You seem to be using some external criterion in relation to which you can say that something else is unnecessary.

CTR: I don't see that there's any problem. Why not? Because there is a problem; therefore, things are as they are. When we say "unnecessary," we are not *complaining*, particularly.

S: I was actually thinking of the yogachara one-mind teaching. From that point of view, all phenomena are irrelevant, arbitrary— just accidental expressions of the one mind.

CTR: From this point of view, which may be entirely different, the notion of one mind isn't needed at all. Even that expression is unnecessary. Things are happening quite smoothly all the time, in their own way, so imposing rules and regulations seem to be out of the question. However, now something has actually taken place. That something takes place out of the atmosphere—or the spirit, rather—of wasting time. So the point we come to is that maybe it is necessary to waste time.

S: Is that the big dose of leap you were talking about before?

CTR: Yes. That leap is also redundant, in some sense—but maybe you have to take another leap. Maybe it is redundant to waste time, but somehow that makes everybody happy. That is the diplomatic approach. Everybody has something to do, including the scholars.

S: If wasting time is redundant, where does practice come in?

CTR: Practice comes along with that, obviously, sitting and doing nothing. Maybe that goes against the Protestant ethic; nevertheless, it frees from Protestant neurosis.

S: When you spoke about speed, you connected it very much with expansiveness and a sort of explosion. You talked about losing track, that the speed becomes so fast that you are standing still, so there's no ground for distinction of speed or not speed. In the past, when I've heard that analogy, it usually referred to your confusion speeding so fast that you think you are standing still. In that sense, it is just an intensification of your confusion. Here there doesn't seem to be any idea like that at all.

CTR: I think it is saying the same thing. We are talking about the unnecessariness of a boundary between samsara and nirvana at this point. So whether we say that your neurosis is so fast that it stays still, or your wisdom goes so fast that it stands still, we are saying the same thing.

S: I was doing a more hinayana interpretation of the idea of speed, which is that your mind is reeling. But that doesn't seem to apply here.

CTR: Let me make the whole thing absolutely clear—let us not regard the word *speed* as a pejorative term. Speed is a descriptive and neutral term. We do not regard New York as having a problem with speed, particularly. In fact, a certain form of speed may be necessary; it's an expression of pragmatism.

S: You seem to be using the term *speed* positively, as part of the expansion.

CTR: Yes. I think we are changing gears at this point.

S: How don't you waste time? What is time?

CTR: Again, when we talk about wasting time, we are not talking pejoratively. It is not that if you waste time, you have screwed up or you are terrible. We are not using judgmental language. Instead, when we talk about wasting time, it is absolutely neutral. We are saying that a particular time does not have any goal or immediate results, so conventionally speaking, it could be said to be a waste of time. But we are not particularly looking at that situation in a pejorative or prejudiced way.

S: What produces the flash from the space, or the click? Is it some sort of tension building up between the space folding in on itself?

CTR: I think it's a question of seeing one's own back. You are running around so fast and you're not getting anything out of it, except yourself. That's very simple, nothing particularly mystical about that! However, that particular experience is called enlightenment.

S: It sounds like it could be the click of something snapping in your neck while you're trying to see your back.

CTR: I don't think so. It's very, very ordinary. It is not particularly biting your own tail, however, it is seeing your own back. It's an anthropomorphic analogy.

S: Is that moment also an expression of transcendental fear? I mean, are the wasting of time and the speeding expressions of fear that gets to the point at which it is so intense that it transcends?

CTR: Not necessarily, because as I have said already, wasting time is not taken as being naughty or needing punishment. Wasting time is regarded as somewhat necessary. It's like having to take a pee in your toilet: you're wasting your pee, but you have to do it, anyway. Obviously, you're wasting your pee, you're flushing it down to the sewage system—but doing that is not regarded as bad. We have to understand that wasting time is not a pejorative, negative, prejudiced term.

S: You said that practice is inseparable from wasting time, but practice also seems to increase one's own fear.

CTR: That goes on all the time. At this point, the pain and pleasure that derive from practice are regarded as absolutely equal. It is not as if getting some pleasurable experience is a sign of one's development and feeling painful experiences is regarded as a regression. That approach does not apply anymore. Everything is on equal terms. Pain and pleasure are the south and north poles of one world.

S: It seems like this flash, this stopping, could happen at any time, and it could happen again and again.

CTR: Infinitely, yes, all the time. It's not like a fisherman waiting for a fish to catch. If you take that attitude, the whole thing is very poverty-stricken. Nevertheless, it happens all the time.

S: But once that flash happens, it doesn't imply that everything is okay. I mean, the flash happens—and then it's not happening.

CTR: Not happening is okay too. That in itself is one of them—because of its unnecessary quality, or indivisible quality.

S: So there would be no notion of clinging to the flash?

CTR: If you cling to it, that breeds more samsara, which is a necessary part of the whole thing; however, *that* necessary *is* pejorative.

S: Rinpoche, are you talking about egolessness in terms of not differentiating between this and that?

CTR: It is unnecessary to discuss egolessness, actually. The notion of egolessness is very heavy-handed and it makes people extremely guilty. You feel that you're being a bad girl or boy, and now you should do something about it. You feel that there's a better version, egolessness, and that if you give up your thingy, you'll be a freer and a better person. However, we are looking at things from an entirely different viewpoint, which comes from a different space-time perspective. If you constantly approach things from this level, the notion of egolessness doesn't apply. That question does not apply anymore.

S: You talked about this perspective being intuitive rather that experiential. Does that intuitiveness develop through your sitting practice? Because I don't feel very intuitive.

CTR: I think that is saying the same thing. In other words, sitting practice *is* that, rather than intuitiveness being something that would develop *through* sitting practice. From this point of view, sitting practice is not regarded as a process of cultivating something, or as a technique, or means, to develop something else. Instead, sitting practice is in itself the goal. The goal and the path are one. Therefore, sitting practice is no longer regarded as training. The sitting practice of meditation has become just simply that in itself, acting out what is there already.

S: Rinpoche, in describing the experience of running faster and faster, are you saying that you are running so fast on one side of the coin that it flips, or are you saying that the coin is flipping so fast that you can see both sides of the coin at once?

CTR: It is the second, that you can see both sides of the coin at once, not the first.

S: The click that you described as dharmakaya, as enlightenment—is that an experience or only a description?

CTR: It is both; they are the same thing. However, I wouldn't use the term *experience,* actually. *Experience* would be the wrong term to use, because when we talk about experience, that automatically has a confirmational quality. We experience something, we register that, and finally we make it a part of our life—and then we remember that. In contrast, that click is unconditional panic. That panic doesn't register in your mind, although it is an actual experience in your life. But you experience it without making a case history out of the whole thing.

S: Then why did you begin by describing the quality of *expansiveness,* or going so fast that you are standing still, and then say that there's a completely accidental click, which is dharmakaya. Why isn't the state of expansiveness dharmakaya? Is it because the contrast is needed?

CTR: It is, in some sense, obviously. Nevertheless, that contrast comes with a great volume of infiniteness. When you experience a greater and greater volume of infiniteness, eventually you get so much that you can't handle the gigantic volume anymore. You have to burst your particular balloon. So you burst your balloon—and then you stand still. That is an expression of everything getting out of control and the infiniteness beginning to take over the whole thing. Do you see?

S: Is that only a momentary click?

CTR: It is a click in the sense of beyond control, rather than a click like a flash bulb flashing on your face. It is a moment of having to give in to something. One has to give in to something. From that point of view there is a click, a stillness. It is as if somebody in back of you suddenly surprised you—you don't actually stop still, but you tend to click.

S: What is the relation of vajradhatu and dharmakaya? Earlier you talked about vajradhatu as the experience of basic positivity, the big picture. Now you are talking about a perspective in which you see the basic condition—or the basic lack of condition. Is the first level vajradhatu and this level dharmakaya? Are they different moments of enlightenment?

CTR: I think we could say that the form—or the intelligence, if we could use such a word—exists out of its own speed. When you find vajradhatu speeding immensely, you find dharmakaya. As a matter of fact, the scriptures say that vajradhatu is like milk and dharmakaya is like churning butter out of that milk. Because the milk has been worked up, finally some kind of solidity takes place. So from that point of view, you could say there are two levels: vajradhatu and dharmakaya. Nevertheless, butter *is* milk, in some sense. In dharmakaya, there is still that basic space. It is continuous. Basic space happens continuously.

S: Is there a difference between dhatu as seed and dhatu as space? What is the relationship of those two concepts?

CTR: That's an interesting point. Dhatu, which literally means seed, also means space. That is, dhatu, or seed, is an analogy for space—outer space, the space in the room, the space in a cup. Space has its fringe and center, at once, constantly. There are seeds everywhere, which create space, center and fringe simultaneously. It is a constantly overlapping process. Overlapping the fringe, or boundary, is another center; and that boundary overlaps another center, which overlaps another boundary, which becomes a center, as well. So center and fringe are saying the same thing. In other words, there is no center and no fringe anymore—it's equally space. The whole thing is like a gigantic pancake. Everything is in the center as well as on the fringe.

S: As you talked about the dharmakaya experience, Rinpoche, I kept relating it to my own experiences with acid, in which the ego reaches a state of panic. There's a tunneling experience and a back and forth between complete awe and panic. I have often thought that LSD experience must be the dharmakaya. I'm trying to relate all this to what some of us may have experienced—or maybe I'm looking for a confirmation of that experience.

CTR: I don't think it's the same, because that kind of drug experience happens purely by artificial means. Because it is based on hallucinogenic drugs, it is known as a shadow experience. There is intense excitement and extensive depression, and that also tends to bring an immense sense of spaciousness and highness. However, what we talking about here is free from physiological conditions. It is a purely psychological experience. In fact, we can't even pinpoint it as a psychological experience—it is a sense of totality. This experience is on another dimension. We have never tapped this particular area; nevertheless, we are dwelling in it. We are surviving in it, yet this particular experience is unconditional. It is called unconditional because you can't pinpoint it. If you try to pinpoint it, it's so loose; at the same time, if you try to experience it, it is so vivid.

S: You have often differentiated between experience and achievement. When one experiences this sense of enlightenment, or dharmakaya, is it an achievement that will stay with one, or is it an ephemeral experience that will just become another thing in one's past.

CTR: It is unconditional experience, which does not need to be recorded, but takes place constantly—unnecessarily.

S: When you leap, how do you step down again?

CTR: Once you have leapt, you are already on the ground, so you don't have to step down from the leap. The leap is from the space to the ground. You actually begin to sink into the mud or the sand of the ground. There's no platform built for you. It's a big plop!

S: In talking about seeing things as they are, without dualism, you mentioned that the dualism is unnecessary. Then you said that when you see the unnecessariness, it becomes necessary. I was confused about that point. Could you explain that a little further?

CTR: I'm glad you got confused. Because of that we have something to work on together. That seems to be the basic point.

S: A few moments ago you explained the origin of dharmakaya as basic space speeding so fast that it solidifies. That doesn't seem to make any sense. How could basic space speed or not speed?

CTR: In order to survive in space, you've got to do something about it. It has to be very efficient and organized. So one corner of space gets crammed into the other corner of space. One corner begins to get the message of the other corner, so panoramic efficiency takes place.

S: Why dharmakaya?

CTR: Because for the first time, some kind of division between this and that—in a very embryonic sense—took place.

S: Is dharmakaya developed from *that* level, or is it just a reflection from *our* level?

CTR: Dharmakaya developed from *that* level!

S: You seem to be saying that it's necessary.

CTR: Unnecessarily necessary.

S: You keep referring to *necessary* and *unnecessary,* and I don't understand them. Necessary and unnecessary in terms of what?

CTR: It is unnecessary to raise the question at all; however, because it is there, because that question *does* exist, it had to become necessary. In other words, the question in itself is hollow, transparent;

however, in order to express the transparency of the question, one has to ask the question. You see?

S: No.

CTR: For instance, in order to celebrate a coronation, you have to have the empty chair of the king to begin with. It is necessary in some sense, but in another sense, it is obsolete.

3

Self-Existing Grin

THE NEXT SET of patterns is that of unceasing energy. Conventionally, if we have energy, we try to manipulate it and work it into particular work projects and purposes. We feel that we have to create further projects and processes in order to maintain our existence. But in this case, the question of energy could be looked at in an entirely different way. That is, if energy is unceasing, there's no need for manipulation. We can't—and we don't have to—sort out anything. It is needless to sort anything out or to look out for anything at all.

The basic ground, the dharmakaya principle, exists as a fundamental necessary measure. Since that has taken place and developed already, it seems that the next process, the sambhogakaya process, is not to question that but to proceed along. The word *sambhoga* means "enjoying pleasure," or literally, "interested in pleasure." It has a slant towards opportunism and it also has a hint of indulgence, as far as the terminology goes. Beyond that, the whole thing is natural and simple, just dealing with energy. It is simply energy—energy which need not be sought; energy which need not be worked with, but energy to *be* with, basically. There are a lot of ideas, and a lot of insights and perceptions as to how can we do things without completely speeding along and trying to get something across from a pragmatic point of view. The point is that there is lots of room, a lot of space.

There's immense intensity in dealing with the world of existence—so what is the point of trying to intensify this world further? One of the attributes of sambhogakaya is play. Basically, play has the qualities of mischievousness and humor. However, in this context, a sense of humor does not mean cracking jokes or trying to be funny out of embarrassment. Humor is not another mask or facade we put on, and it does not mean turning everything into a big joke. Particularly when there are shortcomings or irritations—with oneself or with whatever comes up—we turn everything into a big joke. If a person is brave enough, quite possibly he says, "This joke is on you, not on me." But that's quite far out, in the sense that he is going too far.

In contrast, the sense of humor associated with the sambhoga-kaya principle is light. It is light as opposed to heavy. Such humor also has an uplifting quality, although that particular phrase has been overused. Nevertheless, in this case we are using "uplifting quality" in the proper sense, as a quality of light-heartedness. When we say "uplifting quality," we do not mean being relieved that everything is getting better or feeling that things are finally becoming humorous enough that they don't bother us. We are using upliftedness in the sense of light-heartedness. It is a quality of light-heartedness beyond ego's heavy-hearted level, rather than light-heartedness in the conventional sense of ultimate frivolity.

To review: The question of dharmakaya's existence is that it need not exist at all at the beginning. It's too bad, too good, whatever. Then, after that, a fantastic upsurge of humor comes along. That humor arises not in the nasty sense of making fun of everybody else or making fun of oneself, but as a self-existing grin. That self-existing grin takes place all the time—throughout our sleep time, when we sit on the toilet seat, when we are confronted with challenges. Throughout everything that goes on in our life, we have that self-existing grin. That grin takes place all the time.

I am not saying this to cheer you up or to make you into more productive good guys and stronger people. The British might have said, while they were going through the Second World War, "Everybody should keep a stiff upper lip." But we are not talking about that kind of humor, particularly, that sort of heavy-handed ha-ha. Such humor can only develop when you are in national chaos or personal chaos. For instance, I hear that at this point in the economic crisis, such humor is coming up. It is not that we finally become human beings because we are imprisoned within our human condition facing warfare and depressions of all kinds; therefore, we should stick together and cheer each other up. We are talking about an entirely different kind of humor. Sambhogakaya humor is not the result of depression, and it is not as if you are pressed between two lead plates and someone is trying to make an impression out of you. We are not talking about a depressed situation or being pressed between two objects.

The closest description I can think of for this kind of humor is some kind of light in the atmosphere. The point is not that the flying-saucer people are going to save us, nor are the Mahatmas from the theosophical world going to save us, nor is Jesus Christ going to save us—nor the Buddha, for that matter. Such lightness is not involved with any savior mentality. Usually whenever we talk about light and grace and upliftedness, we approach it from the level of poverty. Although we have been such bad people and the world is in such poverty—we think something good will come down and dawn on us; we think something is going to save us immensely and let us rejoice. But that style of rejoicing is extraordinarily depressing. We are substituting pleasure for pain—that seems to be the only result of such an approach.

There is nothing wrong with the traditions of Christianity and Judaism, but people's attitudes to such great traditions have cheapened them. That is the biggest problem. In talking about light-heartedness and light and love, everything is based on somebody who is going to save you. If you smile, everything's going to be okay in the name of Shiva or Krishna. That's absurd! We are still looking for a transcendental nipple or baby bottle. That approach has been a constant problem all along, throughout our lives. In contrast, when we talk about cheering up—or the ultimate, if we may say so, love and light approach—it is well founded in reality. It is a realistic approach, which is that you are *already* rich. Since you have immense richness in you already, you don't have to ask for somebody's pardon or somebody's loan. Organizationally we do, but spiritually we don't have to.

The notion of feast, or celebration, is very difficult to understand. Should we just try to cheer ourselves up, because there is a lot of richness taking place around us? Not quite. That's still a poverty approach; there's no individual personal dignity involved. Whenever there's personal and individual dignity, *asking* seems to be unnecessary—you just take advantage of that richness. That is what's known as "vajra pride." Poverty mentality means experiencing the lack of something or other, then trying to get it from somewhere else. But we don't have to experience that lack—we could actually experience a sense of richness.

Approaching our whole experience as if somebody will save us from bouncing our check is very sad. It needn't be that way at all. It is so obvious that doesn't have to happen. Where that mind came from, I don't know. It's ludicrous! The closest guess I can make is that some fundamental theistic inclination begins to tell us that we should feel little and the other should feel bigger, great, glorious. That's just a rough guess. This isn't an attack on the theistic disciplines, particularly. Maybe it is the human condition that human beings like to worship somebody, out of their poverty, including hungry, ego-centered emperors and kings.

Rulers of the world have that same problem: they feel that they are cheap and that they haven't fulfilled their wishes and their kingdom to the level that they should. In contrast, the sense of humor depends on a humanistic attitude. In talking about a humanistic attitude, we do not mean humanistic psychologists or pragmatists. Instead we are talking simply of the ape level. Having a humanistic attitude means accepting our ape qualities—being willing to grunt and not trying to be too genteel. I suppose that our desire for union with God is that we a want to be better persons, we have higher ideals. Such rubbish! We would like to be Him or Her, that great fantasy that evolved. We want to boycott our apeship.

All of these perspectives of mind, all of this material, provides an enormous bank of potential humor—not humor in the sense of looking down upon something, but humor in terms of what *is*, basically speaking. We begin to feel that the sense of humor is what *is*, what actually is, fundamentally speaking. The sense of humor is not cracking jokes; it is not trying to cheer ourselves up; and it is not having connections with somebody higher or greater than us. The sense of humor is what is.

By being back to square one constantly, we find lightheartedness in the ultimate sense. Such humor is not the regular, ordinary level of humor, as we usually understand it. In this case, the concept of humor is a sense of celebration. That celebration cannot happen unless we are willing to give up the territories that evolve around us. Territory means that you would like to have things *your* way. You think what you are doing is great, but at the same time, there is a faint doubt. Maybe you are not doing everything wholeheartedly and properly. Maybe you cannot make it up to the prescribed level. You can't be a good meditator, a good sitter, all the time. You can't constantly keep up your humor all the time. You have your weak moments. Your

weak moments show. Of course! Why not? That's part of the celebration! Otherwise, there's nothing to celebrate. If you don't have your
weak points, what's left? Just blank white, without even a dot of ink,
on the sheet of your life.

You can celebrate because all kinds of things are involved with
your life; therefore, it is a source of celebration. There is contrast—
this and that, that and this—and things can't be sorted out properly
and put into proper perspective. So let it be that way! That seems to
be the source of celebration, in fact! What we are discussing comes
out of no logic, by the way. There's no logic at all for that particular perspective. Definitely there's no logic for that. In studying this,
maybe the Sanskrit or Tibetan linguistics student might find it very
hard to accept, in terms of scholarship. However, it is the flat and
hard truth.

Talking about flat truth is like talking about flat water. If your particular glass of drinking water does not have a fizzy quality, it's just
flat water. When we talk about hard truth, we are talking about vajra.
You accept that you are going to bump into this big blade of crys-
tal-clear vajra, this diamond sword. If you push too hard, it is going to
cut you into pieces. There is the sense of humor for you! It's not very
pleasurable and it is not particularly entertaining—but I'm afraid it is
all-pervasive. That hard-core vajra diamond blade is very powerful.
It's like swallowing babies that have lots of spines—porcupines! Baby
porcupines! Swallowing baby porcupines! That is the sense of humor.
You could laugh at that, if you like, but that is very meaningful.

Why would anybody want to swallow a baby porcupine, anyway?
The point is that there is a sense of delightfulness in the whole thing,
although it is very demanding. It is extremely demanding, actually;
but you might find even *that* is extraordinarily delightful, for the very
fact that you are not completely wrapped up in the situation. When
you finally think of that demand, you find that it is usually quite

spacious at the same time, because with such a demanding situation, there's room to have fist fights with the world. You can fight and you can argue. You can put things into proper perspective, rather than feeling that you have sunk into the situation, that you have no choice, and finally, you are completely bound to that particular situation, which is very hellish.

The question seems to be very clear. When you hear about having a playful attitude but at the same time being extraordinarily solid, you think you would never make the mistake of swallowing a baby porcupine down your throat—so why do you? The question that comes up again and again and again is why we are doing all this, obviously. Why *should* we do all this? The answer to that, roughly speaking, is that there is *no reason* why we should do this! That is the answer—because there is no reason. If you ask why we should do this, there is absolutely no reason, absolutely not!

The principle behind this approach is that we are not presenting dogma of any kind at all. We are not looking for ways to convert you to our truth. We are not saying, "If you get involved with us, you are going to have a good color television, you are going to have wall-to-wall carpet, you're going to lead a happy life, you're going to be meeting very interesting people throughout the world, and you're going to have a gold Cadillac." We are not talking in those terms at all! Because of this lack of glamour and lack of promises, a lot of people might find this approach absolutely depressing, extremely depressing. Usually, telling the truth is very depressing. If you mix the truth with a bit of lying, if you add a bit of salt and pepper by lying, you find it more delicious—but somehow our lineage doesn't allow it to happen that way. Nor is this particular spokesman, a holder of the lineage, particularly inspired to do things that way. So things are black and white, straight and square—and *because* of that, there is a lot of humor. That straightforwardness and bluntness is very cute.

On the whole, we are not discussing what you *could* be or what you *should* be, but what you *are*. People have never heard that type of truth before. There's always a tinge of salesmanship involved with telling the truth: "That is what you are, of course—but we can help you!" On this particular earth, there are a lot of such spiritual trips.

The consecutive trips we find or dream up could fill the whole universe—and each one of those trips begins by telling us, "That may be what you are, but you shouldn't worry about that. *We* have the remedy for you." In each of those spiritual trips we are told, "No matter how terrible you are, you could be okay, we could save you. It is terrible, absolutely terrible. Nevertheless, we know that, and we are going to save you. You should take our medicine and pay us more money. You should come to us and join us; then we will have something to say about that whole thing. If you take refuge in us and if you trust us, then we can save you." Somehow, however, in approaching all this from the angle of and according to the ongoing intelligence that exists through the blessings of the lineage, we cannot say that. Instead, we say, "You are *not* going to be saved. You have your problems—that's fine, everybody knows that. Let it be that way. If you could improvise something along with that, maybe that would be good—but at the same time, one has to stay with one's own problems." That is the only demand we can make at this point. It is not particularly a money-making venture, but more a lightening of the air, so to speak.

There's a need to develop a sense of humor. That sense of humor seems to be the point of the sambhogakaya level. The preliminary approach to the sambhogakaya is celebration and indulgence. The sambhogakaya is the level of pleasuring constantly. It is the level of celebrating one's life, which comes with a sense of humor. Humor is the constant flow or thread that runs through one's life. Without that you cannot celebrate. If there's no humor, you cannot celebrate, and the party begins to become a drag, as we know.

Student: The sense of humor of the sambhogakaya level seems to develop out of an extreme hard-headedness, extreme vajra-headedness, extreme non-indulgence. Is that right?

Chögyam Trungpa Rinpoche: Yes.

S: Such humor comes about not because something is funny, but because there seems to be no choice. There seems to be nothing else but this humor.

CTR: That's right. You have choiceless humor.

S: I don't understand why, at the vajradhatu level, space, in order to survive, must do something. You said that one corner of space wondered what the other corner of space was doing. I don't understand why space would wonder at all. What prods the space or makes the space move at all?

CTR: That's quite a serious question. Why should things happen that way—or any way at all? We do not know; we have no idea about that. That's why we need a path, or journey: we have to figure out it out by ourselves. If all the riddles had been solved at the beginning, we would have nothing to work with. The whole journey would have been made already, so there would be no point in saying anything at all. In that case, we might as well go to Disneyland. We might as well go to sensory deprivation programs or get into a tank and take LSD. There is no point.

That *why* seems to be the path. We can't solve these problems on the spot. At the beginning level, the approach is to tell us all this is possible. We have been told that there are possibilities of this nature and we might be involved in very intriguing situations—but let us find out. That seems to be the basic approach. The journey is what is important.

Every talk does not have to be a confirmation. If listening to your student or to your teacher had to be a confirmation, it would be extraordinarily boring. If the speaker were telling you the complete truth all the time, probably it wouldn't make any sense. That is why the truth is not told all at once. To do so would be a completely big flop. Instead one tells just a fraction of the truth—one-quarter of the truth, one-hundredth of the truth—which allows people to seek *further* truth and take the journey. In any case, even if we tried to tell the whole truth, since it is known as self-secret, you probably couldn't understand anything at all. You have to make the journey, in fact. That seems to be the point.

S: On the mahayana level, it seems that compassion is always moving the Buddha toward talking to you, toward even bothering. That doesn't seem to be the same.

CTR: I think that's saying the same thing: compassion is being willing to let you get into it. We don't look down upon you as being a bastard, particularly.

S: I'm trying to follow your development from dharmakaya to sambhogakaya. What I understand is that the dharmakaya question of unnecessary wasting time is developed further, in the sambhogakaya, to the point at which it's drowning you. You're actually drowning in the wasting time. You're caught up in it emotionally. It's like sentimental music that should be too corny for you to be involved in, but you begin to cry anyhow, although you shouldn't. The fact is that you *are* drowned, and there's no right way of swimming. It is like drowning and being lost in sentimentality—and that's the way it is. I suppose that's where the sense of humor comes in. Does that sound like an accurate picture?

CTR: That sounds perfect, sir. Let's share that world together!

S: Could we say that the sambhogakaya produces the sense of humor about this mess that is our life?

CTR: We could say sambhogakaya *is* the sense of humor. That sense of humor is the cause of the world of art and of all kinds of expressions. If we don't have sambhogakaya we don't have any communication. Because of sambhogakaya, we can shape things into forms, we can try painting different colors.

S: Should this sense of humor develop naturally? I really have problems with it, because I take things too seriously. I don't see the humor in things.

CTR: When you begin to realize you are taking things seriously, then that is it.

S: But it's so painful—how can you laugh at it?

CTR: Whenever there is pain, work with that. It's not a question of cracking jokes, making things light, or making things funny. Instead, a general perspective of choiceless humor always comes along with that pain. Usually we are so involved with general principles, ideas, and achievements that we do not pay attention to the details of what is happening in our life. We want to eat our apple, but we don't regard the core. We don't ask how the core feels about the whole thing, we just eat the apple and throw the core in the garbage. But that could be a very humorous situation. We do a lot of things without consideration. We drink our cup of tea, not considering the cup and the plate and what's left behind—the tea leaves and everything.

Things are done in such a blind way all the time, and the sense of humor doesn't work—but that doesn't necessarily mean you are *incapable* of humor. If you pay more attention, there is more humor. So when you walk out onto the street, if you pay more attention to the passersby, your own steps, and your state of mind at the time, you find there is a lot of room for everything. Everything you find is so dharmic, every gesture—including large scale, small scale, medium-small scale, and small-small scale domestic details. You find there is lots of room, immense room for everything—and once you begin to see that, you also begin to be able to appreciate puns.

S: Does vajra pride or confidence have any ground, and what is that ground?

CTR: Vajra pride doesn't seem to have any realm. You are not bound to any particular world; you do not have to relate with any particular world. People of vajra pride do not pay income tax to the realm of the buddhas or the realm of human beings or the realm of hell-beings. Vajra pride is free. But in order to develop vajra pride, you have to supersede karma, so that you don't have karmic debts.

S: Is there a sense of richness?

CTR: I think so, yes, naturally. Needless to say.

S: Does the sense of humor enable you not to be so trapped by your neurotic behavior, or would you just as likely continue speeding along on the same neurotic path?

CTR: I should be very careful and clear here. Humor is not the saving grace that is going to help you all over the place. Absolutely not! You have things you have to work out yourself, so there's no room for that kind of magic—but the sense of humor *does* bring perspective to the whole thing. The sense of humor could be a troubleshooter and a consultant. You don't go looking for anybody else; instead you could develop your own sense of humor, your own troubleshooter. That saves a lot of energy and money.

S: Pride seems to be more a problem than a promise. How is the regular kind of pride we seem to indulge in related to vajra pride, and how is that related to dharmadhatu?

CTR: That's a big question. Vajra pride has nothing to do with the arrogance of ordinary pride. Although it's called by the same name, that's just for convenience's sake. As for ordinary pride, you know as much as I do. Basic pride has inquisitiveness, or intelligence, in that you are looking for alternatives in order to win your particular position. That type of pride hurts immensely. It is very painful because if you do not compete properly and you fail, your whole trip is going to go down the drain. So in ordinary pride, that kind of pain takes place as well. On the whole, such pride is anti-humor. In fact, when there is pride, there is no humor—that relationship is very direct.

When humor takes place, when you are able to see things lightly— not airy-fairy lightly, but lightly in the sense of realistically—things are not as bad as all that. When you begin to see that, you begin to see through the pride. Pride is usually an experience of complete desperation. You are so desperate. You feel so poor and hungry and penniless. Although you might be a millionaire; nevertheless, there is the attitude that you should fight for the universe to give you justice because, "I'm so poor." So, on the whole, I think that such pride is actually aggression and anti-humor.

S: How is all that related to vajradhatu being pre-dharmakaya or super-dharmakaya? And is dharmadhatu synonymous with those terms, or does it have something to do with the sambhogakaya?

CTR: The space of vajradhatu is unbiased space that is willing to accommodate the pre-dharmakaya level as well as the dharmakaya level. Vajradhatu is willing to accommodate everything. That's why it is known as indestructibility, because it has no bias towards anything. It has no bias for either samsara or nirvana or for pre-samsara or pre-nirvana. So the whole thing is completely covered, a diamond field.

Dharmadhatu seems to be related with the sambhogakaya process. Dharmadhatu is somewhat connected with the experiential mind world, although this particular term has been used by all kinds of people expressing philosophical metaphors of all kinds. In a secondary way, dharmadhatu may be involved with the world of pleasure, that is to say, the world of sambhogakaya. As an extension of that, the dharmadhatu could involve the nirmanakaya and all the worlds that exist beyond that.

S: How does dharmakaya relate to the mahayana concept of shunyata, or emptiness? Does it come out of emptiness?

CTR: Shunyata is mahayanist jargon, and we are not even touching that, because we are so snobbish at this point. Shunyata is simply a perspective in which students begin to feel a sense of nonexistence and a sense of everything being full at the same time. There are lots of *little* humors involved with shunyata, but since we are talking about a larger world, greater business, so to speak, discussing shunyata does not seem to be particularly worthwhile. Shunyata is a lesser form of vajradhatu, of much less extent.

S: You said that *sambhogakaya* means "pleasure body," yet it seems that the sambhogakaya sense of humor is not particularly enjoyable, but rather, an appreciation of feeling needle points.

CTR: You are right. It is pleasure in a larger sense. Usual pleasure, conditional pleasure, requires a lot of conditions to maintain that pleasure. It requires security. But this pleasure does not need any kind of security at all; therefore, it is free pleasure. In the ultimate sense, pleasure does not have any conditions. That's why this particular pleasure principle is connected with freedom or enlightenment. Enlightenment also means freedom. You are finally let loose, liberated, free.

S: We are sometimes told to really and fully get into the sense of hopelessness and pain of samsara, to pay particular attention to that. Where in that is there room for a sense of humor?

CTR: That *is* the sense of humor! When you begin to feel a sense of helplessness, you find yourself humorous, because there's nothing that you can do to get around it. Earlier we talked about the British sense of humor, the stiff upper lip they kept up during wartime. That kind of humor differs from this, in that this is an *ongoing* condition. It is constant: when you feel helpless, you don't feel hopeless, but you feel humorous. Because you feel humorous, you begin to develop confidence. Then, as you develop more confidence, you begin to develop fearlessness. So you go along in that way. Without humor, there is no way to conduct the whole path, no way to join the two opposite situations together. That seems to be the basic point.

S: Is it the awareness of the situation that makes the difference?

CTR: Not only awareness, but awareness with humor. If you're just aware, you might dig your own grave; whereas if you are aware with some kind of irony, or humor, then you are not quite digging your own grave. There's lots of room for everything. It is fascinating, inquisitive.

S: So we could celebrate our confusion?

CTR: I wouldn't exactly promise that, but something *does* happen. Let's put it vaguely: something takes place. It doesn't solve all our problems, but actually, there is a Star of David shining on the horizon.

To begin to understand the material in this seminar, it is important to practice sitting meditation. Meditation practice is extremely important, so that we do not pollute the world by our intellectualization of the dharma. It is very important that we begin to kill the unnecessary pollution of intellectualizing the teachings. We can begin to feel what is meant by all this by sitting properly, following the example of Lord Buddha.

4

Light-Heartedness

AT THIS POINT, we have descended from the space of the dharma-kaya level to the energy of sambhogakaya. In the transmitting process from the dharmakaya down to the sambhogakaya, the first impulse of the sambhogakaya principle seems to be a sense of humor and energy. Energy and humor begin to develop and materialize as basic common sense. In this case, basic common sense does not simply mean being rational or pragmatic or mechanical, like a computer's mind. Instead, it is the basic sense of perspective that keeps us alive. The sambhogakaya perspective is that there is a kind of centralization or energizer. There's a sense of fountain, sun and moon, and torch. From that, a lot of luminosity or light can shine through.

Luminosity is the sense of celebration that comes with the sense of humor. Humor and celebration are indivisible at this point: celebration *means* sense of humor. Celebration means a sense of delightfulness, an uplifting quality. We could use all sorts of jargon, but fundamentally speaking, celebration is a sense of *earth*, actually celebrating the earth, and a sense of earth and space making love together. Humor comes from space, or sky, and earth is the celebration. When the earth begins to celebrate, space begins to make love to the earth—that's the meeting point of earth and space. They begin to mate together in a very solid and definite and humorous and delightful way. There's nothing particularly funny about that, in terms of jokes. Everything seems to be very straightforward and simple. Earth blossoms and sky begins to pay attention to it. Sky begins to shine all kinds of light over the earth and accommodate it with its space to grow flowers or trees, to maintain rocks, waterfalls, skyscrapers, and highways—whatever we have on this earth.

We don't have to be particularly romantic about it. We're not just talking about *nature*, we're talking about *reality*. In terms of *reality*, earth produces pollution, and sky or space begins to make love to it. Space begins to get into the solidity of the whole thing—so the hardcore earth begins to make love to the light-handed space. The meeting of the two takes place constantly. Such humor and delightfulness is not dependent on good or bad—that particular philosophical outfit. The whole thing is purely a phenomenological process; it is about things as they are, in the very basic and subtle sense.

The question arises, "What are we doing with all this? What is the purpose?" This is like asking, "What is the purpose of life?" or, "How's life?" for that matter. It is the same question. And the answer is that there is not very much purpose—life operates on its own accord. Life is operating purely for its own sake, every moment, in every individual situation. That may be the purpose of life, so far as the present situation is concerned. However, even that is questionable.

The purpose of life does not exist—or it exists eternally—and the relationship between those two is how a moment of life begins to click with itself constantly. If it doesn't click, then you have no purpose in life, you are a bastard. However, if you begin to feel that the purpose of life is to click with itself, and some kind of spark takes place, then the purpose of life is fulfilled. It doesn't go further than that. There is nothing very profound, deep, metaphysical, or philosophical about it; and no enlightenment questions are involved. Let's take that very heavy light-hearted approach! In that way, the purpose of life is to exist. It is to keep the pot from boiling over. We keep watch that the pot doesn't boil over, keep everything under control and regular. That may be terribly depressing, but that's what we do.

What's the big deal about it? What is this all about? Well, there's nothing. There's nothing! If anybody tries to make meaning out of life, there is nothing. People try to say that you are leading a life and that your life is a profound life, that it means a great deal, an infinite number of things. People say, "Let me explain to you how your life works, and what is the meaning of your life." Everybody likes to interpret. They love to tell you about the line on your palm, how it goes this way a little bit up, this way a little bit down, and therefore this means something to you. Or they say that you have this particular star connected with your life, and this is a little bit off, this is a little bit in; therefore, your life's meaning is *immense!* The way you behave, the way you speak, the way you yawn, the way you sit—this is the purpose of life. It means something to you.

We are constantly discussing futuristic plans. We are talking about our *futures* all the time—we are not at *all* talking about our present state. We are not discussing this present state at all, so we have no humor. Watching our palm, we are concerned, we grin, we make faces: "I wish I had this line a little bit off from that line, then I would be exactly what I wanted." Hard luck! Too bad! You were never made up that way, obviously. That's the answer. The theists would say, "Trust God. He made you." A nontheist would say, "Who cares?" In any case, however, it seems that we are involved with the present situation, very much so. The present situation involves us with the sense of humor, and that sense of humor tends to bring all kinds of light-heartedness—not in the pejorative sense, but in the very personal, pragmatic sense. Light-heartedness means taking things gently, rather than aggressively. That brings all kinds of possibilities, all kinds of situations and locations. With that in mind, we can begin to relate with the various types of light-heartedness that exist.

Light-heartedness is traditionally known as luminosity, which is the intrinsic quality of the sambhogakaya level. The sambhogakaya is the level of enjoyment, the level of celebration; and celebration is equal to the sense of humor. In the sambhogakaya we have a kind of basic wisdom, which is made up of five wisdoms brought together—and light-heartedness seems to be the preparation for that wisdom. The five wisdoms are traditionally known as the five buddha families. These five buddha families are five expressions that exist in our system, our state of being. Those expressions are our innate nature in the present moment, the *immediate* moment. Rather than having the *potential*—if the line on your palm says so, you're going to be rich or you're going to marry a dark handsome man in three years' time—in this case, it is very *immediate*. It is apropos in the *present*. It is your personal situation, which takes place *on the spot*!

A lot of us have a fear of that. Often we have a *lot* of fear, *immense* fear, of that. We don't want to relate with the present moment, because we haven't had any opportunities to practice or prepare for all this. We don't want to have a sudden gush of wind that demands our attention and sucks us in or blows us out. I think that approach is what is known as bullshit—and actually, that is happening all the time.

Depending on your composure, or your level of deception, you manage to block all sorts of things out. For instance, you may have had a big blow-up; but when you come to the next room and deal with your colleagues, you say that everything's okay, everything's fine: "Nothing's wrong, and what can I do for you, sir?" Somehow, we have been trained that way, to keep two faces. We may feel highly disturbed, absolutely disturbed, but we don't want to show that sort of thing. That is the moral, ethical, set-up of the theistic traditions.

The reason the theistic traditions bring that approach is that our own personal relationship to God is extremely depressing. We know that we are not adequate to match up with God, not adequate to get near to Him. On the one hand, we can shift gears by saying that God is magnificent, powerful, fantastic, and extraordinary. We can think about those qualities. On the other hand, a meeting of the two never takes place, although there is electricity. That electricity is explosive and, at the same time, destructive. Sometimes such explosiveness could be taken advantage of; it could be creative. But one never knows the face of God—it's a mystery to us.

Since we have no understanding of the face of God at all, making friends with God means that we are constantly taking a chance. If you are a good friend of His, He might decide to blow you off or He might decide to take you in. That kind of uncertainty is constant in the Judeo-Christian tradition. There's a long-lasting tradition of such a love/hate relationship to God. It goes on all the time. Sometimes people don't want to reflect that hatred to God. They don't want to blame Him, so instead, they blame the world. However, the world is His extension, His creation, so if you blame the world, you are blaming God—and then you might feel some powerful reaction from God.

That approach has become a very serious problem. It leads to a lack of humor, basically speaking. Spiritual traditions are supposed to develop a sense of humor, not fear—particularly if you are an accomplished person. But that tradition provides mostly fear, rather than humor. Maybe that has something to do with the individuals who look into it rather than the actual doctrine. We are not debating or discussing the basic theology of any particular tradition. Instead we are talking about our approach to our world, whether it is the world of gods, the world of pleasure, or the world of pain. So we are talking at a very personal level, at this point, an extremely personal level.

In preparation for discussing the five types of buddha family*; to

---

*Vajra, ratna, karma, padma, buddha. For discussion of the five buddha families, see chapter 5.

begin with, we have open space, general open space, completely open space. That open space is full of all kinds of personal experiences. Those experiences could be said to be dualistic ones; nevertheless, that's not particularly a consideration here. Open space is concerned with vibrating energy, with very powerful solidity, and with the electricity that goes between the two. Open space can provide an immense wind between the two; open space can provide immense waves of water between the two. That is what we are concerned with. We are concerned with all of those elements and all of those forces of energy.

There is energy above, which is watching and glaring at us; there is energy below, which is completely yielding, opening, and at the same time, somewhat threatening and solid. Between the two are created all kinds of sparks. So energy in immense measure is taking place. Those energies seem to be very valuable and valid. At the same time, they are what they are. They function all the time. We might hope they don't function, but they still do function constantly. Sometimes we attempt to reverse the process and change the universe forward-backward. However, if we are tempted to do so, we find that the only thing we can do is write about the theoretical possibility of that—we are unable actually to do so properly since we are not Lords of the Universe and we haven't evolved ourselves into that type of cosmic power. That has become a problem, an immense problem. But there is an immense sense of freedom at the same time, in that we finally give up trying to remold the universe and its structure. Instead we find ourselves giving in, opening, and letting go. We just remain as corpses lying in a charnel ground waiting for the vultures to eat us up.

Student: In my experience, fear seems to be a direct reflex of that energy, as the energy arises and knocks you about. Is there nothing we can do about that fear, no specific way to deal with it?

Chögyam Trungpa Rinpoche: The point is that we have not quite made a connection with the larger scale of the world. We usually feel that if we kill our enemy, that will be the end of discomfort. We think that if we do something to him, then he or she will go away and we'll feel comfortable, since we have gotten rid of our little enemy. However, things do not happen that way. Everything happens on an absolutely larger scale.

Once we begin to feel the logistics of the whole thing, we might feel ourselves completely belittled, just a grain of sand stuck in the midst of a gigantic world. So the first fear is the fear of being little, that we are not powerful enough, like the analogy of the mouse and the elephant. The second fear is the fear of fear itself, which begins to become problematic. As for dealing with the fear, developing ways to deal with it means we are not actually getting into the fear properly. Instead, we think we could outsmart fear—and that's not possible. We can't deal with it at all, so before we do anything, we have to *give up* that we can deal with it. That may be the first way of dealing with fear.

S: Isn't it possible to be in the charnel ground and have the vultures come down and devour me, only not completely devour me, because I get up and walk away? It seems that I do that all the time: I get partially devoured, then I run. How do you keep yourself in that charnel ground to the end?

CTR: Keep sitting, I suppose.

S: How do you keep sitting to the end?

CTR: That's what we do: we sit dathüns, we sit nyinthüns, we keep sitting. Sooner or later these vultures begin to come along, when they are hungry. They may not come to you when they are not hungry, but sooner or later, when they are hungry, they want to eat you up and they *will* come—from all over the place.

S: Do you think that all the deceit, stupidity, and lack of direct, complete, total enlightenment that takes place among humanity is due to the teachings of the theistic tradition?

CTR: I wouldn't say that, particularly. What do you have in mind, sir?

S: Then why do you keep suggesting that?

CTR: I think it has to do with family structure. That is, in any nontheistic approach to spiritual discipline, you have to give up your home life to begin with. You have to go to a desert, or to a monastery, a nunnery, or an abbey. You have to go to all kinds of places. That suggests giving up home, giving up parental figures. That is the first step of the nontheistic approach.

S: You say that we are not debating the basic doctrines of the theistic tradition. However, theism isn't so stupid as to be just relating to a father figure. Certainly it's gone beyond that. Theism is much more sophisticated than that. Even *babies* have gone beyond that!

CTR: I quite agree with you. I think that all of our sophistication may have become a problem.

S: I mean, people are two-faced all over the world, even if they're Confucian!

CTR: Whatever you say.

S: When you describe these difficult subjects, you do so in terms of analogies and metaphors. Do you mean for us to relate to those literally? And in terms of the things we experience in our meditation—are those experiences glimpses of what you are describing?

CTR: That's very difficult to say. When you hear all this, at some point you have to take things very literally. When we talk about thirst, you have to hear it in relationship with your ordinary thirst, being in the desert. When we talk about the burning heat of passion—or anger for that matter—you have to take it very personally. Things become very vivid to us through these means; and if there's enough humor, things become spacious as well as vivid. That is the point we have been making—the spaciousness in the humor or the celebration. We are not talking about your being on the battlefield, but about leading your life.

S: Could you say more about what the five buddha families have to do with all this?

CTR: They have to do with personality and how we relate with our basic ground. We relate with our aggression, we relate with our passion, and we relate with our all-space—or our spacelessness—all over the place. If we begin to relate with those processes in term of the five buddha families, they become different colors that can manifest in mid-air, like a rainbow. So we are talking about rain and clouds and showers and sunlight and space. Once we talk about those, then we can talk about their manifestations very easily, which brings us to the five buddha-family principle.

S: Is it helpful to relate to a particular family that we identify with, or is it better to be aware of all five?

CTR: Working with the five buddha families becomes more like an astrological chart-making process if you begin to look at it as personal identification. The five buddha-family set-up is not personal identification but a general perspective. For instance, in order to drink a cup of tea, you have to have cold water and hot water and fire and tea leaves; otherwise, you can't make a cup of tea. The five-buddha-family set-up constitutes everything within our realm of experience. In our experience there are highlights, lowlights, and energies. Everything is involved with the five buddha-family setup, so I don't think it's all that specific or all that personal. However, on the whole, that combination might become personal.

S: Let's go back to the vultures. I have a feeling that sometimes it is rather stupid to let the vultures devour you. Is this purely defensiveness? Is there's another way of reacting to the vultures besides letting them devour you, or is it always wise to let them devour you?

CTR: Interestingly, when you begin to see the vultures, you may think you have a feeling, but actually you don't have a feeling—you are petrified. You are completely spaced out and you don't have any feeling. Intellectually and personally, everything's completely frozen. I'm sure that people who are involved with an emergency situation such as a car crash or jumping or falling from a high building don't have feeling. In a situation like that, you are suddenly stuck with a challenge, which you can't manipulate at all. Your intellectualization begins to wear out and your sense of openness becomes frozen, so the whole area becomes a solid block. You are stuck in the midst of an ice block. That seems to be the case even if that catastrophic situation happens on a small scale or only for a few seconds. You are still a block of ice in the midst of a block of ice. That experience takes place constantly, and it is not particularly a problem. One doesn't have to get rid of that experience or cultivate that experience—it just happens. It is not particularly a mistake—or even intentional, for that matter—it's just something that generally happens, something that takes place.

S: Isn't getting caught up in your thoughts also very vivid?

CTR: It is the same thing.

S: Is it because you still think you *have* something that the paranoia or fear comes in? If you've got nothing, you've got nothing to lose; therefore, the paranoia is overcome.

CTR: I think so. Yes.

S: That's why you should be eaten completely.

CTR: Yes.

S: Then they won't come back for any more!

CTR: Completely! Absolutely!

S: About the corpse lying there—how does that relate with the sense of not feeling guilty about having something to rip out?

CTR: That depends on your attitude. We are talking about a regular corpse.

5

Loose and Awake

THE SENSE OF humor provides enormous background and perspective—not only for practitioners, but on the level of cosmic plan, so to speak. The five wisdom energies can only be worked with through basic lightness, combining a light touch and wholeheartedness. In our lives, when things become too serious, too well-meaning, we find that we don't have any room to do anything at all, there is no creativity. We might be working very hard in our particular job, and we might be devoting constant attention to facts and figures; however, there is something lacking. We might blame that lack on our colleagues, our employees, our boss, our environment, or our particular social set-up. However, in doing so, we only find that we are becoming gigantic banks of complaints rather than actually achieving anything, properly speaking. Such is life. That is always the problem. So how is life?

With an understanding of basic principles, and realizing our shortcomings or longcomings, we begin to click to humor. We see that things are not actually as rigid and tight as we expected. Instead, they begin to become passive, workable, and playful, which is precisely the meaning of sambhogakaya—that playful and pleasurable aspect. We could extend that vocabulary by saying, "transcendental indulgence." Of course, at the sambhogakaya level, that playful or indulgent aspect takes place in terms of transcending both pain and pleasure simultaneously.

When that general sambhogakaya quality of playfulness and pleasure begins to take place, we find that there is a sense of room. Everything is not limited to our own inadequacy, but the whole process becomes workable. It is like being on top of a mountain: we have the perspective of the surrounding hills and lesser mountains, and we could watch the distant clouds and the mist rising. We have a sense of complete joy and complete freedom. At this level, the question of indulgence is not one of becoming more and more decadent and aggressive, more completely involved in the passion, blood, and dirt of neurosis. Instead, indulgence is the sense of utmost celebration. There is light-heartedness because the things that happen in our life do not mean very much. They do not mean all that much, and at the same time, they mean a great deal. Because of that, a lot more fun and a lot more inquisitiveness takes place in our life. With this perspective, every pine needle—how each pine needle behaves when it is swayed by wind—is an exquisite vision.

Sometimes we are too involved with the aesthetics of the world. For instance, if we are watching the moon and the clouds running across it, we would like to associate more with the clouds than with the moon—so we find that the moon is moving rather than that we are moving or the clouds are moving. However, that whole process becomes very powerful and refreshing. It is refreshing in the sense that this is the very first time we have experienced a love affair. Although we might have been involved in a love affair for a long time, or maybe we are in a love affair all the time, each time it is refreshing—and permanent, in some sense. That's the illusion.

That process of delight should make one's heart light and one's breath gentle, one's neck loose and one's jaw relaxed. Things don't become one hassle on top of another hassle all the time, and we no longer hold a constant grudge against our life and the unworkability of whatever it may be. Instead, it becomes a natural process. In fact, there is no point in holding a grudge against anything at all! Not only is there no point, it is needless! There's no *need* for *anything*! There's no point in shedding tears unnecessarily for our particular situation. Instead, the process becomes very loose, but at the same time, extraordinarily responsible, because we are so awake.

Looseness and awakeness tend to make an ideal person, and that ideal person is known as a sambhogakaya person. *Sambhoga* means "enjoyment" and *kaya* means "body," "person," or "individual." A sambhogakaya person is an individual who possesses all kinds of attributes, immeasurable facets. He or she has a sense of depth and a sense of width; a sense of heaviness and a sense of lightness; a sense of extreme weight and a sense of floating; a sense of being utterly dull and a sense of being utterly, extraordinarily colorful. Those facets and combinations can take place all the time, once there is the basic establishment of what it is all about altogether. There is no problem at all. In fact, we don't have to associate ourselves with one particular aspect alone—we can encompass *all* of those facets at once.

The various types of sambhogakaya persons are described in five different ways, known as the five buddha families: vajra, ratna, padma, karma, and buddha. The vajra family is connected with the notion of immeasurable intellect. The intellect of the vajra family cuts through any other intellect with a sense of joy and relaxation. It has the sense of clear-seeing. By clearly seeing all principles, all metaphysical systems can be seen through and cut through. On the one hand, all metaphysical principles could be regarded as unnecessary; on the other hand, all metaphysical systems could be regarded as worthwhile. Nevertheless, that cutting quality constantly takes place. The vajra approach is very cool, like a crisp, wintry morning, and not particularly friendly. The only friendliness that exists is a celebration and feast of the mind. In the vajra family, a feast of prajna takes place constantly

The ratna family has a sense of immense richness, a richness that can continue forever. It is the richness of earth and its fermentation to the level of shit—or diarrhea, for that matter. That fermentation or shit can be accommodated as magnificent incense, as fragrant incense that can serve the buddhas of the ten directions. Ratna is extremely potent. It is not particularly cutting. Ratna is the elemental process of consuming. Ratna consumption is like fire, which slowly touches, contacts, and consumes, and finally, begins to make something out of something else. It's like the process of fermentation. When something is fermented, that process does not allow any room, none whatsoever. Ratna consumes the whole area and absolutely covers the entire ground. Along with that, there is also a sense of delightfulness. Ratna is not particularly unfriendly. There is a sense of awake. It is as if the active chemical ingredients, which are very awake and intelligent, know exactly what to do with the whole process.

Padma is a question of magnetizing. At this level, earth and sky meet and begin to make love. Through that proclamation of love, all other lovers are inspired and made to be horny, so to speak. The trees and flowers, rocks and vampires—anything that exists in the world—are made horny, so they are inspired to make love. In talking about making love, we are not particularly discussing sex, although sex is usually the first thing that comes into our mind. The padma process is more than that. It is beyond that level, although it may include that level as well, of course. Padma is the meeting point. Padma is magnetization that is improvised constantly and thoroughly.

In the padma family, perkiness, or intelligence, takes place as well. There is a sense of perspective, so when there is a meeting, you do not become completely intoxicated and blinded by it. You are not completely wrapped up in your particular copulation process, metaphorically speaking. Likewise, the sky and earth do not get frustrated by their instant copulation—which takes place for years and years, thousands of millions of years. Sky and earth have been copulating all the time; nevertheless, both the sky and the earth have their momentum: time to create summer, time to create autumn, time to create winter, and time to create spring. So their copulation doesn't become just simple possessiveness. It is not like being bound, or an imprisonment—instead, it is a delightful dance. In that dance, no bureaucracy is involved and there is no calculation. When the time for snowfall happens, it takes place. Both earth and sky agree upon that; nobody is overpowering either of them. When it is time to rain, time to create a hailstorm, or time to produce crops or greenery, it happens. The whole process becomes extremely natural and workable—a dance takes place.

In the case of the padma family, the word *copulation* refers to pragmatic situations, rather than to sexual intercourse alone. For instance, you could talk about the copulation of the contents of a building, like those of us sitting here, and the building itself. This copulation works in such a way that there's no complaint on the part of the building that too many people are sitting on the floor, and the floor doesn't drop down. That process slowly begins to work its way through our system altogether and throughout the universe. An immense magnetizing process of accommodating one another is taking place constantly.

We have to be quite clear that padma is not purely bounded by the level of sex, or seduction. It is not a salesman's mentality, and it is not like walking into a whorehouse, where you feel the vibration of sexuality the minute you walk into the doorway. Padma is slightly more open-minded than that. In fact, the other would be imprisonment. It would be a painful process and a disgrace, in some sense. Padma is very clear and open: whenever a dance needs to take place, that magnetizing process takes birth. From the point of view of earth and sky, up and below, east and west, south and north, that dance takes place simultaneously. That magnetizing is constantly active. In the padma family there is a constant panoramic magnetizing process. That seems to be the basic point.

The karma family is one of constant activity. Activity, here, does not mean that somebody is constantly speeding along, having to achieve his or her particular job or idea. The karma principle is not about being an utter busybody and making enemies all along. The definition of the karma principle is that it offers fulfillment because all activities are *already* fulfilled. What one has to do is to instigate that particular message to the rest of the world. So in the case of the karma family, activity is there already, a process is already happening; whereas, in the other approach of speeding along, that process is not yet happening. You might find it difficult to relate with that, so you try to shout. You are trying to run a project, so you pull everybody out of their bed in their pajamas in the middle of the morning and make them work. That seems to be the wrong approach. It is not at all karma-family activity. It is just some kind of hellish trip.

In the case of the karma family, plans have already happened. Political understandings have already taken place. There are reasonable situations taking place constantly, so the only way to act is to acknowledge that and to look into it and what's happening around it intelligently and very simply. By doing that, the process becomes very natural—and every project initiated in this way actually *does* get fulfilled. Such projects become absolutely successful projects because your project, your plan of work, and your vigor are not based on the idea that you have to initiate the whole thing, you have to think cleverly, or you have to go against the grain of the sand. Things actually do exist already, so you do not have to be particularly smart in order to initiate something. You can only be up to that if you are awake enough to see what's already happening. When the gun is loaded, you don't have to be a busybody about guns; the only thing you have to do is pull the trigger. That seems to be the general idea of the karma wisdom of accomplished action, or karma activity. The gun is already loaded—all one has to do is aim it and pull the trigger.

The sense of humor pervades the entire five buddha-family process; otherwise, we are in trouble. Within that sense of humor, or basic intelligence, the buddha family energy is the process of being solid and noncommittal, which tends to bring immense dignity. It brings immense magnetizing, immense pacifying, immense destroying, and immense enriching, as well. And once again, as far as buddha energy is concerned, let me remind you that it is a natural process.

In the case of the buddha family, you don't say anything and you don't act out anything at all. Instead, by *being* so, by *being as it is*, you begin to create some kind of infiltration. Instead of being completely verbal, in the buddha family the gesture begins to become the message. That seems to be the basic process. Things can develop or not develop, but whatever happens, you are not moved. In fact, you are not swayed by incoming messages of any kind. You have immense dignity. The buddha family attitude is that things have already been fulfilled—they are immensely fulfilled already, from that point of view.

In describing the five buddha families, I have come across a lot of people asking why there are only five. There is no particular logic as to why there should be five or six or ten thousand millions. The buddha families are part of your mind. Similarly, we could ask why there are five primary colors or five directions. There are five buddha families because all potential human energies are included in those five principles. But that does not necessarily mean that those five families are the only energies that exist. All kinds of things can be included in what we are as human beings. There are also borderline situations, in which two families or three families are mixed together, which might be considered another family. But if we look thoroughly, fully, and clearly, we find that there are only five main principles or potentialities taking place. Research and study on the five buddha families has been done within the 2,500 years of the existence of Buddha's teaching; and we have a lot of trust in those people's research work, practice, and understanding. Our point of view is that we can't question that—not because it is the complete truth of the Bible, but because it is the complete truth in terms of practice experience.

The five buddha-family process has provided immense friendly guidance to a lot of us. It has been one of the main ways to subjugate immense aggression and uptightness. Such aggression is taking place all the time. Usually, we are pissed off at our world. We have lots of complaints when things don't fulfill their function in our life—our husband is not being properly husbandly, our wife is not performing her duties, our brothers and sisters are not properly behaving, our friends are not helping us, and our guru's not being kind to us. We have lots of complaints, all kinds! We could begin by being pissed off at little sand flies brushing our cheek, and from that level, we could interpret our complaints to the infinite level: "It was the fault of my father that that sand fly sat on my cheek and ate me up. It was the fault of my guru. My guru led me to this miserable life."

Although all kinds of problems and all kinds of angry situations take place immensely, all the time, that doesn't mean that you are a special case, at all. There are no special cases, none whatsoever! You are part of the world. Everybody is part of the rest of the gray world, absolutely. Nobody is a special case. Nobody has some special potentiality for attaining enlightenment, any more than anybody else. Nobody has the particular potentiality of being a reject. We all are made out of these five types, these five different buddha family processes. That's why we need to understand that every situation is always workable.

You don't have to change your personality, your sambhogakaya manifestation. You don't have to try to make an angry person into a peaceful one, and speedy people do not have to become slower. That approach seems to be based on the Christian ethics of reforming or final conversion. In this case, we are not asking for a change or shift; instead, you maintain your existence. You try to evaluate your existence, your level of experience, personally and properly. That seems to be the basic point. The question doesn't arise of: "I'm out of samsara, I'm into nirvana." If you think in those terms, you need more sitting practice. You have to think more. Your approach is premature and too primitive. You are still approaching things at the preparatory school level. You have to relate to yourself at the level of humor in the sambhogakaya process—much more so. Once that space and sense of delightfulness is taking place, there is no problem—none whatsoever—in tuning yourself into those five buddha family principles.

Again, I would like to mention that it is not particularly that you have to belong to one particular buddha family, as in an astrology chart. You have the potentials of all five buddha families. However, they work together in such a way that you might have different buddha family expressions, or manifest more in one way than another way. On the whole, looking from the neurotic angle, all those processes might be regarded as hang-ups. But they are not hang-ups, they are promises. Or maybe *potentialities* is a better word.

To summarize: If there is a sense of rejoicing and being willing to work with yourself, rather than purely wanting to change the situation, then I think you are ready to have a glimpse of the sambhogakaya principle. Otherwise, you are still going through immense blockages. It is not that you don't possess potentiality, but your potentiality has been blocked—by *you* personally. You won't let yourself give you a good time anymore. The idea is to experience all of these buddha families as a celebration of life. The whole message of the sambhogakaya principle is that sense of celebration. The sambhogakaya principle brings a sense of celebration and a sense of magnificent pride. If you feel you are inadequate to that, then something must be screwed up, fundamentally and basically. You should go back to the hinayana level, if that happens. But you still have a chance!

Student: I was wondering, presuming that you're talking on a psychological level and also on a larger level of cosmic description, what the "body" quality of the kayas is. Why are they described as "bodies"?

Chögyam Trungpa Rinpoche: Basically, body is a reference point to what's happening. If there's no body, there's no reference point.

S: Is the body, in that sense, a container?

CTR: Yes, you could say that. It is a receiver, a container, an editor.

S: There seems to be a relationship between the first four buddha families and the four karmas, and the buddha family seems to combine them.

CTR: I think so, yes. That's how it should be, in fact. Although the vajra family is related with the vajra neurosis of anger or aggression, it is also related with the opposite, the karma of pacifying.

S: In what way is the buddha family energy destructive as well as pacifying?

CTR: Basically, it is destructive from the point of view of ego. Ego suicide tends to happen constantly. If you indulge your particular character, if you nurse that and you become a superstar—finally you commit suicide in a hotel bedroom, or you become a great fighter and you are killed on the spot. That's just a general, primitive analogy, but the fundamental idea is that you are building a gigantic kingdom of egohood, and in doing so, you are using your potentialities as crutches. You may have vajra intellect abilities, or karma fulfillment abilities; but you try to use those in your own way, rather than share with anybody else. You don't want to give to anybody. You would like to preserve your territory. You don't even want to give into any of your colleagues or to share your space. You would like to hold onto your particular world and your particular territory.

S: I have found it useful to work with the buddha families as a way to give me more perspective. For example, in looking at or describing a situation, I find myself feeling that's the way it is, and I relate to the particular buddha family style or quality that characterizes my description. But then I realize that that's only one way of describing it, that I can think about it in other ways, such as in a padma way, a vajra way, or a buddha way. Do you think that's a useful way to work with the buddha families? I find that that it allows me to give the situation some space. Instead of feeling that my way of describing it is *it*, I am able to see other points of view. Do you think that's an appropriate way to use the energies?

CTR: I wouldn't make a big deal out of it, because things exist in their own way, anyway. Whatever you do, others are going to do it in their own particular style. So, at this point, using the five types of approach is arbitrary. You're going to approach things that way, anyway. It seems to be a very natural process, not a big deal. The whole thing needs to have some humor or scope. It is like behaving like a Gentile or a Jew. Either is okay, whichever way you behave, but there might be some problems coming along with that style. If you don't have humor around what you are, you're going to be involved with troubles and fights.

S: This sense of delightfulness transcends birth, pain, and death, but at the same time it never loses touch with these, right? It never gets wrapped up in its own quality of enjoyment or humor, but it stays on the ground, in touch with the pain.

CTR: Why not? Pain is the most valuable learning lesson we have. Without pain we would not be here, for that matter, to discuss anything. On one hand, there are millions of people waiting to come here too, because their pain is so intense. On the other hand, people run away from here because it's too painful—or they are just about to, they're thinking about it.

S: Suppose you suddenly feel a loss or change of identity in which you play a role that seems appropriate, but there's nothing cozy about it and nothing familiar about it, and you don't exactly know who you are—can your buddha family style change in midstream?

CTR: You're not expected to change.

S: No, but it seems to happen.

CTR: If that comes up, let it go that way. I mean, we can't just say, "This is right. I'm not going to change. You can't impose a new role on me. I am a Virgo and I'm going to remain a Virgo because my birthday says so." It's quite different than that. There is a process, which takes place simply and constantly. Let that process be so, whatever it is. Good or bad doesn't matter.

S: You emphasized that the five buddha families are especially connected with the immediate present. I was trying to understand whether it's a matter of trying to avoid thinking of them as past and future or whether we could in each situation, from moment to moment, try to discover within ourselves all of the buddha families or some combination.

CTR: The point is that whatever is taking place on the spot is the particular principle that you have to work with. If something comes up, you have that particular style and you have your own particular style of dealing with the whole thing. So you develop your tactics and mentalities. That takes place on the spot, definitely. You could also take humor in that and pride.

S: Why are you talking about the buddha families in connection with the sambhogakaya? Are they especially connected with that body, or kaya?

CTR: Very much so, yes. They are particularly connected with the level of somebody.

S: Is that a pun?

CTR: Somebody, or sambhogakaya—as opposed to dharmakaya, which is nobody, and nirmanakaya, which is everybody. Policy making, how you handle yourself, takes place in the sambhogakaya. Sambhogakaya is the policy-making process. When you are already *there*, at the level of nirmanakaya, you have already made your policy as to how to handle your life. It's already happening. The nirmanakaya is different in that the only requirement then is awareness. At the level of sambhogakaya, you are just making acquaintance with your policy-making. It's like landing on the ground: before you land on the ground, you have to choose which ground to land on. That is when your five types of buddha energy begin to take place.

S: Is the descent from the dharmakaya level down all part of the cosmic disaster?

CTR: Everything!

S: So all the kayas, starting from the pre-dharmakaya level, are just increasingly more of a disaster?

CTR: I think so. The whole thing began with the dharmakaya. The dharmakaya is the first disaster, which initiates the rest of it. It is not particularly necessary. Nevertheless it happened, and we have to go along with it.

S: You said that you experience joy at the sambhogakaya level in working with yourself and a sense of celebration. You said that if you can't do that, at least there's the hinayana level left. I guess that must be the nirmanakaya level, where the Buddha is actually here in a physical body. This sounds quite bleak to me. Previously, it didn't seem like such a disaster, that the Buddha was in a human body.

CTR: We are not just talking about having a body, but about having such a dualistic *idea* of the whole thing. We have to have black and white, good and bad—the samsara and nirvana syndrome. That we have to discuss this at all is unfortunate. It's terrible! However, since we are in this boat already, we might as well go along. There is no choice. That's why the dharma is so full—and we have the best of it!

S: Then am I to understand that primarily what we have is just an increasing awareness of the process? And that awareness can go on and on and on, without any particular change, just awareness itself making movements?

CTR: Sure. So what?

S: There is a famous psychologist who has a theory that the cosmic disaster was the seeding of this planet by DNA, and now it's time for us to build our starship and go back to the center.

CTR: There is no center. Every area is the center. There's no center to go back to. There is no home, home is everywhere.

S: Rinpoche, in terms of the appreciation of detail and the sense of humor, I was wondering if it might be possible to get really trippy about it, and get so caught up in trying to pay attention to every detail of everything, that you would not be able to do anything. Does that happen, or is there a safeguard?

CTR: I think you can appreciate details, provided you have some sense of the whole project being based on egolessness, some sense that you are not supposed to have any feedback or anything particularly prescribed. That seems to be okay. However, if you begin to get into trips of all kinds, your attention-to-detail awareness begins to become hollow, purely a game. So I think it depends on how your general attitude has evolved.

6

Buddha Is Everywhere

THE SAMBHOGAKAYA is twofold: the sambhogakaya that is experienced and manifests in the form of the five buddha-family process and the sambhogakaya that deals equally with the nonstructured mind world, or the world of the five buddha families, and the body world, the world of music, voice, or speech. At this level, the sambhogakaya principle is the initiator of anything that happens in our life—constantly. The sambhogakaya is the *instigator* of everything that takes place in our life, rather than life itself. When something occurs in our life that is subject to panic, the sambhogakaya principle acts as panic. For instance, when there is discontinuity and noncommunication between mind and body, suddenly something pops up, and all at once there is communication. At that point, when the mind and the physical world communicate together, panic begins to take place. The sambhogakaya principle is also how our body and mind relate with words—how mind and body combine together in the physical manifestation of verbalizing, or making noises. At the ape level, it is grunt; at the sophisticated level, it is music; at the mystical level, it is mantra.

The sambhogakaya principle leads to the nirmanakaya principle. It seems that we don't have any choice about that. The sambhogakaya process begins to take place constantly; and from there, we are approaching the nirmanakaya. That is to say, we are approaching the earthly, physical, bodily situation. The nirmanakaya is the physical, bodily state of existence. It is everything we experience in the audio-visual world in the very ordinary sense. The sun rises, the pine trees hiss in the wind, the rock sits, and waters flow—all those processes are manifestations of the sambhogakaya principle. The sambhoga-kaya is being transmitted into the nirmanakaya as a real life pro-cess. Everything we go through in our life is a manifestation of the sambhogakaya principle.

Also included in the nirmanakaya are actual representations of the sambhogakaya principle: actual physical images are made, the actual voice of dharma is heard, actual living human teachers exist on this earth. All of those are manifestations of sanity coming down—unnecessarily, from the point of view of dharmakaya, of course. Still, those unnecessary processes become necessary at some point. It's like collecting maple syrup from a tree. The first drip descends into the branch, then the branch begins to collect drips, next the drips begin to fall into the bucket, *finally* you have maple syrup in your bucket.

Finally, at the nirmanakaya level, something's actually taking place. Those long-winded descriptions and ideas, those intangible, unbi-ased, unconditional ideas and thoughts of enlightenment are finally captured in this particular sieve of the human mind. You can actually see the physical guru and you can actually prostrate to this physical guru and touch his or her feet. You could worship that particular person, who represents *all* those unconditional processes and *all* of that basic sanity. Immense space, created through the process of enlightened awareness, is finally manifested on earth. That seems to be the basic point.

In regard to the nirmanakaya, there are various types of nirman-akaya. For instance, the Buddha Shakyamuni, Gautama Buddha, was one person. He was born and raised in India, educated in India, and he attained enlightenment by meditating wholeheartedly, and so forth. We also have other examples, other great teachers who are following that particular principle and approach. We have various teachers, masters, gurus of the lineage, who all represent that process. Most of all, we have a sense of earthy touch taking place, a panoramic experience within everyday life. When somebody has heard of the teachings, then that particular person begins to look into every aspect of our life, from the loftiest ideas of philosophy to very manual, basic, ordinary things, such as sitting on a toilet seat. Everything's covered.

The nirmanakaya principle exists in every situation. The nirmanakaya principle exists in a baby's diaper. It exists in our pencils and pad. The nirmanakaya exists at the level of our money. It exists in the flat tire on our motorcar and in the police checking on our speeding. The nirmanakaya principle exists in every situation of our life. So the nirmanakaya principle is related with the ordinary minds of individual students who care to relate with their lives properly. Instead of worshipping some higher principle, in the nirmanakaya, people who are into the dharma properly begin to find a sense of worship, sacredness, gracefulness and grace in everyday life. That is, the nirmanakaya principle exists in our everyday lives.

As a matter of fact, every activity that takes place in our lives is nirmanakaya expression. That nirmanakaya expression has two types: the confused version and the enlightened version. The confused version is regarded purely as a hassle, or an expression of neurosis; and the enlightened version is that within all that there is a sense of sacredness. So having a sculpture or painting of nirmanakaya buddha or being involved with graphic situations and experiences in our everyday life are both regarded as nirmanakaya. If you have a graphic experience such as a car crash or running a red light—the very directness of whatever is taking place in your life is regarded as nirmanakaya expression. The cosmic approach, the larger metaphysical and enlightened approach that takes place in our life, is included in the nirmanakaya—and the petty little details that exist in our life are included in the nirmanakaya, as well. Expenditure . . . exposure . . . encompass . . . space.

The process of nirmanakaya tends to become very powerful at times, because of its claustrophobic quality or watchfulness. Everywhere we turn, around every corner, there is nirmanakaya. We can't just hang out loose. In other words, everything is a reminder of all kinds of things. But that's not particularly regarded as a phenomenological situation—it is just the basic awareness that the nirmanakaya cannot be avoided. In other words, buddha can't be avoided, buddha is everywhere. Enlightenment possibilities are all over the place. Whether you're going to get married tomorrow, whether you're going to die tomorrow, whatever you might feel, that familiar nirmanakaya awake quality is everywhere, all the time.

Some systematizing of this whole process has developed throughout the history of Buddhism, the twenty-five hundred years of Buddhist reign in this world on this particular planet Earth. There is constant pressure that people should sit, meditate, and lead their lives in the Buddhistic way. That is actually adopting just a *fraction* of nirmanakaya activities. The rest of it relies highly on awareness and devotion. In this sense, devotion means being willing to face the possibility that the all-encompassing space of nirmanakaya takes place eternally in our life, whether we want it or we don't want it.

Student: Is there any difference between phenomena in general, all phenomena, and the expression in the phenomenal world of the harmonious relationship of the three kayas? Are the three kayas like the footprint of Buddha in the phenomenal world?

Chögyam Trungpa Rinpoche: I think everything is a footprint, actually, including the basic spaced-out experience we might feel and the sense that we are split in our personalities. It is not that we are schizophrenic, but we are split into five types of personalities, five different expressions. We also have the sense of relating with every detail in life, seeking answers, questioning, looking into life as it is. From this point of view, everything is a footprint, anything that goes on, whether we regard it as sublime or ridiculous. Everything we do—breathing, farting, getting mosquito bites, having fantastic ideas about reality, thinking clever thoughts, flushing the toilet—whatever occurs is a footprint. That is why enlightenment is referred to as en-*lighten*-ment, rather than as a big gain of freedom. It is further *luminosity*; it *illuminates* life. Up to this point, we had a very bad lighting system; but now we are getting a better lighting system, so we begin to see every curve of skin, every inch of our world, properly. We might get very irritated by such sharpness and precision, but that seems to be part of the perspective.

S: Does that mean that there's no such thing as a bad poem?

CTR: That's right! If you look it from that angle, not talking from an editor's attitude, but in terms of cosmic style, bad poems are very cute. In their own way, they are fantastic!

S: You talked about how nirmanakaya always comes up in all these day-to-day experiences. I'm curious as to why you used the term, *nirmanakaya*, as opposed to dharmakaya or sambhogakaya?

CTR: Nirmanakaya is the physical situation; sambhogakaya and dharmakaya are the level of mind.

S: Would it be wrong to say that the sambhogakaya produces the nirmanakaya, or that nirmanakaya is the outcome of the sambhogakaya?

CTR: I don't think that the sambhogakaya produces the nirmanakaya. Nirmanakaya is a self-existing situation. Dharmakaya is like the sun; sambhogakaya is like the rays; and nirmanakaya is like the rays hitting the objects on the earth. So it is a self-existing situation.

S: Lama Govinda used the terms *seed, subtle,* and *gross* in describing the relationship of the three bodies: dharmakaya as seed, sambhogakaya as subtle, and nirmanakaya as gross. Is that an error on his part?

CTR: I wouldn't say that dharmakaya is a seed, particularly. Dharmakaya is more than a seed—it's all-pervasive. Calling it a seed is a poverty-mentality approach to dharmakaya. Instead of shooting a rocket into the atmosphere, you shoot a gun, which doesn't have any sense of confirmation or expansion. Secondly, the sambhogakaya is not all that subtle, it is very obvious. For instance, the five buddha-family principle is obvious. Finally, the nirmanakaya is not at all gross. It is the most refined form that one could ever think of in the universe! It is seeing things as extremely subtle and as extraordinarily sophisticated as we can ever appreciate. It is the highest of class, if you would like to call it that, the highest form of sophistication. So it's *far* from being gross! Lama Govinda's approach seems to be slightly different, bless his heart.

S: Would you say more about the efforts to systematize nirmanakaya? Is that what Buddhism is all about? That's what occurs to me.

CTR: I think so, definitely. Ordinarily, we can't say that everything's okay because there's chaos, things don't make any sense. So we have to begin somewhere. We have to learn to think properly, which is meditation; we have to learn to walk, which is also meditation; we have to learn how to behave. Learning to behave in a certain way is a very rough guide to the nirmanakaya, a nirmanakaya-*type* of approach. We are actually copying the behavior of Buddha. The way Buddha walked, the way Buddha talked, the way Buddha thought— we are just copying that, very simply. There are no trips involved, there's no philosophy. We just simply take Buddha as the example. We are simply doing that as ordinary people. That is Buddha-ism, I suppose we could call it.

S: You said dharmakaya and sambhogakaya were unnecessary, but you haven't said that about nirmanakaya.

CTR: We've done that already, so we can't even bother to say that it's unnecessary. Nirmanakaya has expanded its own world altogether, so we have a very elaborate samsaric world set-up. That has happened already, and we have to go along with it.

S: Is nirmanakaya equivalent to the samsaric world?

CTR: It's getting very close. We are sharing the samsaric world finally, rather than having lofty ideas.

S: You said that in going from sambhogakaya to nirmanakaya, you choose your ground. Could you say something about choosing ground?

CTR: In that case, we were talking about choosing ground because you have *no* ground. Usually when we choose ground we have one ground and then we choose another ground, which doesn't make any sense in the short run or the long run. I don't think we can speculate too much on that, it would be purely a waste of our time.

S: There's a Zen story in which a Zen master asks his disciple to demonstrate his understanding. The disciple shakes a tree, and the master says, "You understand the function but not the essence." I'd like to know if that is related to the three bodies. Is the dharmakaya the essence and the nirmanakaya and sambhogakaya the function?

CTR: Very much so—and I think we are concerned with the function, definitely.

S: Is that sambhogakaya?

CTR: That is nirmanakaya. It is how things work rather than why things are there. People constantly ask, "Why?" like a two-year-old child. But somehow, persons begin to learn the lesson of *not* asking why things are as they are, by throwing the question back to themselves. The nirmanakaya level is purely functional, how to survive. Beyond that, we don't have to be concerned too much with the dharmakaya and sambhogakaya, they just come along. They do exist. If you are interested in the why of their existence, the answer is: because they don't exist, that's why they do exist. That is a pragmatic answer rather than a theoretical one.

S: When you said that you use it every day, but you don't pay any attention to it, like being able to move your arm, for instance, I took that to mean the life force. Is that nirmanakaya or sambhogakaya or both?

CTR: Well, that's a bit tricky. One has to pay attention to it, but one shouldn't; one needs to, but one shouldn't. But when you are told you shouldn't, you actually pay *more* attention, because you want to find out.

S: The Sixth Patriarch says that samadhi is the body of the buddha and that prajna does not exist apart from the three bodies. Would you say something about that?

CTR: I think that's quite true. I agree with him. Good luck for him, the Great Sixth One!

S: Is the sense of sacredness the same as the sense of celebration?

CTR: I think they are identical, definitely. That's a good question.

S: I was very moved by what you said about everything being a footprint. It sounds as if, in order to appreciate the real significance of things, you need to see that there is something beyond, encompassing what is apparent. It is sort of like a poem rather than prose—not the content, but the resonance.

CTR: Mm-hmm. It's a hoofprint.

S: Rinpoche, the kayas are called the three bodies of enlightenment. Are they levels or styles of enlightenment? Because I have the feeling that they are also descriptions of the world.

CTR: They are various functions of enlightenment. It is like having a heart, a brain, a muscular system, and limbs: all of those are operating at the same time. Likewise, all three kayas are operating at the same time. It is like having a motor and a driver and wheels: they function in the same way. It's wrong to look at it in terms of a case history—that one comes first, then the second one comes, and then the third one. The three kayas have been presented that way in many cases, and it is true, in some sense, technically. But in terms of presentation, that approach is a mistake, because people will tend to think that if you get the dharmakaya, you don't need the rest. They will think that you can get rid of the others, the bothersome nirmanakaya and sambhogakaya, and just dwell on dharmakaya. But, somehow, that never happens.

There is an expression, *kusum yerme*, which means "the indivisibility of the three bodies." That indivisibility seems to be the basic point, particularly advocated by our particular lineage of Kagyü. In the Kagyü tradition, it is always said that the three kayas come simultaneously. In your system, as you operate your life, those three principles happen at once. You are always working with all three of them in that way. I feel that's true, and I think that's a good attitude. Let's stick to our lineage.

S: The dharmakaya was very hard for me to get any understanding of at all, but the nirmanakaya seems *too* simple. It seems too simple to say everything is the buddha or the dharma. I've heard that a lot and I've never quite understood it. It seems like *everything* is nirmanakaya. So is nirmanakaya just a fancy word for the entire world and absolutely everything in it, and that absolutely everything is an expression of the dharma?

CTR: Yes.

S: I don't understand how absolutely everything can be an expression of the dharma.

CTR: Dharma in this case is some kind of cosmic plan, but it is not the idea of a God as the maker and creator of the universe, particularly. Instead, anything that goes on has a particular makeup or conditions, which is that everything is transparent and nonexistent— and at the same time, existing. It is like the space that accommodates the world. The quality of space exists in earth, water, fire, and all the other elements; it is part of all those ingredients. In order to make things function—in order to have cosmic lubrication, so to speak— things have to have that kind of nonexistent, unconditional quality. Otherwise things can't exist; it is against the law of logic, the law of functioning. So in order for things to exist, therefore, things have to *not* exist. Nonexistence provides lubrication, functional growth, and the atmosphere for things to blossom.

Everything is known as dharma, enlightenment, or the buddha principle, because the buddha principle is free of any conditions; and at the same time, it creates further and greater initiative. I think there has been a problem in the past with theistic traditions that say there is something that exists, something that heavily conquers the whole universe. That theistic principle or belief, called God or the Divine, has complete dictatorial power. It doesn't allow any nonexistence or unconditionality.

The mystics were probably an exception to this view, but since they were very smart people, they may have begun to realize that if they stuck to their theory it would be suicidal, doctrinally, so they began to cop out. They got into something else, a more humanistic approach. In fact, throughout the history of Christianity, the mystical schools have been banned because they promote nontheism. The mystics subtly produced little bubbles here and there of a nontheistic tradition, and that was not very well accepted. A lot of mystics suffered execution and all kinds of persecution. I think that is a problem, actually. In this case, when we say everything contains dharma, or the buddha principle, we are not saying that something other has been inserted into our world, or the universe—we are talking about unconditional transparency. Because of that unconditional transparency, things can happen. There is constant lubrication, cosmic lubrication.

S: How is buddha nature related to the three bodies? Is it dharmakaya or is it all three?

CTR: All three, hopefully.

S: I don't want to harp too much on one thing, but would you be willing to say, in terms of what we've been discussing, what makes a good poem?

CTR: What makes a good poem? On the one hand, nothing makes a good poem, actually. What is a poem, anyway? On the other hand, one can make good poems if there is more reliance on the lubrication. When there's no lubrication, everything's just a stack of bricks. Poems become bad poems because there's no sambhogakaya humor anymore. Poems become very steep and trippy. From that point of view, excessive aggressive poems written on the idea of war and excessive peaceful poems written on the idea of peace are equally bad, because there's no humor in them. For that matter, excessive poems written on religion and on inspirations of any kind also do not have any humor. Poems are like bread dough: you have to have flour and water, you have to knead properly, and finally you make good bread out of the whole thing. You bake poetry. I think good poetry is very hard to come by—and so is good baking.

S: You said that if you push too hard, the vajra diamond sword will cut you to pieces. What did you mean by pushing too hard?

CTR: What do you think? Have a guess! First thought is best thought. Take a guess!

S: I don't know. I've been thinking about this for a while. Is it trying to get everything at once?

CTR: Something like that. I think that might be the case, actually.

S: If the sword doesn't get you, then the vultures will?

CTR: Not quite. If the sword doesn't get you, your suicide will get you. You're doomed to be destroyed in any case, so it's better to commit hara-kiri. Very heavy.

S: In the meantime, you celebrate?

CTR: Well said! Good luck, madam.

S: If we were never here in the first place, how come we've had such a good time?

CTR: That's a corny thing to say. However, we are corny, as we are, and we are here. So what?

S: If you are cut down by the vajra sword, or have the feeling you are being cut, what's the process after that? Do you pick yourself up—pick your parts back up—or do you just stay cut?

CTR: Nothing.

S: You just stay cut?

CTR: Nothing.

S: Nothing?

CTR: Absolutely nothing.

S: It sounds horrible.

CTR: Whatever. It's not particularly nice and not particularly bad— it's *nothing*. I think we are getting into tantric koan, at this point.

S: Every time we talk about anything, such as what is the footprint of the Buddha, every time we ask questions, we seem to make everything very, very complicated and complex. It all seems much more simple than that.

CTR: I sympathize with us. So what's next?

S: Nothing.

CTR: Yes, I quite agree with you, two hundred percent! That is a problem, I suppose. Otherwise we wouldn't keep meeting so late. This whole thing is somewhat absurd. We want to *know* rather than to actually *experience*. That's the problem with the speech principle.

S: It's very unnecessary, but it's very necessary.

CTR: Yes, you said so. That's right.

S: In wanting to experience rather than wanting to know, I've been noticing the last few days that when I'm very tired, I'm not very aware of the space, and I have a lot of trouble seeing the humor in situations.

CTR: That's good! That *is* humor! Just take a *little* leap after that. That's it!

Sources

Glimpses of Mahayana. Edited by Judith L. Lief. Halifax: Vajradhatu Publications, 2001. © 2001 by Diana J. Mukpo. Based on the seminar "The Complete Teachings of Mahayana," given at Tail of the Tiger (now Karmê Chöling) in Barnet, Vermont, March 29–April 4, 1973.

"The Bodhisattva Vow" on pages 65–67 from *The Way of the Bodhisattva* by Shantideva, © 1997, 2006 by the Padmakara Translation Group. Reprinted by arrangement with Shambhala Publications, Inc.

Glimpses of Shunyata. Edited by Judith L. Lief. Halifax: Vajradhatu Publications, 2005. © 2005 by Diana J. Mukpo. Based on the seminar "Shunyata," given at Tail of the Tiger (now Karmê Chöling) in Barnet, Vermont, April 1–4, 1972.

Glimpses of Space: The Feminine Principle and EVAM. Edited by Judith L. Lief. Halifax: Vajradhatu Publications, 1999. © 1999 by Diana J. Mukpo. Based on two seminars: "The Feminine Principle," given at Karmê Chöling in Barnet, Vermont, January 1–4, 1975, and "EVAM," given at Karma Dzong in Boulder, Colorado, April 5–11, 1976.

Glimpses of Realization: The Three Bodies of Enlightenment. Edited by Judith L. Lief. Halifax: Vajradhatu Publications, 2003. © 2003 by Diana J. Mukpo. Based on the seminar "The Three Bodies of Enlightenment," given at Karma Dzong in Boulder, Colorado, February 28–March 6, 1975.

Acknowledgments

THIS BOOK IS based on a series of short seminars presented by Chögyam Trungpa Rinpoche in Colorado and Vermont in the 1970s. Like other books I have edited, it is a result of the dedication and hard work of many people. In particular, I appreciate the fact that the Vidyadhara's early students were farsighted enough to keep a meticulous record of his teachings in the form of audio- and videotape recordings and transcripts. To this tireless and devoted crew of volunteers we owe much gratitude and appreciation.

The collection of recordings, transcripts, and photographs held in the Shambhala Archives is an incredible treasury of teachings. They are the raw material for books such as this—and there are still more treasures there to be uncovered and offered to the world. Thanks to the many people involved in the creation and management of the Shambhala Archives: the sound recorders, videographers, transcribers, and archivists.

There have been so many dedicated people who made this book possible that to mention them all would require a very long list. But I would like to thank three people in particular: Carolyn Rose Gimian, Gordon Kidd, and Diana J. Mukpo. Carolyn has been a fierce advocate for the Shambhala Archives, tireless in her support and instrumental in conveying the importance of this precious collection to potential donors. Gordon Kidd has been steadfast in his work at the archives, especially with the audio and video collection. And last but not least, Diana Mukpo has graciously given her permission to edit and publish this material and has been supportive and encouraging of such work for many decades. It is due to the dedication and persistence of all these people that we are able to make these teachings available to the wider public.

Judith L. Lief, Editor

Resources

FOR INFORMATION about meditation instruction or to find a practice center near you, please contact one of the following:

Shambhala International
1084 Tower Rd.
Halifax, NS B3H 2Y5
Canada
Phone: (902) 425-4275
Website: www.shambhala.org

Shambhala Europe
Kartäuserwall 20
50678 Köln
Germany
Phone: 49-221-31024-00
E-mail: office@shambhala-europe.org

Karmê Chöling
369 Patneaude Lane
Barnet, VT 05821
Phone: (802) 633-2384
E-mail: reception@karmecholing.org

Shambhala Mountain Center
151 Shambhala Way
Red Feather Lakes, CO 80545
Phone: (970) 881-2184
E-mail: info@shambhalamountain.org

Dorje Denma Ling
2280 Balmoral Rd.
Tatamagouche, NS B0K 1V0
Canada
Phone: (902) 657-9085
E-mail: info@dorjedenmaling.com

Gampo Abbey
Pleasant Bay, Cape Breton, NS B0E 2P0
Canada
Phone: (902) 224-2752
E-mail: office@gampoabbey.org

Naropa University is the only accredited, Buddhist-inspired university in North America. For more information, contact:

Naropa University
2130 Arapahoe Ave.
Boulder, CO 80302
Phone: (303) 444-0202
E-mail: info@naropa.edu

Audio recordings of talks and seminars by Chögyam Trungpa are available from:

Kalapa Recordings
1084 Tower Rd.
Halifax, NS B3H 2Y5
Canada
Phone: (902) 420-1118, ext. 121
E-mail: recordings@shambhala.org
Website: www.shambhalamedia.org

The Chögyam Trungpa website
www.ChogyamTrungpa.com
This website includes a biography, information on new releases by and about Chögyam Trungpa, a description and order information for all of his books, plus links to related organizations.

The Ocean of Dharma E-Newsletter
Sign up for the Ocean of Dharma e-newsletter and receive a quote from Chögyam Trungpa Rinpoche every week. You'll also have access to a growing archive containing hundreds of other quotes taken from Trungpa Rinpoche's works. Go to www.OceanofDharma.com.

Index